WITHDRAWN
UTSA LIBRARIES

D1707307

RECLAIMING *Heimat*

RECLAIMING *Heimat*

Trauma and Mourning in Memoirs by Jewish Austrian Reémigrés

Jacqueline Vansant

WAYNE STATE UNIVERSITY PRESS   DETROIT

The following publishers have given permission to use extended quotations from previously published material. From *Von der Kunst, Österreicher zu sein* by Hans J. Thalberg. Böhlau Verlag Ges.m.b.H & Co. KG. From *Das Wunder des Überlebens* by Ernst Lothar, © Paul Zsolnay Wien 1961. From *At the Mind's Limit* by Jean Améry, courtesy of Indiana University Press. From *Jenseits von Schuld und Sühne. Bewältigungsversuche eines Überwältigten* by Jean Améry. Klett-Cotta, Stuttgart 1977. From *Die hellen und die finsteren Zeiten* by Hilde Spiel, © Paul List Verlag, München 1989. From *Welche Welt ist meine Welt?* by Hilde Spiel, © Paul List Verlag, München 1990. From *Rückkehr nach Wien:* by Hilde Spiel, © 1968 by Nymphenburger in der F.A. Herbig Verlagsbuchhandlung GmbH, Munich/ Hilde Spiel, Rückkehr nach Wien. From *Shanghai Passage* by Franziska Tausig, Verlag der Theodor Kramer Gesellschaft. From *The Traveling Years* by Elisabeth Freundlich, English translation of *Die fahrenden Jahre,* courtesy of Ariadne Press. Every effort has been made to secure permission for copyrighted material used in this book.

Library of Congress Cataloging-in-Publication Data

Vansant, Jacqueline, 1954–
Reclaiming Heimat : trauma and mourning in memoirs
by Jewish Austrian reémigrés / Jacqueline Vansant.
p. cm.
Includes bibliographical references (p.) and index.
ISBN 0-8143-2951-9 (alk. paper)
1. Jews—Austria—Biography.   2. Jews—Austria—Identity.
3. Refugees, Jewish—Austria.   4. Austria—Ethnic relations.
5. Holocaust, Jewish—Austria—Influence.   I. Title.
DS135 .A9 V36 2001
943.6'004924'0092—dc21   2001002029

To the memory of
ERIKA SALLOCH

Every corner, every little square breathed of memories.
Hans J. Thalberg

Contents

ACKNOWLEDGMENTS

Reclaiming "Heimat" has been a long time coming. Without the institutional and individual support I have received over the past ten years, this project would never have come to fruition. I am very grateful to the Fulbright Commission and the Austrian government for a research year in Vienna, 1990–1991, when I first began work on the memoirs. In 1997 I was able to gather additional material for the project when I was awarded a grant from the German Academic Exchange Service (DAAD) to conduct research at the Leo Baeck Institute in New York. I have also received generous support from the University of Michigan-Ann Arbor and the University of Michigan-Dearborn; a combined grant from the two campuses allowed me to spend several months in 1998 researching at the Deutsche Bücherei in Leipzig in the special exile collection. That year I was also awarded a summer grant from the National Endowment for the Humanities to begin writing my book. The two-month support was invaluable in the conceptualization of my study. In 1998–1999, I had sabbatical leave, during which I finished the first draft of my manuscript. For this year I am most grateful to the University of Michigan-Dearborn.

During my numerous research trips to Austria, I have received help and advice from a variety of institutions and a multitude of people. I can mention only a few. I thoroughly appreciate the support of the Literar-Mechana. When I began work on this project, Peter Eppel, then at the Dokumentationsarchiv des österreichischen Widerstands, aided me in my preliminarily research. The staff members of the Literaturhaus, especially Ursula Seeber, have been very generous with their time. Ingrid Schramm of the Österreichisches Literaturarchiv in the Nationalbibliothek guided me in my investigations of unpublished texts by Hilde Spiel. Most recently, Ulla Fischer of the Bildarchiv at the Nationalbibliothek,

9

Regina Wonisch of the Verein für Geschicte der Arbeiterbewegung, and Ingrid Schramm helped me obtain photographs for my book. Erika Thurner of the University of Innsbruck and Helga Embacher of the University of Salzburg have assisted me with their expertise in the area of memoirs. In New York, Barbara Motyka of the German Academic Exchange Service was most helpful. The expert advice of Diane Spielman of the Leo Baeck Institute was vital.

While working on this project, I imposed on many friends both in Europe and in the States. To my many friends in Austria, I am indebted for hospitality, ideas, and legwork. I am particularly grateful to Craig, Eva, and Olivia Thorpe for their hospitality as well as their introductions to members of the Austrian resistance. I thank Gabriele Kolar, who always made her guest room available to me. Moreover, her interested questions helped me reach clarity in my thinking. I also appreciate Lotte Rieder's help in securing photographs. During my stay in New York, Gwynedd Cannan was a gracious hostess. She also offered her expert advice as an archivist in my never-ending search for materials.

Writing a book has been a true learning process. I have come to realize more than ever that for me writing is a collaborative process. My thoughts have truly evolved through the questions raised by my colleagues and friends. For his careful reading of numerous grant proposals, I would like to thank Jonathan Smith. Kathy Wider, Ruth Sanders, Maria-Regina Kecht, and Linda Adler-Kassner offered valuable comments on the original prospectus. The comments of Linda Adler-Kassner, Carolyn Kraus, Jacqueline Lawson, Lora Bex Lempert, Maureen Linker, Elizabeth Mittman, Helga Schreckenberger, Amy Schulz, Diane Shooman, and Patricia K. Smith took my thinking to higher planes. The real and imagined conversations I had with Helga Schreckenberger and Diane Shooman always filled me with renewed purpose. I especially want to thank Gloria Eli and John Lennington, two badminton compatriots, who asked to read the manuscript and served as a valuable and supportive lay audience. And a sometimes reluctant reader, Ron Garrett, my partner on and off the badminton court, read multiple versions of the manuscript even though it had nothing to do with badminton or computers. For his close readings and continuous support, I am forever in his debt. Thanks also to my colleague Gabriella Eschrich, who took time out of her busy schedule to translate an article from Italian into English for me. I would also like to thank Mary Fahnestock-Thomas for doing such a good job on the index.

In addition to learning the dialogic nature of writing a book, I have also come to realize the importance of not taking myself too seriously when working on a very serious project. This insight I owe to my brother James Vansant and my mother Eleanor Tikiob Vansant.

Although it will not be obvious, the seeds for this project were sown long ago when I began my adventure in German with Erika Salloch at Washington College in Chestertown, Maryland. To her memory, I dedicate this book.

Introduction: Reclaiming *Heimat*

This book is a study of a select body of memoir literature written after 1945 by Jewish Austrians who returned to Austria from exile and resettled there permanently. Their attachment to Austria—as much as the events of 1938, forced exile, and the Holocaust—profoundly shaped their lives and their life stories. Consequently, the memoirs are moving accounts of the loss of *Heimat* (home/homeland) and self, and of the acute desire to recover that loss by returning home, something very few of the approximately 130,000 exiled Jewish Austrians did.

Because not all exiles persecuted as Jews identified themselves as Jewish before 1938, they were not registered with the Jewish Community Organization (Jüdische Gemeinde), a major source of statistical studies concerning Jewish Austrians.[1] And not all Jewish reémigrés necessarily registered with the Jewish Community Organization upon their return, making it impossible to calculate the exact number of returnees.[2] Estimates range from 4,500 (Pauley 1992, 301; Embacher 1995, 112; and Wilder-Okladek 1969, 34–40) to 12,000–15,000 (Pauley 1996, 493).[3]

The impossibility of establishing a more precise number of returning Jewish Austrians underscores the diversity of the Jewish population within Austria as well as the problematic nature of the label "Jewish." For the purposes of this study, "Jewish" refers in the broadest sense to a group bound together by the state-sanctioned anti-Semitism of the National Socialists after the *Anschluss* (the incorporation of Austria into the German Reich in March 1938). Despite their varying relationships to Judaism, the memoir writers studied here were defined as belonging to the same group regardless of gender, class, educational background, profession, political affiliation, or even the religion they practiced. The events following the *Anschluss* imposed a group identity upon those determined to be Jewish by the Nuremberg Laws. As a result, their individual life stories reflect group experiences that are notably absent from the collective memories of the general Austrian population.

By the same token, the memoirs offer only a limited perspective on Jewish identity and the life of Jews in Vienna. As historian Harriet Pass Freidenreich writes, "Viennese Jewry comprised an extremely heterogeneous group. They differed significantly among themselves with respect to wealth, culture, and religion, as well as politics and place of origin" (1991, 2).

The memoir writers—all from moderately well-off to well-to-do families—are products of the acculturation or assimilation of Austrian Jews in the late nineteenth and early twentieth centuries described in numerous studies on Jews in Austria before 1938.[4] When Jews in Austria were granted "equal civil, political, and religious rights with all other Austrian citizens" in 1867 during the reign of Emperor Franz Josef, this theoretically promised integration and acceptance for Jews into all aspects of Austrian society (Rozenblit 1983, 10–11). Consequently, many Jews developed a sense of loyalty to the monarchy and Austria. By the memoirists' parents' generation, their families had attained respected positions within Austrian society. The fathers of the memoirists included a chemist, a director of a ship firm, businessmen, and lawyers. Politically, these families tended either to be members of or sympathetic with the Liberal or Social Democratic Parties.

Typical of the Jewish cultural elite, the memoir writers came from families that had at most only very loose ties with Judaism.[5] As historian Steven Beller writes: "It was the assimilation, the giving up of specifically Jewish forms of life and thinking, which had made possible this great participation in the surrounding culture" (1989, 84). Only one of the memoirists writes of Judaism as part of her identity. Two of the memoirists were raised Catholic, one was baptized as a Protestant as a young boy, and for the others, religion was not described as central to family life. Beller argues that the cultural elites' distanced relationship to "a traditional, religious Jewish upbringing" (84) reveals the "consciousness of the problem of being Jewish" (74), which is confirmed in these memoirs.

If the memoir writers identified themselves as Jewish at all before 1938, this was only secondary to their identification with Austria. However, for those who did not view themselves as Jewish before 1938, their perception of themselves as Jews changed retrospectively in light of the brutality that followed the *Anschluss* and the mass murder of the Holocaust. Yet there is no fixed, monolithic Jewish identity to be found in the memoirs. The writers' configurations of their identities are undeniably multifaceted and contingent on the "we"s to which they belonged over time. Not surprisingly, the memoirists' (Austrian) identities are constructed through, among other things, the filter of the individual and collective experiences of exile and return and being an "I" in a real or imagined Jewish "we." The memoirists' identification as part of a Jewish "we" is most obvious in their depictions of the struggles to escape the clutches of National Socialism, the hardships of exile, and the loss of family and friends. However, rather than directly study these most obvious points of rupture, I focus on the memoirists' attempts to reconnect to an Austrian "we" and the challenges inherent in belonging to a real or imagined Jewish "we."

Setting Parameters

In this study, I concentrate on nine memoirs by seven Austrian reémigrés. They are Ernst Lothar's *Das Wunder des Überlebens* (1960; The miracle of survival), Stella Klein-Löw's *Erinnerungen* (1980; Memoirs), Hans J. Thalberg's *Von der Kunst, Österreicher zu sein* (1984; The art of being Austrian), Minna Lachs's *Warum schaust du zurück* (1986; Why look back) and her *Zwischen zwei Welten* (1992; Between two worlds), Franziska Tausig's *Shanghai Passage: Flucht und Exil einer Wienerin* (1987; Passage to Shanghai: A Viennese woman's flight and exile), Hilde Spiel's *Die hellen und die finsteren Zeiten* (1989; Light and dark times) as well as her *Welche Welt ist meine Welt?* (1990; Which world is my world?), and Elisabeth Freundlich's *Die fahrenden Jahre* (1992; *The Traveling Years*, 1999).

The memoirists experienced the *Anschluss* as life-threatening and were all adults at the time they left Austria. Lothar, Klein-Löw, Lachs, Freundlich, and Spiel had completed advanced degrees at the University of Vienna and were pursuing careers. Lothar was working as the director of the Theater in der Josefstadt, Klein-Löw and Lachs were both teaching, and Freundlich was working in theater and film. Spiel, having fled fascist Austria, was trying to establish herself as a writer in England. (Although she left Austria in 1936 to emigrate to England, her memoirs are nonetheless included in this study. The events of 1938, forced exile, and the Holocaust shaped her attempt to reconnect to an Austrian "we" in ways similar to the other memoir writers and her memoirs can justifiably be included in this study.[6]) Thalberg had completed his *Matura* (high school exit and college entrance exams), had begun study at the

Hochschule für Welthandel (College for International Business), and was working in a textile firm. Tausig's husband was firmly established in her father's firm and Tausig was a full-time housewife and mother.

After the *Anschluss* in March 1938, it was abundantly clear that Austria had become a death trap for Jewish Austrians. Lothar and Freundlich left the country within days. Thalberg and Lachs both escaped in September 1938. Tausig and Klein-Löw stayed long enough to witness and experience the brutal November Pogrom. Also known as *Kristallnacht,* the "spontaneous" attacks on Jewish synagogues, shops, and citizens were organized by the National Socialists supposedly as a reaction to the assassination of Ernst vom Rath at the German embassy in Paris by the Polish Jew Herschel Grynszpan on November 7, 1938. Those who remained describe panicked scenes and desperate attempts to leave Austria.

Even after the memoirists escaped the immediate borders of the *Ostmark* (the designation for Austria in the Third Reich) and Germany, the danger from Nazi Germany did not disappear. Before Lothar, Freundlich, and Lachs reached the United States, they were faced with harassment and the threat of deportation by immigration officials in Switzerland and France. For those who remained in Europe, their chosen "haven" often became unsafe as Hitler's army advanced. Thalberg first fled to Yugoslavia; when that became unsafe, he smuggled himself into France, and after internment there as an enemy alien and numerous other dangerous adventures, he escaped to Switzerland, where he remained until the end of the war. Both Tausig and Lachs describe the voyages to their countries of exile as harrowing and fraught with danger.

Once they reached apparent safety, the memoir writers all had to struggle at first for simple material survival. Finding employment was not easy, and these highly educated Austrians were initially underemployed in jobs ranging from domestic to factory work. But with the exception of Tausig, who was in Shanghai—one of the most difficult places to survive materially and physically—the memoirists were able to establish themselves with an amazing degree of success.

However, life in exile remained difficult. The memoirists struggled with feelings of alienation and homesickness. Often they did not know the fate of their families. Klein-Löw and Spiel suffered from the German bombings in England. Those who spent part of their exile in France experienced the shrinking of their refuge with the advance of Hitler's troops, and Tausig was subjected to bombings late in the war in Shanghai.

Removed from their Austrian *Heimat* and brought together with Jews of different nationalities in exile, the memoir writers nonetheless did not perceive themselves as any less Austrian than before 1938. Several were involved in activities promoting Austrian culture both within and outside the exile community. Lothar directed Austrian plays for an exile audience and lectured to Americans on Austrian culture, stressing the differences between Austria and Germany. Klein-Löw was active in the Socialist exile group in England. Freundlich worked tirelessly as an editor of the cultural section of the exile newspaper the *Austro-American Tribune,* which was very concerned with drawing a strict demarcation between Austria and Germany. Thalberg, a struggling student in Switzerland, became active in an Austrian student organization and acted as a contact between the Allies and members of an Austrian underground organization. These activities suggest a continued emotional attachment to Austria and a belief in its right to independence.

The memoir writers returned to settle permanently in Austria between 1945 and 1963. When they made the decision, it was to return as Austrians. They were all professionally and personally integrated into Austrian society and became active as teachers, politicians, parents, civil servants, and writers.

I have chosen as primary texts only published memoirs by Jewish Austrian reémigrés who experienced the *Anschluss* as adults and whose memoirs span their lives from early childhood to return and beyond.[7] By narrowing the focus of my study in this way, I can better explore the influence of social context on the expression of trauma and mourning and examine how these traumatic experiences were integrated into the writers' entire lives. As published expressions of loss and recovery, the stories are told from within a society that has honored its own trauma at the expense of the persecuted. In looking at the memoirists' attempts to integrate the traumatic events of exile and return into their life stories, I uncover tensions between the writers' ethnic and national identities in configuring their very personal experiences. The writers' rhetorical stances and narrative strategies, the tropes of trauma and mourning, and the use of the past to root themselves in an Austrian story highlight the difficulty of reconnecting to an Austrian "we."

I purposely do not include memoirs by Jewish Austrian reémigrés who experienced the concentration camps. The horrors of the camps tend to overshadow all other experiences and shape the retrospective view of the life stories of those who experienced them in radically different ways from those who experienced "only" exile. For example, the memoirs of those Austrians who were incarcerated in concentration camps rarely deal with life in Austria before or after National Socialism. Moreover, as Barbara Foley has noted of concentration camp memoirs in general, "a sense of distinct individuality is signally lacking in most of these narratives" because of the burden of testifying and the rapid progression toward death experienced in the camps (1982, 337–38). In contrast, the memoirs discussed here convey a sense of the writers' distinct individuality, while at the same time relating the fates of others.

The authors of the works I examine represent a limited cross section of returning Jewish Austrians. Yet their memoirs reflect collective memories of the many people persecuted under National Socialism and can help describe the place of Jewish Austrians in Austrian history. These life stories are not only stories of exile and its long-lasting effects but an important part of the Austrian story as a whole. Taken together, the memoirists' lives offer a composite picture of the traumas of exile and return. The memoirs can be seen as enactments of mourning with the potential for reshaping Austrian collective memory.

Introducing the Memoirists and the Memoirs

In his memoir *Das Wunder des Überlebens,* spanning almost seven decades, Ernst Lothar (1890–1974) conveys his deep love for Austria and for the theater—indeed, the professional writer devoted his life to the promotion of Austrian literature and culture, particularly theater. Born Ernst Lothar Müller, the writer spent his early years in Brünn (now in the Czech Republic), where his father was a successful lawyer. He later moved to Vienna to attend school. There he completed his studies and married in 1914 shortly before the outbreak of World War I. After two years of service with the Sixth Imperial and Royal Dragoon Regiment, he worked as a lawyer for the state.

His break into the world of theater came after freelancing as a theater critic. At the time he escaped Austria in March 1938, he was the director of the Theater in der Josefstadt. Lothar, his daughter from his first marriage, and his non-Jewish wife, actress Adrienne Gessner, found safe refuge in the United States. There he became involved in a number of activities promoting Austrian culture. He directed plays by Austrian playwrights and lectured on Austria and Austrian literature. He continued to write and was relatively successful, publishing in the United States with Doubleday. In addition to writing, he taught at a college in Colorado before and during the war.

Lothar was able to return to Austria soon after the war. In 1946 he was assigned to Vienna to work as theater and music officer for the United States State Department. He worked in cultural denazification and handled the cases of conductor Herbert von Karajan and actress Paula Wessely. A naturalized U.S. citizen, Lothar struggled with his

Ernst Lothar (courtesy of
Paul Zsolnay Verlag)

loyalty to the country that provided him refuge and his devotion to his
Heimat. After much deliberation, he applied for and received Austrian
citizenship. After he resettled permanently in Austria in the late forties,
he dedicated himself to a stage revival of the works of nineteenth-century
playwright Franz Grillparzer (1791–1872) and was also active in the
Salzburger Festspiele.

   In his literature, Lothar wrestled with the effects of National
Socialism, Austrian identity, and exile. His novel *The Angel with the
Trumpet* (1944), written in exile and first published in England, was
made famous in Austria in 1948 through the film version with celebrated
Austrian actress Paula Wessely. It chronicles the ups and downs of a piano
maker's family from the late nineteenth century to "occupied" Austria in
the forties and music appears as the embodiment of the Austrian soul.
In his later works, *Heldenplatz* (1945; *The Prisoner,* 1945) and *Die
Rückkehr* (1949; *Return to Vienna,* 1949), Lothar portrays a soldier
and an exile who come to realize the power of their love for Austria.

Stella Klein-Löw's *Erinnerungen,* which appeared in 1980 after its author's long and illustrious career as a teacher and politician, displays an underlying teleological movement toward Klein-Löw's involvement in the Socialist Party. Born in Przemysl in Galicia, one of the easternmost parts of the monarchy, Klein-Löw (1904–1986) writes of her awareness of inequalities at a very young age. As a teenager, she became active in Socialist Party politics, taking an independent political course from her father. Her activities in the Socialist Party allowed her a unique perspective on the riots and the burning of the Palace of Justice in July 1927, the short civil war between government forces and the Socialists in 1934, and aspects of the Socialist resistance after the Socialist Party was outlawed in 1934.

Klein-Löw received her Ph.D. and teaching certification from the University of Vienna. She studied a wide variety of subjects, including psychology with the renowned husband and wife team Karl and Charlotte Bühler. She was hired as a teacher at the Chajes High School, a private Jewish school with state accreditation. She worked there for five and a half years. After fleeing to England in January 1939, she worked first as a domestic and later with disturbed youth. While in England, she was also involved in Labour Party activities. In the forties she returned to Austria, where she resumed both teaching and political involvement. She served as a representative of the Socialist Party in the National Assembly of Parliament from 1959 to 1970.

Hans J. Thalberg's work as a diplomat and his contact with Bruno Kreisky are the major focuses of his memoirs *Von der Kunst, Österreicher zu sein,* and as such the memoirs may appear to have limited appeal. However, the first section is a moving family history. Here, Thalberg (1916–) portrays his family as exemplars of Austrian patriotism and their attachment to Austria as typical of Jewish Austrians. Born in Vienna to a family devoted to the emperor and Austria, the author was the only member of his immediate family who escaped the Nazis. Thalberg first traveled to Yugoslavia, leaving his parents and sister, whom he never saw again. His sister, Marietta, was never seen again by her family after she said good-bye to Thalberg at the train station. She was most likely arrested and deported. His parents were interned in Theresienstadt where his father died. His mother most likely perished at Auschwitz. After Yugoslavia became unsafe, his travels took him to France and then to Switzerland, where he spent the remainder of his years in exile.

While in Switzerland, Thalberg studied macroeconomics and law and made contact with an Austrian underground group. There he also met and married his non-Jewish Austrian wife. Upon his return to Austria in the late forties, Thalberg was recruited into the diplomatic

Stella Klein-Löw with Bruno Kreisky (photograph by Robert Hutterer; courtesy of Verein für Geschichte der Arbeiterbewegung, Wien-Foto- und Bildarchiv der Arbeiter-Zeitung)

service. His diplomatic career took him to the United States, the German Democratic Republic, Mexico, and China. Although he never joined a political party, he was most closely aligned with the Socialist Party.

As an educator, Minna Lachs (1907–1993) viewed her memoirs *Warum schaust du zurück* and *Zwischen zwei Welten* as windows into a distant past that could potentially serve to inform young people. More than any of the other memoirists, Lachs combines aspects of classical autobiography with those of the traditional memoir. In *Warum schaust du zurück*, the author reflects on her personal development, constantly asking what shaped her. Once she reaches adulthood, she focuses almost exclusively on external events. Like Klein-Löw, Lachs was born in Galicia. However, whereas her Galician roots are elided from Klein-Löw's memoirs, in Lachs's text this origin plays a major role in her construction of self. Lachs moved with her family to Vienna to escape the advancing Russians in World War I. As a refugee and

Hans J. Thalberg (courtesy
of Alisa Douer)

eastern European Jew, Lachs was exposed to anti-Semitic prejudice at
an early age. However, until Lachs received religious instruction in
school, she knew little about Judaism. Her father had distanced himself
from his religious background in an effort to emancipate himself from
his own father and what he saw as the oppressive backward ways of
Orthodox Judaism. In contrast, Lachs found solace in religious and
political activities and became very involved in a Socialist Zionist youth
organization.

Like Klein-Löw, Lachs received her Ph.D. and teaching certification from the University of Vienna. And like Klein-Löw, she took
psychology courses with the Bühlers, integrating her interest in psychology with her interest in literature. Before she and her husband fled
Austria in September 1938 with their two-month-old baby, she taught
at a private *Maturaschule* (school leading to college). Their exile took
them first to Switzerland, then to southern France and Spain. American
Muriel Buttinger intervened with President Roosevelt to obtain visas
for Lachs and her family. From Spain, the Lachs family traveled to the

Minna Lachs (courtesy of
Alisa Douer)

United States in 1941 on what the author called a floating concentration
camp. During her years of exile in the United States, Lachs taught in
private schools and summer camps. After her return to Austria in 1947,
she resumed her work as a teacher and later served as a school principal.
In addition, she was very active in UNESCO.

With her memoirs *Shanghai Passage*, Franziska Tausig (1895–
1989) proves herself a talented raconteur. Her focal point of identification remains her family throughout. Born in Temesvar (now in Romania,
then in Hungary) at the childhood home of her mother, Tausig provides
a lively account of her birth and important childhood memories—which
she views as possessions the Nazis could not steal. Married to an officer
at the age of nineteen on the eve of World War I, Tausig relates how
the First World War and the demise of the Austro-Hungarian monarchy
were the first major disruptions in her life. However, she convincingly
shows that the upheaval and displacement of the First World War paled
in comparison with her personal loss after the *Anschluss*.

23

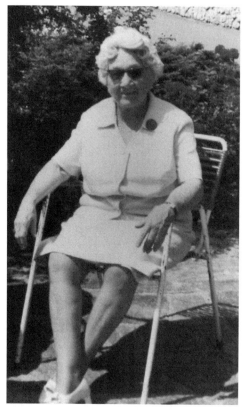

Franziska Tausig (courtesy of
Otto Tausig)

   From a well-to-do family that lost its fortune as a result of the
Anschluss, Tausig began working as a domestic to support the family.
To ensure her teenage son's safety, she and her husband sent him to
England in 1938 on a *Kindertransport,* an initiative that she reports was
organized by the Quakers to save Jewish children. After the November
Pogrom of 1938, she and her husband fled to Shanghai, one of the
few places of refuge that did not require a visa. Her life in Shanghai
was characterized by extreme material and emotional hardship. Her
husband, twice displaced by historical turmoil in the twentieth century,
suffered from depression and died in Shanghai. When her son Otto
Tausig opted to return to Austria, she joined him. She ends her narrative with the reunion with her son in 1947 after an almost ten-year
separation. Because she derived her sense of self and her identification

with Austria through familial relations, she will offer a point of contrast. Tausig connects herself to Austrian culture and history through her father, a successful businessman, her husband, an officer in the Royal and Imperial Army, and her son Otto, whom she describes as quintessentially Viennese.

In her memoirs, writer Hilde Spiel (1911–1990) chronicles her life from early childhood to the late eighties. She highlights historical events and her encounters with some of the most important thinkers of her time, who shaped her life and literary work. Although she was raised a Catholic, she reveals herself as very much a product of the "Jewish Vienna" Beller describes in his book on Jews in Vienna. Beller studies the contributions Jewish Austrians made to modern high culture in Vienna, from emancipation to the *Anschluss* and illustrates the impact of "one of the most important historical events in modern European history," that is, "the integration of the Jews into their host societies" (1989, 12). From her attendance of Eugenia Schwarzwald's progressive school for girls, to the study of psychology with the Bühlers, to her preoccupation with the Vienna school of philosophy, to her flirtation with Socialism, to her interest in Austrian literature, Hilde Spiel was shaped by and part of this "Jewish Vienna."

In 1936 she completed her dissertation, married Peter de Mendelssohn, a young German writer, and emigrated to England to escape the oppressive Austro-Fascist regime. Before she left Austria, she had published and received recognition as a young talent; however, she could hardly have been called an established writer at the time. Once in England, Spiel steeped herself in English literature in her effort to make the transition professionally from German to English. However, it was not until the *Anschluss* that she consciously switched to English in her personal life. After she began writing in English, she concentrated on journalism, a field more lucrative than creative writing and easier to break into as a nonnative speaker of English. She returned to Austria often after 1945 before she settled there permanently in 1963. She was particularly active in Austria's literary scene and is remembered as a critic, essayist, and prose writer.

Like Lothar's, Spiel's experiences of exile and return shaped her literature. Fiction dealing with these topics include her novel *The Darkened Room* (1961), (published in German as *Lisas Zimmer* [1965]), which focused on the long-lasting effects of exile and displacement, and her play *Anna und Anna* (1989), in which the female protagonist splits into two Annas: one flees to England after the *Anschluss,* the other remains in Austria and must struggle with questions of conscience. Her experiences spawned an interest in Jewish contributions to Austrian

Hilde Spiel (courtesy of
Isolde Ohlbaum)

culture, which she wrote about in her histories of Jewish acculturation, *Fanny von Arnstein* (1962) and *Vienna's Golden Autumn, 1866–1938* (1987). Of particular interest for this study is her literary diary of her first return trip to Vienna in 1945, *Rückkehr nach Wien* (1968; Return to Vienna). Written retrospectively in the form of a diary, both the original unpublished English version and the reworked German version expand on insights offered in her memoirs. After being diagnosed with cancer, Spiel raced with death to finish the second volume of memoirs.

In her memoirs, *Die fahrenden Jahre,* Elisabeth Freundlich (1906–2001) traces her development from a sheltered child to a politically conscious person. She draws the reader in with stories of her childhood and anecdotes that portray herself as a lovable imp. She views herself as apolitical until the events of 1934. During the short civil war in February, her father, a lawyer and president of the Workers' Bank, was arrested by the Austro-Fascists. After this, she looked outside Austria for political outlets and became involved in the international peace movement.

Freundlich, who studied German, Romance languages, and theater at the University of Vienna, completed her Ph.D. in 1931. After graduating, she worked at a variety of odd jobs in theater and film until 1934, including a brief stint with filmmaker G. W. Papst. Acutely aware of the danger her parents were in, she convinced them to leave Vienna with her on March 11, 1938, for a brief vacation in Paris. In France, they were awarded visas for the United States through the help of Joseph Buttinger, Austrian husband of American Muriel Buttinger. While in France, Freundlich became involved in a variety of left-wing political activities, including work with Austrian Communists active in the resistance. To support herself in the United States, she studied library science, after which she worked at the New York Metropolitan Museum; she later taught at Princeton University.

After returning to Austria in 1950 with her husband, philosopher Günther Anders, she translated the work of the Irish playwright Sean O'Casey (1880–1964) and was active as a cultural reporter for *Mannheimer Morgen*. Her literary oeuvre includes short stories and two novels. Her most significant work, *Der Seelenvogel* (Soulbird), a novel written in exile but not published until 1986, is an autobiographical family history of her maternal grandparents and mother that provides insight into two generations of a Viennese Jewish family.

Even such a cursory examination of the memoirists' lives reveals a striking number of similarities. Indeed, many of them had contact with the same people, and their paths must have crossed. Particularly in light of the small number of returnees, it seems likely that some of them knew or knew of each other. Nonetheless, the memoirists do not appear in each other's memoirs. Although they became part of a Jewish "we," they did not write about the state of the Jewish community upon return. They viewed themselves as Austrians, returning either as individuals or as members of a political community—regardless of whether this is how they were received or not.

The Memoirs in the Context of Postwar Austria

The publication of seven out of the nine memoirs examined in this study coincided with the rise of critical interest, starting in the late seventies, in the role of Austrians during the National Socialist period. Those who had been persecuted set out in substantial numbers to

Elisabeth Freundlich
(courtesy of Alisa Douer)

reflect on the issue,[8] while creative artists and intellectuals from younger generations also saw the value in exploring this past.[9]

Until the late seventies and early eighties, there were relatively few publications by Austrians directed toward a German-speaking audience on Austria's National Socialist past.[10] Indeed, works that dealt with the National Socialist period (1938–1945)—fictional or nonfictional— were slow to appear in Austria and very poorly received when they did. Numerous personal narratives published in Austria by Austrians who had been interned in concentration camps or prisons immediately after the war were read by so few people that their impact was negligible.[11] Written to inform and act as a bridge between former inmates of concentration camps and prisons and the general public, the personal narratives were soon forgotten. A survey conducted in 1947 revealed that only 14 percent of the entire population read books published after 1945; of that group, only 11 percent read political literature or books about concentration camps (quoted in McVeigh 1988, 105).

28

Unchallenged anti-Semitism surely deterred some from sharing their stories of exile. In the immediate postwar years, government officials denied anti-Semitic sentiment on the part of the government and the population while continuing to make or tolerate anti-Semitic remarks (Knight 1988; Wodak et al. 1990). Despite the virtual elimination of the Jewish population, a series of polls taken after the defeat of National Socialism point to continued anti-Semitism in Austria (Pauley 1996, 493–95).[12] This has become less intense over the years, but in the first two decades after the war, few anti-Semitic incidents drew widespread public attention or protest. On the surface, this might indicate the disappearance of anti-Semitism, but I counter that it suggests either that there was little protest of open anti-Semitism, or that there were few openly anti-Semitic incidents.[13]

During the early seventies, those who had been uneasy with the way in which Austria had dealt with its Nazi past may have believed that Austria would finally free itself from its legacy. A hopeful outward sign seemed to be the success of Chancellor Bruno Kreisky (1970–1983)—a Jew who had been active in the Socialist underground before he escaped to Sweden. He won the election in 1970 despite the anti-Semitic slant of the campaign of his opponent Josef Klaus from the conservative People's Party. One of Klaus's campaign slogans claimed that a vote for him was a vote for "[a] true Austrian" ("Einen echten . . . Österreicher"), intimating that Kreisky, as a Jew and a former exile, was not a true Austrian (Pauley 1992, 313).[14]

Events of the seventies and eighties made people acutely aware that many Austrians continued to misrepresent the past and to deny responsibility for the injustices suffered by Jews, political and religious opponents, and sexual and ethnic minorities. Kreisky's appointment of four former Nazi Party members to his cabinet in 1975, including a former member of the Waffen-SS whose unit had been involved in civilian murders and his subsequent ad hominem attacks on Simon Wiesenthal during the controversy that followed, made it clear that Austria had not yet begun to deal honestly with the past. The reception of convicted war criminal Walter Reder by the minister of defense, Friedhelm Frischenschlager, on the occasion of Reder's return to Austria after being released from an Italian prison (1985) and the Waldheim affair (1986) were further reminders that many in Austria had not distanced themselves from the Nazi past.[15]

By the same token, the scandal surrounding Waldheim, often seen as a watershed, made it clear that the Austrian public was not of one mind with regard to Waldheim's stance toward his wartime military service (Pauley 1996, 500–501). Austrian intellectuals came out in numbers and vocally protested Waldheim's election and his campaign. Scholars and writers reacted with works of fiction and nonfiction that asked questions about Austrian complicity. Moreover, the fortieth and fiftieth anniversaries of the end of World War II and the fiftieth anniversary of the *Anschluss* and the November Pogrom offered the country the opportunity to present pertinent lectures, exhibitions, and publications.[16]

Nonetheless, events in the nineties served as reminders of the continuation and resurfacing of anti-Semitism and xenophobia in Austria. The popularity of Jörg Haider and the direction the Freedom Party has taken under his leadership reflect an intolerance among segments of the Austrian population. In the early nineties, his party garnered support with slogans such as "Vienna must not turn into Chicago" ("Wien darf nicht Chicago werden") and "Vienna must remain the *Heimat* of the Viennese" ("Wien muss Heimat der Wiener bleiben"). In the first slogan, the Freedom Party plays on the image of Chicago as both the city of gangsters and home to the largest population of Poles outside Poland. In the second, the party picks up on the intense and often xenophobic feelings sometimes associated with the untranslatable word *Heimat*.

In June 1991, when Jörg Haider suggested that the employment policies of the Third Reich could be used as a positive model, his reactionary voice did not go unchallenged. This time it was a government official who played a decisive role in taking him to task. The Socialist chancellor Franz Vranitzky was swift to rebuke Haider. He "responded with the strongest denunciation yet of Nazi Germany and the role played by many Austrians during the Holocaust" in a speech he gave in the Austrian Parliament in July 1991 (Pauley 1996, 505). Vranitzky gave a similar but more detailed speech in 1993 at Hebrew University; this speech was followed in November 1994 by the first visit of an Austrian president (Klestil) to Israel (Pauley 1996, 505).

The brutal murder of four Romanies in February 1995 and the ensuing discussion are sad reminders of continued support of the radical Right. Moreover, the most recent political gains of the Freedom Party in October 1999 (it became the second strongest party in Austria), the racist rhetoric of its election campaign (campaign posters warned of "overforeignization" [*Überfremdung*]), and its inclusion in the newly formed coalition government in February 2000 have been cause for concern and evidence that the past continues to be contested territory. However, unlike the postwar anti-Semitic rhetoric, the Freedom Party's racism has not gone unchallenged.

The effect of familial and professional obligations, combined with cultural and psychological factors, contributed to the long silence in Austria. Faced with reestablishing themselves and involved in professional activities, potential autobiographers and memoir writers may not have found time to devote to writing. And, as is clear from the statistical data, the Jewish exiles did not find a public ready or willing to listen to their stories.[17] Moreover, both writers and audience may have needed time to gain an emotional distance from the past.

Because the presence of the reémigrés was perceived as a threat to Austrian claims of victimhood, the reémigrés and their stories of exile were not particularly welcome (Knight 1992). Indeed, they found themselves and their experiences marginalized or denied in both public and private discourse, in which non-Jewish, nonexile Austrians overwhelmingly assigned themselves the role of victims of Hitlerian aggression and Allied bombings. The narratives of victimhood, or "mainstream victim narratives," as I term them, allowed little room for the reémigrés' stories.[18] The emplotment of Austrian "victimhood," a "psychological strategy for coming to terms with individual association with the disastrous enterprise of the Third Reich" by the general population and a means "of integrating potential disgruntled elements" into the state by the government resulted in the evasion of questions of moral responsibility across the board (Knight 1992, 225).

Neither the retrospective nature of the autobiographical memoir nor the Austrian situation alone can account for almost three decades of unbroken silence on the National Socialist years and Austrian complicity. For many, the emotional impact of persecution, the losses they suffered, and the brutality they experienced and witnessed led to the suppression of memories and the subsequent unwillingness or inability to share their experiences for so long after the war.[19] The silence extended even to Jewish communities in Austria, where one would have expected a more receptive audience. Austrian filmmaker and cultural critic Ruth Beckermann comments on the nature of the silence surrounding the history of European Jews:

> The discussion concerning the destruction of Jews occurred at that time [the fifties] in a very abstract and embarrassed manner. Everyone knew something, everyone had noticed something strange about their relatives, but no one knew a coherent family history. Everything having to do with the time of persecution was bound up with great fear and shame. It was a wound no one wanted to touch, one that had to be covered and hidden. (*Unzugehörig* 120)[20]

The enormity of events silenced survivors. In the case of the former exiles, they may have also suffered from the feeling that "nothing exceptional" had happened to them in comparison to the pain and suffering of those in the concentration camps. They had to gain the sense that their stories were worth telling.[21]

In the eighties and nineties, the confluence of several key factors led to the increased publication of autobiographical literature by those persecuted by the National Socialists. Disturbed by the persistent refusal of the general population as well as high government officials to take an honest look at the past, a growing potential audience skeptical of Austrian claims to victimhood began to seek information on these years. Concomitantly, those who had been persecuted and had remained silent saw this history, which existed only in their memories, as endangered. If they had previously been reluctant to talk about this period, they were now motivated to write autobiographical accounts or to release unpublished personal narratives by the realization that the memory of their experiences was in danger of dying with them.

In many cases, the titles alone of the memoirs draw a direct connection between the texts and Austria's National Socialist history. Ernst Lothar's *Das Wunder des Überlebens* (The miracle of survival) was the earliest of the exile memoirs, published for the first time in 1960 and reprinted in 1961 and 1965 before the awakening of a more critical consciousness; its title suggests the precariousness of his situation after 1938 and the subsequent trauma of exile. Minna Lachs's *Warum schaust du zurück* (1986; Why look back) and Hilde Spiel's *Die hellen und die finsteren Zeiten* (1989; Light and dark times) both indicate that this painful Austrian history is an important part of their memoirs. It becomes immediately clear upon reading these texts that Austria's suppressed past has cast a shadow over their lives. The titles of Lachs's *Zwischen zwei Welten* (1992; Between two worlds) and Spiel's *Welche Welt ist meine Welt?* (1990; Which world is my world?) conjure up feelings of personal and cultural displacement not uncommon among exiles and émigrés. Franziska Tausig's *Shanghai Passage: Flucht und Exil einer Wienerin* (1987; Passage to Shanghai: A Viennese woman's flight and exile) clearly signals the centrality of her time in exile to her narrative. Elisabeth Freundlich's choice of title, *Die fahrenden Jahre* (1992; *The Traveling Years*, 1999), also suggests her desire to highlight the years of exile. Indeed, the title of her memoirs, taken from a poem by her husband Günther Anders, suggests that her exile was more formative than her childhood.

The tone and content of each volume were influenced by multiple factors, including the memoir writers' professions, their gender, their experiences of the *Anschluss*, exile, and return, as well as by their target audience and the societal attitudes current at the time they wrote. Consequently, not all of the texts discussed in this study can be seen as being exclusively directed at this lacuna in Austrian history. This, too, is reflected in the titles. For example, Stella Klein-Löw's choice of title, *Erinnerungen* (1980; Memoirs), offers little insight into the tone and content of her work. It is clear in reading her memoirs that she interprets her life in terms of her development as a Socialist. Nonetheless, Austrian anti-Semitism and her years in exile play a significant role in her interpretation of the past. Similarly, the title of Hans J. Thalberg's memoir, *Von der Kunst, Österreicher zu sein* (1984; The art of being Austrian), offers no clear clues about the emphasis of his book. The memoirs are primarily aimed at an audience interested in Thalberg's work as a diplomat and his relationship to Bruno Kreisky. However, the story of his family and youth as well as the impact of the *Anschluss* and the loss of his family as a result of the Holocaust profoundly shape his life story.

The overt engagement of others in bringing the threatened histories to the foreground underscores the cooperative aspect and cross-generational involvement in four of the memoirs. Klein-Löw mentions Ermar Junker, whose encouragement spurred her on and who had the manuscript typed. Writer Julian Schutting introduces the second volume of Lachs's memoirs and describes Lachs as a representative of an enlightenment spirit. He situates her book next to Holocaust narratives and claims that Lachs's story may not have been as harrowing but is nonetheless a valuable contribution to an understanding of the past. For Tausig's memoirs, Helmut Oplethal includes a short historical overview of exile in Shanghai to provide the reader with the necessary context. Elisabeth Freundlich's *Die fahrenden Jahre* is perhaps the best example of a cooperative and cross-generational effort. The author maintains that it would have never occurred to her to write her memoirs if a friend had not encouraged her (1992, 7). In addition, the editor Susanne Alge introduced and wrote an afterword for the volume, situating Freundlich and her work within the silencing of the "other" in postwar Austria and providing readers with a tabular overview of her life and works. She also highlights Freundlich's work as a journalist with the inclusion of samples of her articles.

Attitudes have certainly changed in the span of over thirty years during which these memoirs were published. When Ernst Lothar's memoir *Das Wunder des Überlebens* was published in the early sixties, Austrian society was still steeped in self-pity, and the topics of exile and Jewish persecution were taboo. In the eighties a nascent interest in these stories was evident. By the time Elisabeth Freundlich's *Die fahrenden Jahre* and Minna Lachs's *Zwischen zwei Welten* were published in 1992, an audience open to hearing the stories of persecution and understanding them as Austrian stories had emerged. If most Austrians were at best uninterested and at worst hostile toward the stories of Jewish réemigrés in the sixties, by the nineties there was a growing audience.

With *Reclaiming Heimat* I hope to contribute to the general discussion on memory and remembering, and more specifically to remembering the National Socialist past and its relationship to national identity in Austria.[22] I read the memoirs as textual manifestations of the traumas of exile and return and the process of mourning the loss of *Heimat* on rhetorical, metaphorical, and thematic levels. In order to construct a useful framework for exploring connections among emotional processes, social context, and the expression of such processes through language, I synthesize recent work on trauma and mourning, identity construction, individual and collective memory, and autobiography. By examining the memoir writers' attempts to reconnect to an Austrian "we," to reconstitute a traumatized self, and to mourn the loss of self precipitated by exile and return, the emotional depth and complexity of these works are revealed.

✎ I ✐

"How Much *Heimat* Does a Person Need?"

In his autobiographical essay "How Much Home Does a Person Need?"[1] (1966), Jean Améry claims that the one lesson he learned from exile was the impossibility of return. "Anyone who is familiar with exile has gained many an insight into life but has discovered that it holds even more questions. Among the answers there is the realization, which at first seems trivial, that there is no return, because the re-entrance into a place is never also a recovery of the lost time" (1980, 42).[2] Born Hanns Maier in Austria in 1912, Améry grew up celebrating Christmas although his parents were Jewish. He felt at home wearing traditional Austrian garb, a practice outlawed for Austrian Jews after the *Anschluss*.[3] Améry's sense of self was inextricably bound with his identification with Austria. He greatly admired Austrian writers and he saw himself as part of Austria's cultural and historical landscape. His German name and regional dialect were essential parts of his identity. Although his family never hid the fact that they were Jewish, Améry maintains that it meant little to him. He felt a connection neither to Judaism nor to a Jewish cultural heritage. His main source of group identity, of being an "I" within a "we," was his identification with Austria. This sense of belonging was shattered with the *Anschluss* and lost forever as a result of his experiences of exile, torture, and Auschwitz.[4]

After his liberation from Auschwitz, Améry returned to Belgium, where he had previously lived, and worked in a resistance group while in exile. There he set out to construct a new identity and a non-Austrian self, romanizing his first name to Jean and anagrammatizing his last name to Améry. His name change was much more than simply an adaptation to his adopted Belgium home—it was an expression of his irreparable alienation from his Austrian self, while it nonetheless acknowledged a connection to this earlier self. Although Améry was offered a job in Austria and visited the country on numerous occasions between his first return visit to Vienna in June 1946 and his suicide in October 1978 in Salzburg, the traumatic, irrevokable nature of the loss of *Heimat* made it impossible for him to resettle in Austria.

It may seem odd, then, in a volume on memoirs by Jewish Austrian reémigrés, to begin with a writer who chose not to return permanently and who ultimately committed suicide. However, Améry's sociopsychological understanding of *Heimat* will help frame the discussion of the textual manifestations and representations of trauma and mourning in the memoirs. Améry's concept of *Heimat* is shared implicitly if not explicitly by the memoirists, and it is *Heimat* in Améry's sense of the word that they strive to reclaim.

Loss of *Heimat* and Exile as Potentially Traumatic

During the Third Reich, the term *Heimat*, which can be only inadequately translated as "home" or "homeland," had been perniciously misused for political purposes. For the National Socialists, *Heimat* "was a synonym for race (blood) and territory (soil), a deadly combination that led to the exile or annihilation of anyone who did not 'belong' " (Kaes 1989, 165–66).[5] Améry provocatively reappropriates the highly charged, ideologically laden word, defining it ultimately in sociopsychological terms from his position of profound loss.[6] In the most basic sense, according to Améry, *Heimat* is security:

> Home is security, I say. At home we are in full command of the dialectics of knowledge and recognition, of trust and confidence. Since we know them, we recognize them and we trust ourselves to speak and to act— for we may have justified confidence in our knowledge and recognition. The entire field of the related words loyal, familiar, confidence, to trust, to entrust, trusting belongs in the broader psychological area of feeling secure. (1980, 47)[7]

The security of home is derived from the bonds to community implied by the field of etymologically related words, linked by the roots true (*treu*) and trust (*trauen*). This security is lost when one is expelled from the community. Repercussions for individuals can be particularly severe if their sense of self is bound up with the community that has excluded them.

For Améry, possession of *Heimat* is inseparable from his concept of selfhood. Consequently, he experienced himself in exile as diminished. No longer a part of an Austrian "we," Améry found that saying "I" was just an empty phrase. "I was a person who could no longer say 'we' and who therefore said 'I' merely out of habit, but not with the feeling of full possession of my self" (44).[8] Understandably, this membership in the "we," and consequently the validity of the "I," are predicated on one's acceptance into the community by others. Améry relates the story of the Jewish German poet Alfred Mombert, who ceased to be a German writer, Améry contends, because the larger German community considered him neither German nor a writer. "In order to be one or the other we need the consent of society. But if society repudiates that we ever were that, then we have also never been it" (60).[9] Because of state-sanctioned anti-Semitism, Améry felt as if he had never been a part of the society with which he had so much identified and he could not fool himself into believing that he was still part of an Austrian community.

In Améry's discussion, full possession of *Heimat* is contingent upon a series of interrelated connections between an individual and a collective; such connections are realized linguistically, spatially, and temporally. Reflecting on the experience of German-speaking exiles, Améry claims: "We were shut out from German reality and therefore also from the German language" (52).[10] Because Améry conceives of language as an integral part of the social web constituting *Heimat,* his expulsion from the Austrian "we" and the racist policies estranged him from the German language and himself. When a soldier from the German army came to his door in Belgium and spoke Améry's regional dialect, Améry found himself in a paradoxical and terrifying situation. On the one hand, he felt an emotional connection to this person from his *Heimat,* but, on the other, he realized that revealing this "kinship" could be fatal for him. It was yet another reminder that he was no longer a part of a larger Austrian "we." However, Améry's alienation from the German language and consequently himself was more gravely affected by the exclusion of his experiences in the general usage of the German language. Reading the *Brüsseler Zeitung,* the newspaper of the German occupation, Améry was reminded of his expulsion and its dire consequences for him:

Daily, in spite of extreme aversion, I read the "Brüsseler Zeitung," the organ of the German occupying power in the West. It did not ruin my language, but it also did not help it along. For I was excluded from the fate of the German community and thus from its language. . . . The meaning of every German word changed for us, and finally, whether we resisted or not, our mother tongue became just as inimical as the one they spoke around us. (53)[11]

Jewish Germans and Austrians had not only been transformed into a disease attacking the German body by the anti-Semitic rhetoric of the National Socialists, but their reality was denied by the absence of its objectification through language.[12] Realizing the full implication of the dynamic between language and the collective, Améry recognized that he and fellow Jewish Germans and Austrians no longer existed in language as part of a "we" and had thus lost ownership of part of their reality (53–54).

In addition to severing linguistic connections to *Heimat,* exile disrupted spatial ties or spatial identity, according to Améry. If individuals are securely rooted in *Heimat,* they have the ability to "read" their surroundings—they have developed a type of spatial semiotic competency. This ability Améry describes is unconsciously acquired and as much a part of a person as one's mother tongue. "Just as one learns one's mother tongue without knowing its grammar, one experiences one's native surroundings. Mother tongue and native world grow with us, grow into us, and thus become the familiarity that guarantees us security" (48).[13] The full impact of this competency on the integrity of the individual can only be understood from the position of loss. In Belgium, lifted from his usual surroundings, Améry finds himself unable to "read" his environment. "Faces, gestures, clothes, houses, words (even if I halfway understood them) were sensory reality, but not interpretable signs. . . . I staggered through a world whose signs remained as inscrutable to me as Etruscan script" (47).[14] Améry concedes that with time one can acquire the semiotic competency just as one acquires a second language; however, the relationship to that language, culture, and space can never have the same intimacy.[15]

Améry's sense of self was further diminished by what he viewed as the loss of his past. Reflecting on his sense of self in exile, Améry lamented: "I was no longer an I and did not live within a We. I had no passport, and no past, and no money, and no history" (44).[16] He generalizes this loss to Jewish Germans and Austrians and then compares it to the loss of *Heimat* by ethnic German refugees fleeing Eastern Europe after 1945. Because he understands *Heimat* in broader terms than simply loss of place, Améry argues that exile for Germans and Austrians defined as "Jewish" by the Nuremberg Laws was consequently much more personally devastating than expulsion from their *Heimat* for ethnic Germans. As a Jewish exile, he was not only robbed of the right to live in his country but was forced to view his relationship to the land and his fellow (but non-Jewish) Austrians as an illusion. "We, however, had not lost our country, but had to realize that it had never been ours. For us, whatever was linked with this land and its people was an existential misunderstanding" (50).[17] The "existential misunderstanding" meant that his past and his memories of the past did not belong to him and were fraudulent. If the refugees from Eastern Europe could gain solace from their memories of their *Heimat,* this was not possible for Améry and others like him.

The loss of *Heimat* or total severing of linguistic, spatial, and temporal connections to an Austrian "we" resulted in what Améry labels *Heimweh* (literally, "home hurt" or "home ache")—homesickness.[18] Elaborating a pathology of exile, Améry very explicitly ties possession of *Heimat* to selfhood. The first time Améry uses *Heimweh* he equates it with "self-alienation," connecting his estrangement to his lost past. "[O]ur homesickness was alienation from the self. Suddenly, the past was buried and one no longer knew who one was" (43).[19] What he thought had been his history was no longer his; the landscape he had seen himself as so much a part of had become an alien planet (42–43, 48). As a result, he tried to forget his memories of Austria's history and its landscape. However, because these were so integral to his self-image, a consequence was a diminished sense of self. Because there was no relief, his *Heimweh* went beyond self-alienation and turned into self-destruction, both brought on by his troubled relationship to his past. "Genuine homesickness was not self-pity, but rather self-destruction. It consisted in dismantling our past piece by piece, which could not be done without self-contempt and hatred for the lost self" (51).[20] Exile then precipitated not only a diminished sense of self, but also a loathing of the fraudulent self. How could you love a part of yourself that was so bound up with the country that had rejected you?

Améry's equation of loss of *Heimat* with *Heimweh* is echoed and developed more fully along psychological lines in the discussion of migration and exile as potential traumatic events by the Argentinean psychoanalysts León and Rebeca Grinberg.[21] In their book, *Psychoanalytic Perspectives on Migration and Exile,* the Grinbergs suggest that the notion of trauma does not apply only to "single, isolated events . . . but also to events which may be prolonged for greater or lesser periods," including migration and exile (1989, 10). They go on to say that "migration as a traumatic experience comes under the heading of what have been called cumulative traumas and tension traumas, in which the subject's reactions are not always expressed or visible, but the effects of such trauma run deep and last long" (12). Logically, exile as a forced migration can have even graver consequences than voluntary migration (156–65).

The Grinbergs's study confirms the validity of the connection Améry draws between *Heimat* and selfhood. They claim that the traumatic experience of exile and migration "threatens the integrity of the personality" (1989, 11) because of the resulting interference in the ways in which "one's sense of identity is developed through one's connections to others" (130). The Grinbergs view identity construction in terms of "continuous interaction among spatial, temporal, and social integration links" that "function simultaneously and interact among themselves" (130, 132). Their spatial, temporal, and social integration links overlap with Améry's concept of multiple connections of an "I" to a "we" through space, time, and language. According to the Grinbergs, "[*s*]*patial integration* refers to the interrelations among parts of the self" and "lends the person cohesion and allows him to compare and contrast objects" (131–32). On the other hand, "[*t*]*emporal integration* connects the different representations of self over time and establishes continuity from one to the next," and "[*s*]*ocial integration* . . . helps create the feeling of 'belonging' " (132). They argue that exile interferes with the healthy interaction of these links and can thus profoundly affect one's sense of self.

What the Grinbergs describe in clinical terms, Améry poignantly illustrates with his discussion of *Heimat* and the impact of its loss on him. For Améry, it was not one single experience that proved traumatic, but a series of events that alienated him from his language, his past, and himself. The *Anschluss*, in legitimizing the exclusion of Jewish Austrians from the larger community, lifted Améry out of the world he had seen himself as so much a part of. The realization that he and his reality were excluded from the German language, the feeling that his memories were fraudulent, and the inability to "read" the world into which he had been thrown led to *Heimweh* or disorientation and self-destruction—logical consequences of exile. The cumulative traumas of exile, compounded by torture and Auschwitz as well as the failure of the Austrian people to rise up against Hitler, made recovery of *Heimat* impossible for Améry. He and his life story had been lifted out of the Austrian story, and his wounds were too deep to make reintegration possible—and too profound to heal. Indeed, time and memory seemed only to exacerbate them:

> Remembering. That is the cue, and our reflections swing back on their own to their main topic: the loss of home by an expellee from the Third Reich. He has aged and, in a time span that now already runs into decades,

has had to learn that it was not a wound that was inflicted upon him, one that will scar over with the ticking of time, but rather that he is suffering from an insidious disease that is growing worse with the years. (57)[22]

For Améry, time brought with it not healing, but the realization that he would never heal. The severing of the bonds with his *Heimat* resulted in an "insidious disease" that ate away at him, underscoring the devastating impact that the cumulative traumas had on Améry's sense of self.

As a rule, the memoir writers, too, fiercely identified with Austria and experienced exile as self-alienation and even self-destruction. However, unlike Améry, the memoirists discussed here chose to return, suggesting that the original cumulative traumas were not as profound or as profoundly felt. Certainly the fact that they did not experience torture or the death camps made return a more viable possibility. Nonetheless, as we will see, becoming a part of a postwar Austrian "we" was potentially a cause for further self-alienation.

The Trauma of Return

Drawn by the cultural and geographical landscape, by political and professional activities, or by familial ties, the memoirists still felt connected in some way to their Austrian *Heimat.* For them return held the possibility of regaining a part of *Heimat* and themselves that would have otherwise remained inaccessible to them. Because of their professional and personal achievements, the memoir writers were able to reestablish themselves in Austria. However, this does not mean that return was not experienced as traumatic or that return afforded them the possibility of totally recovering the lost *Heimat.*

The decision to repatriate was no doubt difficult. The refugees were returning to a place that had once been their home, but had become a death trap for them and their families. Moreover, repatriation was not supported by the majority of the exile community. Using the United States as her main example, historian Helga Embacher describes the discussion revolving around return. She paints a picture of great debate among factions in the exile communities (1995, 116–19). Indeed, many viewed such a move as evidence of a lack of character (118). How could people return to a country that had thrown them out and murdered their friends and relatives?

The exiles who did return were typically "forty years of age, mostly baptized, married to gentiles, and reluctant to learn a new language in a foreign land, or they entertained (naive) hopes of recovering their businesses" (Pauley 1996, 493). The greatest number resettled in Austria between the late forties and the sixties (Embacher 1995, 112–13). The memoirists only partially fit this profile. While most of them were over forty and returned between the late forties and the sixties, none returned to Austria to resume a business. Moreover, most of them had adapted linguistically and at the time they returned to Austria they had jobs commensurate with their professional qualifications. The motivations for their return lie elsewhere.

In his research on three generations of Jewish Austrian returnees, sociologist Christoph Reinprecht writes that motives for return cannot be narrowed down to any one single factor (1992, 46). However, usually one factor predominates in reémigrés' justifications for return. Committed to rebuilding Austria in the image of their party's doctrine, a significant number of returning Jewish exiles were Socialists and Communists (Embacher 1995, 119–23). Their political beliefs provided an Austrian "we" to which they could return.[23] For those Jewish Austrians who returned for political reasons, their political identity represented a personal choice, whereas their Jewish identity was often not only incidental to them, but something from which they distanced themselves. It certainly was of no consequence to them in their political vision for a new Austria.

Reinprecht's study suggests that *Heimweh* in combination with one or more factors motivated many exiles to return (1992, 43–46). For those returning, their emotional attachment to Austria and Austrian culture must have played an important role. If political ideology alone had been their reason, political reémigrés could have remained in their country of exile and become involved in politics there. As Reinprecht discovered: "[h]omesickness had multiple dimensions, above all a sentimental (memories of childhood and youth) and a political-cultural dimension" (44).[24] In her memoirs, Stella Klein-Löw most clearly states that she and other political exiles were returning to Austria as Socialists. However, she hints at an additional emotional and cultural element:

> Why did we want to leave England even though we were aware of the want and cold, hunger and lack of freedom in Austria?
>
> We wanted to live and work as Austrian *Socialists* in Austria, in occupied Austria: personally, professionally, politically. We wanted to adapt the life that had been interrupted by exile to the new circumstances, revive old friendships, deepen existing relationships. The adventure "New Austria— Old *Heimat*" appealed to us and lured us. And we would have also been ashamed to have abandoned Austria, Vienna, Socialism at this juncture to wait for better times. (1980, 165)[25]

In Klein-Löw's vision of a new Austria in the old *Heimat,* she captures a sentimental dimension of return, echoed in most of the memoirs, that extends beyond pure political motivation.

No matter what their motivation(s), even the heartiest individuals found return filled with expected and unexpected challenges. To come home the refugees had to jump through numerous bureaucratic hoops. To begin with, they had a difficult time regaining Austrian citizenship. Once they returned they had to be willing to put up with continued or renewed hardship. Property restitution was made difficult for Jewish reémigrés (Knight 1992, 222). If Austrian exiles were waiting for a beckoning gesture from home, they were disappointed. With the one exception of Viktor Matejka, a Communist city councilman, no official call went out from Austria encouraging exiles to come home. In the November 1945 issue of the *Austro-American Tribune,* Matejka appealed to artists and other members of the intelligentsia to return to Austria.[26]

Indeed, the returning refugees were not particularly welcomed by either the general population or government officials. In a poll taken in 1946, 46 percent of the respondents opposed the return of Jewish refugees, while only 28 percent favored their return (Pauley 1996, 493). Many among the general population viewed returnees as competitors for housing and jobs and as constant reminders of Austrians' moral failings (Knight 1992, 221–26). The governmental efforts to construct a new Austrian identity as well as civilian claims of victimhood resulted in the creation of a non-Jewish victim "in-group" in Austria:

> By claiming the status of victim one could officially refuse to accept any guilt or responsibility that went beyond individual crimes. The efforts of creating an identity consequently led to and leads to a new nationalism. Such an intensified nationalism created new borders, which facilitated the division of the (cognitive) world into a corresponding "in-group" and "out-group," into a "we" and the "others." (Wodak et al. 1990, 24)[27]

Postwar Austrian identity was based in part on the construction of an Austrian "in-group" whose "integrity" was upheld by marginalizing ethnic, political, and religious victims from this discourse. Whereas in the 1930s the conservative Catholic and Communist intellectuals sought to construct Austrians as the better Germans, after 1945 the political leadership of the conservative People's Party and the Communist Party "reimagined Austrian identity as radically *anti-German* in order to disconnect Austria from most of her World War II past and distance the new nation and her citizens from any responsibility for Nazi war crimes" (Bischof 1997, 3).[28]

43

Being of Jewish heritage in postwar Austria brought with it differ-ent challenges than for Germans of Jewish heritage returning to either of the Germanies, despite some similarities.[29] The fundamental differences in the countries' official stance toward National Socialism impacted on the postwar constructions of their national and ethnic identities. Unlike Austria, neither the Federal Republic of Germany (West Germany) nor the German Democratic Republic (East Germany) could have claimed a victim identity.[30] The Federal Republic officially accepted guilt for the crimes of National Socialism, while the founders of the Democratic Republic reinvented themselves as antifascists. Those Jews returning to the West aligned themselves with democratic forces; those returning to the East saw themselves as part of an antifascist, anticapitalist tradition. Jewish Austrian reémigrés were faced with the challenge of constructing an identity in "victimized" Austria. Robert Knight writes of a fundamen-tal conflict arising for them:

> Clearly post-war Austria was a world apart from what had preceded it. Anti-Semitism was no longer a political weapon as it had been in the first Republic, and much less was it the driving-force for mass murder that it had been in the Third Reich. The Austrian state's commitment to equal rights could in many individual cases provide enough scaffolding for those Jews who returned or stayed to allow them to build up a successful life or career. However, what it did not allow them to do was to link their personal experiences authentically with the state within which they lived and with which in so many cases they longed to identify. (1992, 228)

Even if they had not defined themselves as Jewish before 1938, their experiences put them in a much different position from gentile Austri-ans. Those returnees active in politics or the foreign service were faced with unique challenges when expressing an Austrian identity. Strong identification with the state often led to the suppression of their identity and experiences as part of a Jewish "we," or instrumentalizing their Jewish identity as proof of the absence of anti-Semitism in their party and its moral superiority.

Coming back can never be return to an original state. The passage of time and the nature of the historical events in the thirties and forties transformed the memoirists' Austrian *Heimat* into a very different place, which was paradoxically the same place. It was inhabited by some of the same people, but they, too, had been changed by their experiences, just as the harrowing events of the *Anschluss* and exile had transformed the reémigrés. If those who returned hoped to regain their former sense of security through membership of the "I" in an Austrian "we," reenter language as a full partner, reestablish a comfortable relationship with their surroundings, and share a common past, they were bound to find reconnecting to *Heimat* challenging. As the Grinbergs maintain:

> The person who contemplates returning home does not always see clearly that the return trip is yet another migration. When the emigrant returns to his native country he builds up hopes and has expectations of recovering everything he has yearned for. Even knowing that it cannot be, he hopes to find everything—people and objects—just as he left them, as though they had slept in the sleep of Sleeping Beauty, awaiting his return.
>
> But the reality he finds is a different one. When he sees the changes in people, things, habits and styles, houses and streets, relationships and affections, he feels like a stranger. Not even his language sounds the same. Colloquialisms have changed, along with the tacit understanding of words, meanings, shared images, and past references, winks of complicity among the initiated—all the sublanguages that make up a language. (1989, 186–87)

The danger of return lies in the distance between expectations and reality. Return hypothetically offered the possibility of reestablishing those links necessary for the possession of *Heimat* in Améry's terms and for dealing with past emotional injury, but the reality of return was less hopeful.

Faced with both physical and psychological obstacles, reémigrés had to adjust to an Austria very different from the one they had known before March 1938. A common theme running through the memoirists' impressions of their first trip home is the unsettling estrangement from once-familiar surroundings. Klein-Löw recalls her arrival at the West Station. "The West Station in Vienna: Noise, activity, barracks, disorder, chaos. The streets: All familiar, yet foreign" (1980, 167).[31] Hans Thalberg remembers meeting unfamiliar faces at familiar places. "New, unfamiliar people—about whom one moreover could never be sure how they had come to replace those who had earlier occupied their place—met me apathetically on familiar squares" (1984, 152).[32] For him, the incongruence punctuates a certain mistrust of the new faces. In contrast, Elisabeth Freundlich is totally alienated by the lack of familiarity with Vienna when she returns in 1950. "At first we drifted aimlessly through the city; it had become completely foreign to me" (1999, 98).[33]

In her literary diary, Spiel captures this combination of being confronted with strange and familiar:

> Now I have to learn everything anew. I become reacquainted with the cold, dank stone smell of Viennese houses, the porous, worn out granite

steps, the wretched stairwells with the scribblings on the paint peeling off. I get to know the blank look of the building custodians, the curiosity of the old women with the scarves on their heads, and the suspicious, unfriendly smile that was here before the Nazis and will always be here. (1968, 35)[34]

For her, it is the rediscovery of the familiar after years away in England. In Améry's terms, Spiel uses her semiotic competency to rediscover the past and interpret the present:

> There are also new things: the Tirolean hats that everyone is now wearing, even the noblest inhabitants of the city that had once been so elegant; the furs of the small businesswomen who had previously only possessed cloth coats, boots everywhere, unknown in England, from the leather jackboot to the ugly hightop felt models. In my day one wore galoshes in the rain, but now the boot rules and transforms every woman into a camp commandant or a Berlin streetwalker of the twenties. (1968, 35)[35]

She sketches a somewhat comical and dissonant picture. The Viennese have retained certain negative attributes while at the same time they are busy reinventing themselves with a new provincialism—marked by their Tirolean hats—in the hope of distancing themselves from Germany.[36] However, she uncovers their association with Germany by describing their new love affair with boots. In Spiel's mind, boots connect the women either to the concentration camps or to Berlin streetwalkers of the twenties. She also suggests that the black market is blooming with her reference to the new prosperity of the small businesswomen at a time when most are wanting.

In a draft of the author's note to the earlier, unpublished English version of this diary, Spiel captures the mental split not uncommon in those returning as well as the sense of estrangement in returning to one's past:

> A native of Vienna; a subject of the British crown; owning allegiance to the moral truth of England, the aesthetic truth of France, the sensuous truth of Italy, and the most alluring falsehoods of my former country; possessed, then, of the numerously split personality so common to the age, I set out from London less then a year after the war to revisit Europe. Like the wanderer in the legend who enters the sunken city of Vineta which has emerged from the seas, I was to walk through the risen streets of my past. ("The Streets of Vineta," Blatt II)

Just as Vienna and the nonexile, non-Jewish Viennese have been transformed by their experiences of war, so, too, has Spiel been shaped by the years in exile. Alienation from the once-familiar *Heimat* seems inevitable.

Their experiences as part of a Jewish "we" no doubt made them more sensitive to continued anti-Semitism. Ernst Lothar, who first returned to Austria in the service of the United States government to further denazification of the arts in Austria, paints a grim picture of Austria for Jewish Austrians. In his memoir *Das Wunder des Überlebens,* he relates a conversation in which he described the Vienna he found after the war to three Viennese Jewish doctors in New York:

> Anti-Semitism—and at that time the return of Nazi graffiti had not yet made its appearance—dominated as it had previously. That six million Jews had been murdered, the seven million Austrians, presumably, as well as the rest of the world, were about to forget; they took offense at being reminded of that fact, it was perceived as tactless. Certainly, anti-Semitism momentarily withdrew its claws and draped itself with alibis, so that among other things minor positions were awarded to non-Aryans. However, Jews were on principle not or only against strident resistance offered decisive positions. Although no one would officially admit it, there was no demand for returnees, the more recognized the less desired; they wanted to remain among themselves and spare their attacked conscience. (1961, 408–9)[37]

Lothar, for whom return was the only possibility of recovering from *Heimweh,* framed the situation in postwar Vienna as less than desirable for Jewish reémigrés. According to him, anti-Semitism was widespread and only going to get worse. Because of Austria's continued anti-Semitism, incipient collective forgetting of Jewish genocide, and defensive stance toward returnees, full recovery of *Heimat* and self would prove challenging if not impossible.

The difficulties of return were exacerbated by the general population's perception of the returnees. Even if the reémigrés did not perceive themselves as Jews, they once again found themselves constructed as Jewish "outsiders." Reinprecht concludes in his study that the exiles "returned as isolated individuals, but were perceived by the others as scattered parts of an imaginary collective. Their Jewishness, their Jewish identity was, on this level, no longer freely definable, but predetermined" (1992, 100–101).[38] Elisabeth Freundlich explicitly recalls how she and her husband were perceived as Jewish foreigners, a situation implied in other memoirs: "The people were dressed shabbily, too, their glances jealous and mistrustful when we tried to engage them in conversation. We were, after all, the 'rich Americans,' and more than that, Jews. All Americans were Jews; this Herr Rosenfeld, as the

Nazis had called Roosevelt, had caused the poverty and bombed-out cities. They had gotten the chronology out of order" (1999, 98).[39] The suspicion with which Freundlich was met underscores the difficulty of becoming part of a postwar Austrian "we" for reémigrés. Despite her self-definition as an Austrian, fellow Austrians were not deterred from imposing other definitions on her. Seen as an American and a Jew, she was also perceived as someone who now, once again, was the cause of Austrian misery. Freundlich realized that history was being rewritten, and Freundlich's experiences had no place in that new text.

From the perspective of exile, Améry pinpointed the *Anschluss* as the great rupture in his life and the source of his diminished sense of self. With it he realized that the links to "this land [Austria] and its people" were based on an "existential misunderstanding" (1980, 50). In contrast, Reinprecht discovers in his interviews that 1938 and the subsequent exile do not mark the reémigrés' disillusionment with Austria the same way that return does: "In the reports of the interviewed emigrants, the 'existential misunderstanding' that Améry describes is evident, but only then in the emigrants' retrospective evaluations of their decision to return. . . . Apparently, only after return did the experiences take on that disillusioning character that led to that profound injury about which *Améry* speaks" (1992, 44).[40] 1938 may have lifted many out of their sense of security, but they nonetheless held onto the illusion—as Améry would see it—that they belonged to an Austrian "we." If the reémigrés expected restoration of the combined linguistic, spatial, and temporal links to *Heimat* to pre-*Anschluss* Austria, they were most likely sorely disappointed. Arriving with high expectations, the reémigrés could experience return as a renewed loss of *Heimat* rather than its recovery.

The Grinbergs explain how return can be traumatic and experienced as a renewed attack on their sense of self:

> Inevitably, new emotional conflicts erupt when those who return meet those who stayed behind, the welcomers of the returning exiles. Neither those who left nor those who stayed at home are the same: everyone has felt the impact of separation, and beneath the surface, each reproaches the other for having abandoned him. Nearly everything must be rebuilt, like a house after a tempest: fallen trees cleared away, cracked roofs repaired, rubble swept away. And as for the structure itself surely a different house is needed, for the returning person inhabits a different reality. The one thing certain is that he will feel a new kind of homesickness, a new kind of grief. (1989, 188)

The Grinbergs' metaphor of disrepair seems particularly apt for the Austrian situation at the end of the war. Austria's cities and industrial centers had been severely damaged and their destruction was emblematic of the inner state of many Austrian citizens. Many of the citizens experienced the war and the defeat of National Socialism as traumatic and perceived themselves as victims.

Arriving with high expectations, the reémigrés were often met with reactions ranging from indifference to disdain and distrust. Moreover, anti-Semitism was still evident: returnees were perceived first as Jews, and they were even viewed as the cause of Austrian misery. They were often absurdly reproached for having left Austria even if staying would have meant certain death. Thus, if migration and exile proved to be traumatic, then return, too, had the potential of being experienced as a psychological injury. Return confronted the reémigrés most brutally with their alienation from *Heimat* and themselves.

The (Im)Possibility of Mourning

Despite the gradual normalization of life after the war, return usually compounded the emotional injury and rarely was conducive to a mourning process. Return to the site of the original trauma was emotionally explosive. Powerful emotions suppressed in exile as a matter of survival were bound to be unleashed. Moreover, the situation in post-war Austria allowed for little possibility of dealing with such emotions productively.

To discuss more thoroughly the process of mourning and the challenges that return provided, I shall back up a bit and look briefly at Hilde Spiel's description of her emotional state in exile. She offers an excellent example of the challenges that both exile and return posed to the mourning process. In the beginning of the second volume of her memoirs, *Welche Welt ist meine Welt?*, Hilde Spiel notes how she and her husband shut down emotionally in order to function during the war:

> With true haste I reported the course of our life since the beginning of the war in the first volume of my memoirs; however, I did not betray to what extent its dismalness affected me and my husband emotionally. The truth is we had to refuse to give in to our emotional responses. In the face of the atrocity that the daily murder from the sky and the latent danger of a German invasion already represented for us, long before the abyss of human devilry, the "final solution," was public knowledge, we *put on an armor* to the point of *dulling,* to the point of the *numbing* of our senses if not to the point of *lethargy.* (1990, 7; my emphasis)[41]

To function in the face of the reality of war, Spiel and her husband suppress their emotions. Spiel's choice of words, evidence of an emotional numbing, correlate with the first step of the classical description of the mourning process. In his book *Bereavement: Studies of Grief in Adult Life,* Colin Murray Parkes describes stages of the grief process:

> Grief is not a set of symptoms which start after a loss and then gradually fade away. It involves a succession of clinical pictures which blend into and replace one another. . . . [N]umbness, the first state, gives place to pining, and pining to disorganization and despair, and it is only after the stage of disorganization that recovery occurs. Hence, at any particular time a person may show one of three quite different clinical pictures.
>
> Each of these stages of grieving has its own characteristics and there are considerable differences from one person to another as regards both the duration and the form of each stage. Nevertheless, there is a common pattern whose features can be observed without difficulty in nearly every case, and this justifies our regarding grief as a distinct psychological process. (1986, 27)[42]

Although Spiel views the numbing as a coping strategy, it can also be interpreted as part of an aborted mourning process brought on by the *Anschluss* and the loss of *Heimat.* Because of the circumstances, Spiel appears caught in the stage of numbness. She does not show herself as progressing very far toward total recovery.

As someone who had been excluded from the Austrian "we," but who still defined herself in part through her connection to her Austrian past and its cultural heritage, Spiel approached Vienna with feelings of trepidation and estrangement. Expecting a difficult reunion, she prepared herself mentally. "I'm returning to my origins, estranged by the long absence, steeled by some of the losses and ready for a hard, presumably painful, experience" (1968, 15–16).[43] Her steely resolve is slowly worn down during her travels through Vienna. The breaking point occurs when she returns to Pfarrplatz near her childhood home in Vienna:

> In the fading light I stand on Pfarrplatz. Here my soul lies buried. During the past ten years of my absence, whenever I was homesick, it was for this square. Whenever I heard certain parts of Beethoven or Schubert, it appeared before my eyes. A small village square: to the left is a farm house in which the Eroica Symphony was written; another one is on the right-hand side; and in the middle the little St. Jakob's Church. . . . The community news is posted on the wooden door of the church, but it has nothing to do with me. Here, where my roots reach so deep in the earth like no other place, I am a total stranger, so removed in time and space, like a ghostly revenant. (1968, 54–55)[44]

50

This quaint square was full of cultural as well as personal significance for Spiel. After the *Anschluss* and before the end of the war, when return to Austria was impossible, Spiel had projected the essence of her being, her soul, onto this specific geographic location in Vienna. Her memory of this square had been a mental talisman that helped her through hard times. However, when faced with the ultimate estrangement from her self and her past upon return, she succumbs and the floodgates to repressed emotions open up: "All the dammed up feeling, suppressed for years, during which you had to pay the price of courage by putting your feelings on ice—all the sorrow concerning the humiliation of my *Heimat,* all the worry concerning my children in the war, all the pain concerning the death of my father, now pushed its way to the surface" (55).[45] The emotions that she had been holding in check for years finally gain the upper hand. Unable to share her feelings with either her former Austrian countrymen and women or her new British compatriots, Spiel is left alone with her pain.

As the excerpts from her literary diary demonstrate, her first visit to Vienna melted the emotional reserve, but only temporarily. In her memoirs, written over forty years after the end of the war, she again recalls the emotions released by her first return visit to Vienna:

> Even after the end of the long winter when the doors and windows sprang open and we ran out into the pacified reality, we did not give our emotions free rein. Once I fell apart during my first return visit to Vienna at Pfarrplatz, the central square in Heiligenstadt. I had anticipated it. However, the ambivalent situation in which I found myself among the occupiers of my former *Heimat,* the vacillation between confidence and doubt concerning the question of whether we had truly put down roots in England and had unconditionally been accepted by our English compatriots was too stressful to also be felt acutely. As a result everything forced its way to us as through a veil. (1990, 8)[46]

Spiel's metaphor of the emotional suspension as winter and the resurfacing of emotions as a type of spring cleaning suggests a hopeful moment. However, her position of in-betweenness forces her to retreat into her emotional shell and the process of mourning is interrupted yet again.

The possibility of "normal" grieving or effective mourning, psychiatrist Henry Krystal contends, can be inhibited by a number of factors. Based on his work with elderly Holocaust survivors, Krystal argues that "there is a limitation to how much an individual can absorb through grieving and achieve integrity and good-natured acceptance of the past." He explains, "[t]here are both qualitative and quantitative factors in the limitations on what can be dealt with through mourning" and notes

51

that in the case of the Jewish genocide, the "quality or the quantity of losses may go beyond one's capacity to integrate" (1995, 84).

The original loss of *Heimat* in Améry's sense could never be fully restored: the "I" had been indelibly changed. As Reinprecht's research indicates, this became abundantly clear to the exiles upon return. A new kind of homesickness set in, precipitated by the full impact of their loss and the realization of the irretrievability of the past. Return opened up suppressed emotions and simultaneously inflicted new injuries. Moreover, the ways in which the Austrian population instrumentalized its traumatic memories added to their own emotional injury, and the government's construction of Austria as victim allowed little public support for mourning their losses.

Identity and Individual and Collective (Traumatic) Memory

Sociologist Kai Erikson argues that "trauma shared can serve as a source of communality in the same way that common languages and common backgrounds can. There is a spiritual kinship there, a sense of identity, even when feelings of affection are deadened and the ability to care numbed" (1995, 186). The shared traumatic memories of the general Austrian population created a sense of community and served as a cornerstone of a postwar Austrian identity. In contrast, the returning exiles had memories that tied them both to a pre-*Anschluss* Austrian collective and to a Jewish collective. Both groups had suffered from traumatic events, yet the memories of the Jewish Austrians actually questioned the selective use of the memories of the non-Jewish Austrians, who styled themselves as victims. The divergent experiences between those who left and those who stayed consequently resulted in an experiential divide between the returnees and the general population; the moral implications of which side of the divide one was on widened the rift.[47]

Indeed, Elisabeth Freundlich, Hans Thalberg, and Hilde Spiel use the spatial metaphors *Kluft* ("chasm" or "gulf"; literally, "cleft" or "ravine") and *Graben* ("rift"; literally, "ditch" or "moat") to describe an emotional divide between themselves and the general Austrian population so many years after the war. Elisabeth Freundlich tersely comments, "In fact the chasm between those who had stayed—this term also encompasses those who supposedly had clean consciences—and those who had been chased away never closed completely" (1999, 98).[48] The spatial metaphor *Kluft* in Freundlich's memoirs is mirrored in Hans Thalberg's use of *Graben* to describe his first visit to Vienna in 1945. "The city of my birth, yes! But my *Heimat* city? The rift that separated me from the rest of the population was too profound" (1984, 153).[49]

Thalberg suggests that this divide separating the reémigrés from nonexiles is magnified and stabilized by a linguistic divide:

> This was most obvious to me when I spoke with previous or new acquaintances about the recent past. Whenever they spoke of the "catastrophe," they meant 1945. For me, the catastrophe had occurred in 1938, and 1945 was the year of happy fulfillment. People whose political and personal integrity had been above reproach had somehow willy-nilly been a part of the Hitler madness and had shared the fate of Nazi Germany in good as well as bad times. Some had been stationed as officers of the German occupation in Paris, Athens, or Brussels; convinced of their innocence, they naively related stories of these "good" times, not aware of the devastating impression such tales had to conjure up for all of those who had experienced the war on the other side. To be sure, the matter was complicated. It was not easy to celebrate the American bombs that caused the houses over their heads to come falling down on them as a step toward the approaching liberation. But the total ignorance with which Austrians—even today—identify with the fate of the German *Wehrmacht* in the war makes my blood run cold. (1984, 153)[50]

Reminiscent of Améry's thoughts on the relationship between language and the expression of reality, Thalberg argues that the use of words has been shaped by divergent experiences. Thalberg suggests that different understandings of the very same words mark the distance between the exiles and nonexiles. Simple words such as "*Heimat*," "catastrophe," and "liberation" have assumed different meanings for Thalberg; he cannot use them to describe the same concepts or events as nonexile Austrians.[51] As George Steiner argues, "the post-war history of the German language has been one of dissimulation and deliberate forgetting" (1998, 109).

Thalberg does not ignore the complexity of the situation and facilely condemn Austrians who did not experience exile. He realizes that it was no doubt difficult for Austrians to connect the death and destruction caused by the bombings with liberation. Nonetheless, he abhors the narrowness of the perspective of many Austrians and confirms the devastating effect that language and the absence of *his* reality in language has on him personally and which he believes must affect others like him.

The rift or divide Thalberg perceived on his first visit to Vienna did not narrow in all the years since the war:

Quite obviously, no one in Austria has ever completely comprehended what really happened during these war years, how profound the hatred and the contempt are that the world feels toward Hitler's Germany and everything associated with it. Up until the present day, it is more likely that I can find common ground with a Dutch citizen, a Norwegian, or a Yugoslavian than with my own countrymen. An intellectual and instinctive rift separates me in this respect from my country and its people. (1984, 153–54)[52]

Thalberg notices no change in attitude in later years. He continues to be estranged from Austria and other Austrians because of the inability or unwillingness of many Austrians to consider the perspective of those on the other side.

Like Thalberg, Hilde Spiel pinpoints the war experience as the gulf separating her from other Austrians. "However much I grow into the Austrian milieu later in life, this starting position after the lost-won war creates a gulf between me and the other citizens that is never to close" (1989b, 224).[53] Because she does not and cannot consider the end of the war a defeat, she naturally finds herself on the other side of the experiential and linguistic divide. She goes even further in her analysis and suggests that guilt and denial of guilt play an important role in the construction and maintenance of the gulf between exiles and nonexiles:

We weren't to blame for it [the war], nor were the majority of those on the enemy side, or so one hopes. Yet almost all of them over there [in Austria] held it against us later that we had been victims and had not belonged to the world of the perpetrators and that we could not be held responsible for the years of terror under any circumstances. How could we ever be forgiven for this? How could one hope that one day in the far future when one once again stepped upon the soil of the fatherland or settled there anew that this gulf between those who stayed at home and those who left—mostly expellees—would not open up at any moment to the astonishment or horror of those who had perhaps believed the alienation was over forever. (1989b, 176)[54]

Spiel explicitly connects the discourse concerning the war and guilt with the gulf between exiles and other Austrians. As an exile and "Jewish victim," she is a constant threat to most Austrian claims of victimhood. Consequently, she presents the fragility of the returnees' position and suggests that any sense of belonging to an Austrian "we" is ultimately an illusion.

The memoirists' use of the image of a gulf or rift to describe their relationship to the general Austrian population illustrates the connections among memory, language, reality, and identity construction that scholars have studied both generally and in terms of the Austrian situation specifically. Researchers on memory generally agree that even the simplest memory "is constructed from influences operating in the present as well as from information you have stored about the past" (Schacter 1996, 8).[55] Recall of events as memory is determined and shaped by numerous factors. What and how one remembers depends, among other things, on one's subject positions at the time the event occurred as well as that person's subject positions at the time of narration. Recall can also be influenced by the person(s) to whom the memory is being related. Within this matrix of factors, an individual's disposition and personality play a decisive role in recall.

According to sociologist Maurice Halbwachs in his groundbreaking work on collective memory, although only individuals have memory, their personal memories are shaped by the various groups—ranging from family to the nation—a person "belongs" to. By the same token, what is forgotten or left out of collective memory is also shaped by the group. Collective memories, or "intersubjective sedimentation," as sociologists Peter Berger and Thomas Luckmann label it in their work *The Social Construction of Reality,* are those experiences that are shared by a community and incorporated into a common stock of knowledge through their objectification in language (1966, 67–69). They contend that "[l]anguage objectivates the shared experiences and makes them available to all within the linguistic community, thus becoming both the basis and the instrument of the collective stock of knowledge" (68).

This being the case, one could argue that since Austrian anti-Semitism and the humiliation and brutal treatment of Jewish Austrians after the *Anschluss* were not part of the general population's personal experiences, these experiences were naturally not a part of Austrian collective memory and thus did not appear in oral versions of this past. However, in a variety of publications—ranging from studies on the interplay among individual, collective, and institutional memory in Austria, on Austrian involvement in the persecution of Jewish Austrians, on anti-Semitic discourse in Austria, and most recently on Austrians in the German *Wehrmacht*—a common theme emerges.[56] The researchers note that in the majority of the narratives concerning the years of the *Ostmark,* those truly persecuted are uniformly marginalized or effaced with the exception of select resistance fighters, who were instrumentalized by the state in the early days of the postwar Republic.

The distance between the experiences of the two groups objectified in language suggests that regardless of how well the reémigrés were integrated into society, the past divided them from much of the

55

population. What is more, the instrumentalizing of the general population's traumatic experiences did not allow for the original loss to be mourned, but only inflicted additional emotional injury on reémigrés.

Reclaiming and Reinventing Self and *Heimat*

The memoirs of the Jewish Austrian reémigrés potentially serve a variety of functions with respect to the processes of trauma and mourning. The exile situation seldom allowed for institutionalized mourning, which is seen as an important part of the recovery process.[57] To some extent, the texts themselves serve as ritualized mourning, or at least commemoration. If the writers could not bury their acquaintances, friends, and family members, they can commemorate them in writing. Without exception, the writers commemorate in some way those who died. However, more than this, the memoirs offer the former exiles the opportunity to reconstitute a traumatized self within a specific Austrian context.

In much of the theory on trauma, the healing process involves a gradual move from silence to language, from disassociated memories to their contextualization, from fractured self to reconstituted self, from isolation to reintegration in a "we." Trauma researchers Bessel A. van der Kolk and Onno van der Hart describe the transformation of traumatic memory into narrative memory—or those "mental constructs, which people use to make sense out of experience" (1995, 160)—as essential for recovering from a trauma. They contrast the two types of memory: whereas narrative memory is "a social act, traumatic memory is inflexible and invariable" (163). To what extent the traumatic memories are immutable is debatable; however, they do seem separate and incongruent with narrative memory.[58] As such, "[t]raumatic memories are the unassimilated scraps of overwhelming experiences, which need to be integrated with existing mental schemes, and be transformed into narrative language" (176). To transform traumatic memory into narrative memory, the person has to contextualize the memories and infuse some flexibility into the traumatic memory (178).

Autobiography allows the victims of trauma to infuse their traumatic memories with flexibility by interpreting the events of their life and placing them in a larger context. As historian Mary Jo Maynes, a member of the Personal Narratives Group explains, "[a]s an interpretive act, the autobiography is, among other things, an effort to impose order, form, and meaning on the facts of an existence" (1989, 105). The processes of remembering, telling or writing, and mourning do not take place in a vacuum, but within a specific social context. Grieving, although a very individual process, requires reaching out and connecting to a listener. Roberta Culbertson stresses how narrating, by its very nature, forces the survivors of trauma to reestablish the social character of self:

> To return fully to the self as socially defined, to establish a relationship again with the world, the survivor must tell what happened. This is the function of narrative. The task then is to render body memories tellable, which means to order and arrange them in the form of a story, linking emotion with event, event with event, and so on. In so doing it becomes possible to return the self to its legitimate social status as something separate, something that tells, that recounts its own biography, undoing the grasp of the perpetrator and reestablishing the social dimension of the self lost in the midst of violation. (1995,179)[59]

The ability to transform traumatic memory into narrative memory and to reestablish the social dimension of the self is necessary for the process of mourning and reconstituting the "I" as part of a "we." Retelling within the Austrian context poses unique challenges for the memoirists since collective memory in Austria of this period has been shaped largely by non-Jewish, nonexiled Austrians. The memoirists must undo "the grasp of the perpetrator" in the land of the perpetrator.

The traditional memoir form, with certain modifications, appears an especially logical choice from among the autobiographical genres because it focuses on the "I" as "being-in-the-world" as opposed to the "I" "becoming-in-the-world" (Billson 1977, 261). Unlike the classical autobiography, the memoir does not have the inner development of the "I" as the major focus, but rather the position of the "I" in a social web or matrix. Almost without exception, the Austrian memoir writers shy away from an introspective examination of the development of self and choose to focus on the self as a social being, as an "I" in an Austrian "we." Reflecting on their entire lives in their memoirs, the reémigrés place the trauma in a context and reestablish the social character of the self or, in Améry's terms, reconnect the "I" to a "we." This sets their memoirs apart from most memoir literature, in which the memoir writer "relates a segment of his own life that was important to his identity as a social being, e.g. an exile, an imprisonment, the course of a career, participation in war, in politics, in an artistic coterie" (Billson 1977, 267). By doing this, the memoirists define themselves within an Austrian context and as Austrian "social beings."

In the following chapters, I use Améry's definition of *Heimat* as a yardstick for plotting the reémigrés' recovery of *Heimat*: being connected linguistically, spatially, and temporally to an Austrian "we."

The memoirs offer the former exiles the opportunity to reconstitute a traumatized self within a specific Austrian context. If individual and collective traumatic memories divided Jewish and non-Jewish, exiled and nonexiled Austrians, the memoirists seek to change this with their life stories. They also demand their right to an Austrian *Heimat*. As much as the memoir writers want to reconnect to Austria, they want Austria to connect to their stories. However, they do not simply wish to reconnect to an interrupted Austrian story, becoming a coda to the mainstream victim narrative; they strive to transform this story by creating narratives that lead to a more honest understanding of the past—and consequently a more honest personal and national identity.

However, the narrators are telling their stories within a community that had at one time rejected them and that had long marginalized the stories of Jewish Austrians to maintain its position as victim. They are faced with the task of relating the stories in such a way that they will be heard. Moreover, when they write of traumatic events, they are faced with a narrative paradox of expressing the inexpressible. Their life stories are more then their own life stories. As part of a Jewish "we," they carry other stories with them. With their tropes of trauma and mourning, they illustrate the importance of body memory and spatial memories in accessing traumatic memories and reclaiming *Heimat*. With their use of the past, they root themselves in an Austrian story with the ultimate goal of reinventing *Heimat*.

2

Asserting Narrative Authority

To tell their life stories as Jewish Austrians within a society that had long almost exclusively honored the suffering of the general population and soldiers, the memoirists had to reach across an experiential and linguistic divide. Jean Améry maintained that "[e]very language is part of a total reality to which one must have a well-founded right of ownership if one is to enter the area of that language with a good conscience and confident step" (1980, 53–54).[1] Upon return, the memoirists must have found that as far as their experiences as Jewish Austrians were concerned, they had ownership neither of language nor of their own reality. Years later when they demanded ownership of their past with their memoirs, they still could not simply tell their stories. They needed to assert narrative authority without alienating readers. To this end, they assume a variety of rhetorical stances and employ a range of narrative strategies.

In his article on the memoir genre, Marcus Billson argues that memoir writers can assume three different rhetorical stances to invest their texts with authenticity and authority: the eyewitness, the participant, and the "histor," or historian. The stances of eyewitness and participant, which sometimes overlap, lend authenticity to the narrative by virtue of the narrator's proximity to the events. An author, too, may adopt the stance of a histor "whenever he narrates events he has not seen with his own eyes, whenever he tells what he has overheard, read about, or accumulated by research" (1977, 278).[2] Because the "historian" bases his or her findings on documents, that is, on something viewed as factual evidence, this stance or position potentially invests a narrative with additional authority.

Key to an examination of rhetorical stances and narrative strategies—authorial perspectives and ways in which the narrators make their memories into a story—is the relationship of the writer to the reader as well as the relationship of the writer to individual and collective memories. In her study on rhetoric, Karlyn Kohrs Campbell explains that the "rhetors'" stance, the tone the rhetors adopt, the structure of their stories, and the conscious or unconscious rhetorical strategies they employ are all informed by the rhetors' experiences and subject positions, that is, by their positions as an "I" within multiple "we"s (1982, 3–17). Moreover, "[b]ecause rhetoric is *addressed* to others, it is *reason-giving*; and because it is social and public, it uses as reasons the *values accepted and affirmed* by a subculture or culture. In this way, rhetoric is tied to *social values*, and rhetors' statements will reflect the social norms of particular times and places" (6). As Austrians, the memoirists found themselves part of the dominant culture, and as Jewish reémigrés, part of a (sometimes imagined) subculture. In their effort to convince, they simultaneously have to challenge mainstream victim narratives and make their own stories believable and compelling.

Before launching into a discussion of the memoirists' attempts to assert narrative authority and reconnect to an Austrian "we," it will be helpful to examine the rhetorical stances and narrative strategies employed by the Austrian state and the general population to construct an Austrian victim identity. Although sometimes contradictory, public and private discourses concerning these years nonetheless complementarily construct an Austrian "in-group," with those truly persecuted as the "out-group." Propelled by the claim of victimhood, the non-Jewish Austrian "storytellers" assume the rhetorical stances of participant, eye-witness, historian, and at times defense lawyer to legitimize Austria's victim status. In the presence of a perceived or real skeptical listener, the Austrian "in-group" narrator constructs linguistic barriers that disallow criticism. In the process, he or she delimits a clear boundary between the in-group and the out-group.[3]

In an analysis of the semipublic rhetoric surrounding the Wald-heim controversy, an interdisciplinary team headed by linguist Ruth Wodak discusses and enumerates the discursive or rhetorical strategies employed to construct an Austrian victim "in-group" and a Jewish "out-group." These observations build on the team's previous study of anti-Semitic discourse and are helpful in understanding the influence of the mainstream narratives on the memoirists' stories. Arguing from a narrow "we" perspective that excludes others, the "in-group" narrator shifts guilt to another person or group.[4] Other tactics include displacing the victim with the perpetrator, playing up one's own suffering, and playing down or relativizing Jewish suffering (Wodak et al. 1990, 352–54). Such narrators discount the authority of outsiders, which implicitly included the exiles. They uphold their victim status by decontextualizing the past, presenting Austrians as pawns of history, and constructing tenuous continuities between the past and the present. With their defensive rhetorical strategies, they seek to silence criticism, disallow probing questions, and avoid discussion of degrees of complicity. In both public and private discourse, Austrians have coped with the past by "externalizing it," to borrow a term and explanation from German sociologist M. Rainer Lepsius. By "externalizing" this part of their past—by making it "German"—Austrians could avoid dealing with questions of complicity and guilt.[5]

The *Rot-Weiß-Rot-Buch* (Red-White-Red Book), a government document written by an Austrian committee under the guidance of Foreign Minister Karl Gruber and presented to the Allies in 1946, is perhaps the most representative example of the government's attempt to create Austria's identity as a victim. Moreover, the government blatantly effaces the persecution of Jewish Austrians and shuts them out of representations of reality. The authors of the *Rot-Weiß-Rot-Buch* employ a variety of rhetorical stances and narrative strategies to create an "in-group" identity that excludes, among other victims, Jewish Austrians.

The document drafters attempt to discredit critics outside Austria, maintaining that only eyewitnesses within the country can judge it. The government officials also claim to speak from a position of moral authority, pointing the finger of blame at other nations. Assuming the voice of defense lawyer, they invoke destiny, use juridical arguments, and exploit the deeds of a resisting minority. As historians, they include select documents such as Nazi rosters of trials against "Austrians." They assert the inevitability of the *Anschluss* while at the same time they present it as the rape of Austria, observed with complacency by virtually the entire world. The authors of the *Rot-Weiß-Rot-Buch* look back to 1918 and 1938 to frame their argument, suggesting that the unfavorable conditions of the Treaty of Versailles in 1918 necessarily contributed to the demise of Austria. They maintain that when Austria was invaded by the foreign German army in 1938, the situation was comparable to Germany's invasion of Czechoslovakia in the same year. They argue that, since Austria did not exist in an official sense after that date, it could not be held responsible for the war. Finally, by exploiting the deeds of select members of certain politically viable resistance organizations, they attempt to exonerate the general population by association.[6]

Reacting defensively to possible arguments questioning Austria's claim of victimhood, the authors suggest that as effective propagandists the National Socialists greatly contributed to the illusion that Austrians enthusiastically supported their regime (1946, 3, 69). The government officials seek to strengthen their argument by maintaining that those who fault Austria are either uninformed or ill-willed. "Only ignorance of the true situation or ill will can allow one to apportion blame to the Austrian people based on the outward impression created by the atmosphere of these turbulent days" (70).[7] The Austrian officials shift responsibility to someone or some entity outside themselves: in this instance, to those foreign powers who "abandoned" Austria: "The perspective of Austria's critics today is false. During the days that were so difficult for Austria, they sat securely abroad while, one by one, countries shrank back from Hitler. They make themselves moral judges over the abandoned and tortured Austrian people and demand a heroism after the fact that the world did not muster up at the time" (71).[8] The criticism directed at the foreign powers echoes criticism often directed toward exiles; those who abandoned Austria and were secure in a foreign country have no right to point an accusatory finger at Austria and Austrians.[9]

The guilt for Austria's postwar situation is not sought in actions by Austrians; rather, the drafters look outside Austria's borders. Germany was the aggressor and the Allies Austria's tormentors. Indeed, the document drafters minimize Austria's involvement in the war and maintain that Austria cannot be judged on the actions of a few individuals. "It would be unjust if one wanted to evaluate . . . the [German] occupation from the perspective of the personal behavior of individuals or from the spur-of-the-moment suggestion of further circles" (6).[10] The German *Wehrmacht*, though rarely perceived as an occupation army by those Austrians who served, has to be constructed as such officially. The government officials also discourage the Allies from considering the opinions of certain circles. In light of the controversy surrounding Waldheim in 1986 in which the World Jewish Congress was attacked for its criticism of Waldheim, one cannot help but associate "further circles" with the international Jewish community.[11]

The government officials convinced no one of Austria's victimhood with their rhetoric, except perhaps themselves. Indeed, the Russians labeled the *Rot-Weiß-Rot-Buch* "Viennese masquerade" (Jochum 1985, 230), and the favorable conditions of Austrian independence were more a result of the cold war than Austrian rhetorical prowess (Knight 1988, 48–54). Nonetheless, Austria as victim was an unquestioned cornerstone of Austrian national identity for many years—with material consequences for Jewish reémigrés as "the most influential Austrian politicians had always denied any obligation for the payment of restitution" to Jewish Austrians (Bailer 1997, 107).

Like Austria's leaders, the general population saw itself as a pawn of history. However, unlike the official state narrative, which constructed 1938 as the Austrian catastrophe for political reasons—to distance Austria from Germany and make a case for Austrian independence—many of the personal narratives of the general population show World War II and the immediate postwar period as the catastrophe of their personal histories. In her article "Aus Angst, uns ein Bild zu zerstören" (For fear of destroying an image), Karin Berger draws on her own family's stories of the period, which she finds typical of those passed down to her generation. Her relatives warmly remember the early years under National Socialism. The older generation begins to lament when the bombings are recalled, or when confronted with crimes committed under National Socialism. Then, Berger reports, she had to listen repeatedly to the Austrian litany: "We were poor, we suffered, we didn't know anything" (1989, 3). The general population derived its sense of victimhood by focusing on the war years, beginning with the bombardments of Austrian cities and the losses on the eastern front. Former soldiers could exculpate themselves by claiming that they merely performed their duty.[12]

Particularly to an outsider, the logic of these narratives appears obviously flawed. However, the victim narratives and stories of war marked the acceptable parameters within which one could talk about the years under National Socialism in Austria. In the face of these narratives, the reémigrés find that they cannot describe their experiences with the available language—they have to transform language to access and express their stories.

Memory and the Crisis of Truth

The memoir as an autobiographical genre appears both a powerful and logical response to the discursive marginalization and effacement of Jewish Austrians. As Marcus Billson writes, "[t]he memoir recounts a story of the author's witnessing a real past which he considers to be of extraordinary interest and importance" (1977, 261). Moreover, with the choice of the autobiographical mode, the writers engage in what Philippe Lejeune has labeled the "autobiographical pact": an implied contract between reader and author in which it is understood that the author is identical with the narrator and protagonist (1975, 13–14). This autobiographical pact—taken for granted by the readers of

63

memoirs as well as autobiographies—creates an immediacy between events and reader and sets up a relationship of intimacy between the author and reader. The memoirists engage readers with the personal stories, allowing them to experience a real past vicariously. However, the autobiographers' claim of authenticity alone does not guarantee narrative authority within an Austrian context.

SILENCING ENCOUNTERS

As discussed in chapter 1, the memoirists delineated a linguistic divide separating them from their Austrian colleagues when they spoke about the war years. The linguistic divide was maintained not just by words alone, but with a silencing rhetoric the reémigrés encounter upon return. From the position of participants, the memoirists expose the ways in which they were "shut out from language and reality" in their encounters with non-Jewish Austrians, excluded from the Austrian collective "we" and consequently from Austrian collective memory. They illustrate the eliding nature of the rhetorical stances and strategies of the nonexile interlocutors and suggest as a possible motive a desire to avoid discussions of responsibility. As such, their observations echo the findings of the discourse analysis of Wodak's interdisciplinary team.

Commenting on the ways in which they had been silenced, the memoirists demonstrate the power of their linguistic marginalization. In these exchanges, the memoir writers highlight implicit and explicit delineation of acceptable boundaries within which one could talk about the National Socialist past. As social scientists David Middleton and Derek Edwards suggest, "[t]he *rhetorical organization of remembering and forgetting* . . . can be seen in argument about contested pasts and plausible accounts of who is to blame, or to be excused, acknowledged, praised, honoured, thanked, trusted and so on" (1990, 9). The memoirists reflect on these encounters and expose a specific rhetoric of remembering and forgetting, leading the reader to question the veracity of the mainstream victim narratives.

Ernst Lothar recalls his conversation with the building custodian on his first day back in Austria, showing the non-Jewish "storyteller" narrating from an exclusionary "we" position. " 'Well, Herr Councilor, you've got to admit, dropping bombs was nothing short of barbaric!' I should have said 'It was the consequence of barbarity!' Instead I just said good night to Herr Steindl and that's the way our first day back ended" (1961, 305).[13] The building custodian focuses narrowly on the suffering of the Austrians during the war and thus can see the population as a victim. The phrasing of the rhetorical statement "you've got to admit" does not invite a response, but solicits silence, sympathy, or, as in Lothar's case, a banal answer.

At the same time the reémigré Lothar is effectively silenced, he also finds himself and his experiences "shut out from language." Very few people ask him about his experiences. In contrast, the nonexile Austrians appear very eager to recount their own suffering. He finds that his Austrian interlocutors actually tell him about the reémigrés' situation in exile and consequently play down the suffering of the exiles. In a letter to Austrian writer and fellow exile Raoul Auernheimer dated September 8, 1946, Ernst Lothar recounts his conversations with the "victims": "They've totally forgotten the fact that they treated us so shabbily back in March 1938. In these three months almost no one has asked 'How was it for you?' Instead, they say and mean even more clearly than their words express that we did all right for ourselves to have beaten it back then. It was very sly of us at the time" (quoted in Daviau and Johns 1989, 543).[14] Struck by the insensitivity of nonexiles to the fate of the exiles, Lothar also demonstrates that his fellow Austrians have no desire for a true exchange. Lother's interlocutors assume the role of victim while placing the exiles in the role of traitor. Furthermore, they absurdly do not acknowledge that exile was not a matter of choice, but a question of life and death.

Lothar remarks that the exiles waited in vain for their fellow Austrians to ask them about exile, while they, in contrast, were expected to listen patiently to Austrian laments (1961, 302). He does, however, note one exception, a former lieutenant colonel of the Royal and Imperial Dragoons. Baron Putlon is the first to inquire about his fate and that of other exiles. Unlike most Austrians Lothar encountered, he speaks little of himself (312). However, he remains the exception. Moreover, Lothar discovers that when he does bring up the past he is accused of being bitter (318), filled with hate (351–52), and thirsty for revenge (415). By transgressing accepted boundaries of speech, he is stigmatized in these conversations.

Although Stella Klein-Löw does not write of any specific exchange between herself and her non-Jewish Austrian compatriots, she echoes Lothar's experiences. Her summary of the postwar situation shows how the narrow focus on personal suffering allows people to construct themselves as victim and exclude the suffering of Jewish Austrians:

> The people themselves felt that they were innocent, betrayed, persecuted unjustly by fate. If one suggested that they—at least through their silence, if not because of their involvement—shared a smattering, just a smattering of responsibility, of guilt, they would have vehemently objected. They

complained, felt sorry for themselves, envied others for every piece of bread that was bigger than the piece they had managed to get hold of. They knew everything better in hindsight, but they maintained not to have known anything earlier. (1980, 169–70)[15]

Like Lothar, Klein-Löw finds that when her interlocutors speak from this narrow "we" perspective, they can claim that they had been ill-treated by fate. She illustrates that they also actively resist dialogues concerning guilt. Moreover, they have assumed a stance that discourages Klein-Löw from asking questions on this topic. She anticipates a refusal even to consider responsibility. With their defensive stance, they thus effectively silence Klein-Löw to prevent her from challenging their versions of the past.

Klein-Löw's acquiescence to silence appears contradictory in light of the description of her welcome back, her inaugural speech after her return, and her self-stylization as a rebel throughout her memoirs. As noted in chapter 1, Klein-Löw returned to "The adventure 'New Austria-Old *Heimat*'" (1980, 165). According to her memoirs, Klein-Löw was welcomed back into her Socialist "family" and given her *Heimat* again. However, upon closer examination, her acceptance into the *Heimat* appears to have occurred at the expense of an honest and open dialogue about the recent past. When we consider the description of her inaugural speech and earlier comments on her ability to return, we find evidence that she has unconsciously recognized the unspoken sanctioned discursive borders within which she could speak of exile and her experience. In her speech she remains "concrete" (*sachlich*), speaks in general terms about exile, and does not recount her own personal experiences (171). When writing about her motivations for return, she clearly distances herself from other Jewish returnees when she comments, "[w]e did not have a hate complex against *the* Austrians, *the* Viennese, *the* Aryans. We did not allow ourselves to be infected by others. What had happened would and could not be forgotten. But hate is a bad course in a new era" (165).[16] Designating the embittered Jews as the "diseased other," she participates in the marginalization and stigmatizing of Jews and adopts aspects of the anti-Semitic rhetoric. If she were to speak in detail about her personal experiences, she possibly runs the danger of being labeled as someone "infected" by hate like Lothar. If remembered within the proper bounds and in the proper contexts, the explosiveness of the past can be contained.

The more integrated the memoirists were into official Austria, the less clear-cut their position vis-à-vis the linguistic divide. This particularly applies to someone like Stella Klein-Löw, who was very involved with

Socialist Party politics.[17] The party did not welcome back all former
Socialist exiles. Out of political expediency, the party did not seriously
question the mainstream victim narratives in its desire to win votes
of former Nazis.[18] Moreover, the Socialist Party was not immune to
anti-Semitism or anti-Semitic rhetoric. A memoirist such as Klein-Löw
who saw herself as part of the Socialist "we" was forced to negotiate
a linguistic morass within which she herself became mired. By align-
ing herself with a larger political cause that transcended psychological
traumas, Klein-Löw distances herself from other Jewish returnees. In
contrast, Lothar was perhaps able to avoid becoming entangled in such
a compromising rhetoric because his profession did not demand the
same degree of identification with contemporary Austria. He looked
to the past for identification. He nonetheless found himself in the
category of "diseased other" when he tried to relate his experiences
and feelings.

Hilde Spiel reveals the perversity of the situation reémigrés found
themselves in by providing the example of a nonexile Austrian who has
little problem assuming the role of victim in his conversation with her. In
her literary diary *Rückkehr nach Wien,* she describes her first encounter
with a waiter from her favorite café when she returned to Vienna in
1946 for the first time since her 1938 visit:

> I walk out of the light and he recognizes me. Amazement and fear appear
> in his face as if he had expected to see me again only in the hereafter.
> Then to my dismay a scene takes place, down to the last detail, just like an
> Austrian friend of mine who had died in exile had predicted. Sometimes,
> in the internment camp or after his release from the Isle of Man during
> the bomb attacks on London, he had imagined his reception in Café
> Herrenhof.
>
> "Herr Doctor spent the war abroad?" the waiter would ask him in that
> polite indirect manner customary since the days of Maria Theresia. "That
> was smart of Herr Doctor. You saved yourself a lot of unpleasantness.
> If Herr Doctor only knew what happened to us. The suffering we went
> through. How well Herr Doctor looks, really a joy to see!"
>
> Expropriation, humiliation, imprisonment, and the constant threat of
> death, illegal flight across closed borders, years of exile, an enemy alien in
> a country rocked by war—all this would be made to seem like nothing,
> would dissipate in the air, be swept away with a snap of the fingers. Herr
> Hnatek begins the very same way, full of self-pity, to complain about his
> fate and the fate of Vienna whose dust I so successfully have shaken from
> my shoes.
>
> "Frau Doctor did the right thing by going away. The bombings
> alone—three times they set the entire city in flames." (1968, 78–79)[19]

67

In this much-quoted passage, Spiel points to the temporary effectiveness of the non-Jewish interlocutor in keeping her out of the conversation. She also uncovers his defensive stance and counters after the fact with a brief résumé of the experience of exile. By focusing on the bombings and their narrow world, the Austrians can construct themselves as victims. However, Spiel puts this in perspective and shows that suffering and experiencing trauma does not necessarily make one a victim. After Spiel's description the reader must conclude that the waiter was aware of the persecution of Jewish Austrians. His reaction reveals that he knows about the fate of the Jews in the concentration camps. He had already assumed she had been murdered like so many other Austrian Jews. The fear she detects in his face precedes his defensive discourse.

By highlighting their early postwar encounters with Austrians who experienced National Socialism in the *Ostmark*, the memoirists expose the multiple ways they were "shut out from language." Their experiences as persecuted and exiled were either absent from the stories of nonexile Austrians or perverted by their interlocutors. The nonexile Austrian interlocutors engaged in discursive practices that sought to bar or discourage a true exchange. Moreover, clear—albeit unspoken— boundaries of acceptable speech were demarcated in the exchanges. There seemed to be a tacit agreement about what could and could not be talked about. Jewish Austrians who crossed the boundary were labeled "bitter," "revengeful," and "infected."

SALVAGING MEMORIES—DOCUMENTING MEMORIES—MEMORIES AS DOCUMENT

In the melded stances of participant, eyewitness, and historian, the memoir writers connect the past with the present. In order to legitimize themselves as narrators of the past and convince readers of the veracity of their stories, they suggest the painfulness of salvaging past traumas, document their memories, and ultimately present them as documentary material. Because the past in question is tied to their sense of self, the memoirists are personally invested in convincing their readers of the validity of their memories and imparting their emotional impact. Moreover, in writing about their past they not only reenter, but can potentially reshape an Austrian "we." And their memories possibly challenged much of what readers had heard or could point to gaps in the collective memory of the readers. Their memories become "testimony" in a response to what Shoshana Felman labels a "crisis of truth":

> In its most traditional, routine use in the legal context—in the courtroom situation—testimony is provided, and is called for, when the facts upon

which justice must pronounce its verdict are not clear, when historical accuracy is in doubt and when both the truth and its supporting elements of evidence are called into question. The legal model of the trial dramatizes, in this way, a contained, and culturally channeled, institutionalized, *crisis of truth*. The trial both derives from and proceeds by, a crisis of evidence, which the verdict must resolve. (1992, 6)

As "witnesses" in this public arena in Austria's "crisis of truth," the memoirists employ multiple strategies to solicit readers' identification and sympathy and to activate a desire to find out more about Austrian history and the history of exile.

To bring readers toward a position contrary to mainstream victim narratives and closer to the narrated past, the memoir writers do not question the truth value of their memories. The memoirists rarely mention the fallibility of memory, since questioning the veracity of their memories could weaken their challenge to Austrian victim narratives.[20] The vividness of the memories, particularly those of extremely emotional events, is one of the striking characteristics of the memoirs. Well sketched are the farewells from family and friends, which were in many cases the last time they saw these people alive. The scenes of humiliation and escape are also particularly gripping in their sharpness.

Researchers have correlated high memory retention to highly emotional events. The memoirists' descriptions often bring to mind what psychologists have termed a "flashbulb memory"—a memory of "a novel and shocking event" that "activates a special brain mechanism. . . . Even if flashbulb memories are prone to fading and decaying over time, they still might be better retained than memories for more ordinary events" (Schacter 1996, 195, 198). Even though they do change with time, these memories are more likely to be "subjectively compelling." (199). Whether the memoirists remember the events exactly as they happened is not essential: the vividness of the memories conveys an emotional truth.

Sometimes, rather than describing certain events, the memoirists simply suggest that they remember them as if they had happened yesterday. For example, Elisabeth Freundlich explicitly comments on the clarity with which she can visualize the evening before she fled Austria. She begins the chapter entitled "March 1938 in Vienna" with the assertion, "I still see the events before me today with undiminished clarity. Even today, after over half a century" (1999, 55).[21] By maintaining the sharpness of the memory, the author conveys the emotional impact of the events. By not describing it, she suggests the difficulty in translating extreme emotions into language.

Stella Klein-Löw, Minna Lachs, and Hans Thalberg present remembering as extremely painful and their memories as unmediated
truth, independent of themselves.[22] Both Klein-Löw and Lachs employ
metaphors that point to the traumatic nature of their experiences. Klein-
Löw explains that through writing, "a lot also came to the surface that
I would have gladly forgotten, that had been kept in the subconscious
behind lock and key up until that point" (1980, 9).[23] Once released,
the memories take on a life of their own. In the chapter entitled "The
'Brown' Flood: 1938–1939," Klein-Löw presents her memories as independent and separate from her conscious self. "Nothing brings us closer
to people, events, the entire atmosphere than experiences, characters,
episodes sketched without any chronology, just as memory dictates them
into the quill" (112).[24] By showing her memories as having a life of their
own and dictating themselves to her, Klein-Löw holds up her memories
self-assuredly to those of nonexile Austrians and suggests the power of
memories to engage her audience.

Only once in the course of her memoirs does Klein-Löw consider
the possibility that her memories might not be unmediated. She questions her memory of riots in July 1927 when the Palace of Justice was set
on fire. "I couldn't swear whether that was experienced or reexperienced
or vicariously experienced through tales of others. That the newspaper
reports played a role in this memory goes without saying. But—no! The
memory of the mayor's effort to prevent the worst was real" (67).[25] Despite possible "contamination" of her memories, Klein-Löw is convinced
they truly replicate her experience because as she writes she is able to
visualize herself in the scene. "While writing this I closed my eyes for a
moment" (67–68).[26] Much of the study of memory would suggest that
one can indeed remember things one did not experience (Schacter 1996,
200). Nonetheless, her explanations are no doubt meant to convince her
readers and herself.

Klein-Löw strengthens her claim to the veracity of her memories
when she reminds the reader at the end of her memoir that she has a photographic memory. "Whoever is amazed at the exactness of my memories
should take into consideration that I, as already mentioned, have a
photographic memory. My 'memory-photos' reproduce the event either
in black and white or color, according to its own nature" (210).[27] Klein-
Löw thus calls on the reader to understand her memories and memoirs
as photographic representations of the past.

Like Klein-Löw, Lachs also chooses a metaphor of containment to
describe her relationship to memories associated with Nazi rule. If Klein-
Löw kept her painful memories behind lock and key, Lachs imagines her
traumatic memories as a sunken vessel. As with Klein-Löw's "memory

chest," once she retrieves the "vessel," Lachs sets out on an expedition from which there is no turning back:

> The memories come over me—without me having called them up either chronologically or continuously. They rise up from the depths where I forced them and repressed them, as if each of them demanded not to be forgotten. They demand that I translate them into language and give them shape. In my memory, feelings, thoughts, dreams, and realities collide, they hunt and persecute me. I would have to write volumes in order to do justice to each one of these risen up dreams that has forced itself upon the daylight. As if I had raised up a vessel from the deep whose cover cannot be shut anymore. They besiege me to exhaustion, they haunt me until I can stand them no longer. I can only give form to a representative sample. However even this washes me up onto shores where I do not want to land because only undergrowth and boulders await me there. (1986, 185).[28]

Lachs's discussion of memory is pivotal in an examination of the rhetoric of remembering for several reasons. She underlines the fact that she is making a selection from her memories, giving them shape and investing them with meaning. She imparts to her readers the emotional risks she undertakes by recalling this past. And she ultimately shows traumatic memories as autonomous, something beyond her control.

As we have seen with Klein-Löw and Lachs, Hans Thalberg does not question the veracity of his memories; he presents his life story as experienced truth. "I have tried to depict this sunken world with all its virtues and faults just as I experienced it. In doing this I have tried to avoid the reproach of narcissistic self-representation or self-pitying" (1984, 15–16).[29] However, in contrast to Klein-Löw and Lachs, he appeals directly to his reader to forgive emotion when it seems extreme to them. "If, however, pain and bitterness have made their way into the first part of this text, then may the indulgent reader forgive this. I can assure him that the experienced reality was much worse than can be expressed in words" (16).[30] A somewhat contradictory position emerges here. While maintaining the truth value of his story, Thalberg suggests the impossibility of conveying the "experienced reality." He captures the memoirists' dilemma of relating their stories and feelings to listeners who can never comprehend the depth of their loss and emotions. This apparent contradiction arises from the tension in constructing a narrative of such traumatic events. On the one hand, Thalberg desires to construct a tellable story, but on the other hand, the events themselves resist telling.[31]

Once memories are accessed, the memoirists have to sift through them. Only then can they make sense out of their memories or present them to the audience in a palatable form. How the memories are selected and interpreted is tied to the memoirists' position within postwar Austrian society and their position vis-à-vis the mainstream victim narratives. Vividness, immediacy, and assurances of the truth value of the memories alone may not be enough to legitimize the memoir writers' memories and their narrative authority within the Austrian context. The writers therefore document their memories through a variety of strategies.

Lothar, Lachs, Spiel, and Thalberg all mention their reliance on diaries or daily notes. The inclusion of excerpts from journals and diaries could be seen as indirect acknowledgment of the fallibility of memory and the ways in which memories are constantly reconstituted. However, the writers rarely compare the excerpts with earlier memories or use them to reflect on the validity of their memories. They insert the notes much more to confirm and document memory and with them attempt to re-create the past "as it was." This is supported by the use of other documentary materials. Freundlich, Spiel, Lachs, and Tausig seek additional legitimization of their memories in a documentary stance attained through the inclusion of letters, official documents, and photographs, investing their narratives with a more historical tone.

The letters fill a function similar to the journal and diary entries: documenting memory and re-creating the past "as it was." Freundlich and Spiel both explicitly acknowledge the documentary nature of these letters, and Lachs and Tausig imply it. Freundlich quotes extensively from the last letter she received from her friend Otto Heller, who was involved in the resistance in France and ultimately died in the concentration camp at Ebensee (Austria). She explicitly views this as documentary material: "The last letter sent to me, dated March 15, 1941, first mentions his ever-changing travel problems; but as it continues, it reflects so much of the conflicting sensations, and is so much a document of the time, makes so evident the proud, calm behavior of Otto Heller, that I would like to quote it" (1999, 71).[32] She conveys the difficult moral dilemmas facing those who had to choose between leaving Europe and endangering their lives by staying there (96–98). More than this, she documents how love of his Austrian *Heimat* actually led to Heller's death.

Spiel, too, explicitly considers the documentary value of letters her first husband Peter de Mendelssohn sends her from Berlin after the war. "All these letters, ten in all, . . . are of some documentary value" (1989b, 208).[33] Later she includes excerpts from her correspondence with de Mendelssohn during her first trip to Vienna after the war. She does this effectively to capture the feeling at the time and to reflect on her position years later.

By including a letter to her parents, Lachs hopes to re-create the mood at the time of the Hitler-Stalin Pact. "I had brought along a letter that I had written my parents in Israel on September 23, 1939. It reflects the mood that affected not only us political emigrants, but also the Swiss population after the beginning of the *Blitzkrieg* against Poland" (1992, 50).[34] Lachs's letter not only captures the mood, but also illustrates that her memory of this is shaped more by her understanding of herself as a political refugee than as a Jewish refugee.

Tausig quotes from a letter she received in 1948 from the first mate of the ship she traveled on to Shanghai (1987, 65). The letter indicates that the passengers actually underestimated the danger they faced. If the crew had not been able to land, they had orders to kill all the passengers on board. The passengers themselves had feared they would be returned to Germany and sent to concentration camps. Tausig's reaction to the letter and her inability or unwillingness to take up the first mate's offer to meet with her as a gesture of reconciliation also indicate the continuing emotional impact of the harrowing escape and exile.

The most compelling documents are perhaps the photographs. Because readers can relate to photographs on a more personal level than to official documents and letters, they have the potential to bridge a gap between the past and the present. They have the "capacity to signal absence and loss and, at the same time, to make present, rebuild, reconnect, bring back to life" (M. Hirsch 1997, 243). They document memory, simultaneously pointing to its limitations. "They affirm a past's existence" (23), while making us aware of what has been lost. With photographs the writers supplement their narratives and capture their memories visually. Moreover, the combination of text and image enhances the possibilities for reader identification and recognition of the void created by the loss.

In her discussion of the "Tower of Faces" at the United States Holocaust Memorial Museum, Marianne Hirsch writes of the power of family photographs. "[T]hey re-create something of what has been destroyed, even as they elicit and facilitate the viewer's mourning of the destruction. The conventionality of the family photo provides a space of identification for any viewer participating in the conventions of familial representation" (1997, 251). Like the curators of the museum, the writers are engaged in creating post-memory in their readers. The memoirists aim their life stories not at an audience of other exiles or well-informed children of exiles, but at a public with little knowledge of the events.

Both Freundlich and Spiel state explicitly in their narratives that they are poring over pictures and using them to recover lost memories

and knowledge about the past. At three points in her narrative, Freundlich mentions photographs and then describes them. The first is a picture
of an uncle killed in World War I, the second a picture postcard her
mother sent to her father before their relationship became serious,
and the third is a school photograph of Freundlich's class. With the
first photograph, Freundlich compares her emotional distance from a
picture of her uncle killed in World War I to the feelings evoked by his
handwriting to suggest the ways in which emotional attachments shape
memory and responses (1992, 26). Her uncle wrote to her throughout
her childhood and she could reproduce his handwriting while his picture
meant little to her. The second photograph allows her to recover a family
memory before her birth (1992, 29) and discuss class difference and the
ways in which her mother was treated by other girls as an arriviste. She
uses the third photograph to document most explicitly an effaced past
and draw in her Austrian audience. Looking at the photo, a class picture
from 1917, Freundlich can remember neither the names nor faces of
many of her classmates. Part of her past is unrecoverable. Nonetheless,
the picture allows her to speculate on the fates of her classmates and
their actions after 1938: "When the Second World War broke out all
of my former schoolmates must have been a bit over thirty years old.
Was the gentle Toni also thrust into a uniform, did he also have to fight
for the 'Thousand-Year Reich,' did he live through it? And the others
who were of the Mosaic Confession, were some of them able to escape
destruction? I don't know. Their tracks have been wiped away" (31–
32).[35] Through the picture, she connects the classmates' histories and
fates, tying disparate Austrian stories together. She is sympathetic to the
fate of Austrians on both sides of the experiential divide. However, she
clearly delineates radically different fates.

Like Freundlich, Spiel uses photographs to access the past or to
demonstrate the holes in family memory (see especialy 1989b, 27,
29, 32). However, she also connects herself to some of the major
public figures and movements of her time. Scattered throughout the
two volumes are photographs of prominent thinkers of the twentieth
century, usually accompanied by descriptions of her relationship to
these people.

Other documents the memoir writers include in the memoirs are
excerpts from newspaper articles, handbills from a theater performance
and a reading of Austrian prose and poetry in exile, a passport, and
official state department documents from both the United States and
Austrian governments. The memoir writers invest their texts with a
documentary appearance, suggesting the "truth value" of their memories. The sometimes seemingly arbitrary selection of documents hints at

the dearth and one-sidedness of documentary material on this period. Much of the material has been destroyed, and many of the remaining documents are from the Nazis.

If the memoir writers attempt to document memory with the inclusion of photographs, official documents, and letters, they also point to the limitations of such documentary material. Because of the nature of the National Socialist terror, the Jewish genocide, exile, and the destruction of the war, documents of their lives as well as those of others have been eradicated. Thus, memory becomes important "evidence" and a virtual archive. In either retelling their search for traces of their past after 1938 or in the course of writing their memoirs, the memoir writers engage in their own investigations of the past and come to realize that sometimes memory itself is the only remaining connection. For example, Minna Lachs vainly seeks information on the night school where she taught in Vienna:

> After my return to Vienna in 1947 I tried in vain to find out from the Vienna Board of Education and the Ministry of Education what had happened to the college preparatory school "Universum" and whether the name of its temporary director in 1938 could be found out for me. There were no records anywhere, many archives had perished in the flames. I almost fear that the only proof that this "Universum" ever existed in the 9th district at 7 Garnisongasse is the proof of employment that Prof. Nathansky made out for me in March 1938 with the school stamp and date. He himself perished in a concentration camp. (1986, 198–99)[36]

She discovers that except for one document in her possession and her memories, virtually every trace of the existence of the school "Universum" had been destroyed. Lachs illustrates that traditional documents and memories can complement each other for a more thorough understanding of the past, implying that the memories themselves can be viewed as documents of the past.

The memoirists not only have the credibility of their lives at stake, but the memory of others they carry with them. The weight of these memories creates a narrative tension between the forward motion of their stories and the "impeding" or digressive motion of the story fragments or truncated stories of others. The memoir writers often interrupt their own life stories with the stories of others. These digressions allow them to pay tribute to those who helped them, honor a certain admired moral standard maintained by a small segment of the population, suggest areas for further historical investigation, and commemorate family and friends who were murdered.

Tausig's life story is peppered with monuments to those who helped her escape or showed her some measure of kindness. For example, Tausig remembers an unidentified woman who helped her and her husband in Hamburg. Unable to find a hotel that would take Jews, they are stranded on a rainy, miserable night before they leave for Shanghai: "It would be worthwhile to erect a monument to her. A pot of hot tea when you're freezing, a bed in which you can have a good sleep, your clothes, which are drying next to the oven; that can give you the courage to survive. She was much older than we and is certainly not alive. I would like to lay a wreath down here for her" (1987, 35).[37] Tausig's "monument" is a very personal remembrance of personal kindness. Her quiet verbal imagery contrasts with the bombast and hubris of war monuments.

Tausig also includes vignettes of people she meets along the way whom she feels have also been discriminated against, for example, a Chinese prostitute and an African sailor who befriend her. She shows particular compassion for those she perceives to be less fortunate than herself but who nonetheless maintain a sense of human decency.

Thalberg uses his memories as partial documents to call on others to uncover hidden stories of this past:

> When I illegally crossed over the Swiss border from France in October 1942, the motto of the Swiss officials was: The boat is full. I was able to escape deportation and so my life was saved. The commemoration of the many who were not able to escape the barbaric regulations demands, however, that the cloak of silence not be spread over these matters. The drama of those people who were hounded and persecuted and handed over to the henchmen at the Swiss border after great trials and tribulations still has to be written. It belongs to that picture of human brutalization that alone the Holocaust made possible. (1984, 116–17)[38]

He interrupts his story of escape briefly to remember those less fortunate as part of his effort to remove "the cloak of silence" from the past. He, like other memoirists, implicitly and explicitly suggests directions for further historical investigation.

The memoir writers also commemorate the deeds of those active in resistance movements, Jews and non-Jews alike. For example, both Thalberg and Freundlich interrupt their life stories to tell of Emil Alphons Rheinhardt and his contribution as an Austrian expressionist writer as well as someone active in the French resistance who helped many of the exiles. Rheinhardt's story ends like so many others. Thalberg poignantly marks his death and disappearance with the abrupt ending: "Nobody ever heard anything more from him" (1984, 115).[39] In her portrayal of Rheinhardt, Freundlich remains very factual and as a writer shows particular interest in Rheinhardt's literary significance. "His name turns up occasionally in Austrian literary history as a representative of the Expressionists, but the second part of his life has remained largely unknown in Austria: the not insignificant works which he produced in France, his other activities there, and his tragic end" (1999, 61).[40] Freundlich suggests the writer-resistance fighter died a second, symbolic death with the ignorance concerning his oeuvre.

Lothar memorializes Raoul Auernheimer, another cultural figure who he feels has made an important contribution to Austria, but who has been forgotten: "I feel the need to commemorate him here because there are not many people left who received lasting impressions from an encounter with him. And also too few remember his writings and his impact on the Austrian mind. He shared this fate with other superb Austrian intellectuals whom the raging demon banished to the concentration camps" (1961, 160–61).[41] Lothar portrays Auernheimer, who escaped to the United States after his release from Dachau, as an untiring cultural diplomat for Austria. His short memorial, too, largely lacks affect.

Klein-Löw remembers the young couple Hans and Steffi Kunke, whom she first met when they helped her dispose of emergency supplies after the debacle of 1934: in February civil war briefly broke out between the Socialists and government forces. As a result the Socialist Party was outlawed and material that could have incriminated its members had to be destroyed. After Klein-Löw introduces the couple she briefly describes Steffi and then the horrible fate of the couple: "My helpers were Steffi and Hans Kunke. I became friends with Steffi. She was a teacher and a great person: carefree, cheerful, open-minded. She had a beautiful voice. Her large, sparkling eyes spoke such a clear language of affection and enthusiasm. (Both were later cruelly tortured and murdered, he in Buchenwald, she in Auschwitz, where she had been sent from Ravensbrück)" (1980, 90).[42] With few words, Klein-Löw juxtaposes Steffi's vibrancy and vivaciousness with the pointless, horrible murder of her and her husband. With her parenthetical statement, she interrupts her chronological narrative and mini-portrait to point in a very straightforward, unemotional manner to the fate of friends and colleagues whose lives were so brutally cut short.[43]

The memorials to family members and friends range from longer descriptions of individual family members and their fates to very terse mentions of the person. What they share is the absence of affect in relating their loss. In an article on interviewing concentration camp survivors entitled, "Interviewing Victims Who Survived: Listening for the Silences That Strike," historian Sidney M. Bolkosky remarks on the lack of affect of survivors in relating moments where the listener expected "emotional storms." "Perhaps the most startling, even eerie, discovery for interviewers has been the low affect, the unemotional quality of survivor accounts. This exceeds sadness or depression" (1987, 41). Because of the nature of written texts, "writing" in silences and consequently "listening" for silences becomes a unique challenge.[44] If the memoirists found themselves silenced by their non-Jewish Austrian interlocutors on occasion, the silence that is present in reporting the deaths of murdered family and friends can be read as a commemorative silence that poignantly draws attention to their and Austria's profound loss. Thalberg uses the fate of his mother's family, the Kellner family, to introduce his tribute to his family. "The tragic fate of the maternal side of my family was symbolic and typical of the fate of the demise of Vienna's Jewish haute bourgeoisie" (1984, 67).[45] After providing a brief history of the family, he summarizes what remains. "Out of several dozen children and children's children of the fourteen *Kellner children*, only five survived. They live throughout the world and write one another letters occasionally" (70).[46] Thalberg's long "inventory" of family members—their characteristics and accomplishments as well as a description of their skepticism that Hitler could separate them from Austria—stands in stark contrast to the terse two sentences that close this passage.

Klein-Löw provides another example of the stocktaking typical of the memoir writers: "Out of my large, very close family with its many branches, forty-eight people were swallowed up by the Moloch fascism. Among them was Mischa, a year older than I, with whom I spent my childhood, ran races, climbed trees, with whom I horsed around and read books. No, it's better not to think about it" (1980, 166).[47] Like Thalberg, Klein-Löw relates very matter-of-factly how her family was decimated by the Jewish genocide. However, she then focuses on memories of one particular relative with whom she shared childhood memories. She provides the reader with "snapshots" of her memories, which eventually overwhelm and silence her. Tausig, too, sums up the destruction of her family using few words. "It [death] reached my parents in Theresienstadt, where they had been deported. My siblings were killed in Yugoslavia. I alone survived" (1987, 64).[48] Like the other writers reporting on the deaths of family members, Tausig keeps her commemoration very factual, with little outward emotion. The pain of loss can never be conveyed, and she falls silent.

Not only a commemorative silence, the narrative silence woven in the stories within stories can be compared to Henry Greenspan's description of the "stories about the death of stories" evident in the narratives of the Holocaust survivors he spoke with. If death is not "recreated within them," they are cut off by death (Greenspan 1998, 15). This is repeated again and again in the stories of family and friends and most poignantly related by Minna Lachs. A childhood friend of her younger sister has a message for her:

> I have a final message that Monek Katz left for you. . . . He had survived the murder of his wife and two children, now it was his turn. We were sitting in the dark. At that point Monek suggested that each of us should tell the name and address of a particular person to whom—should one of us survive by some miracle—a last message be passed on. (1986, 140)[49]

By passing on Monek Katz' final message in turn to her readers, Lachs points to the vast void created by the Holocaust.

As perhaps the only ones with access to a particular past, the memoirists construct themselves as keepers of memory and their memories as legitimate "documents." As such, their memoirs deviate from conventional autobiography and memoir to become memorials, testimonies, and testimonials.

Conclusion

If the predominant victim narratives derive authority from the stances of participant, eyewitness, and historian often found in memoirs, so too do the memoirs of the Jewish Austrians. In the national victim narratives in public and private discourse, these positions and strategies of authority serve to silence, block out other stories, avoid guilt, promote forgetting, trivialize Jewish suffering, and ultimately avoid dealing with trauma. In contrast, the memoirists draw on these strategies to fight the silencing of the mainstream narratives and contextualize the traumatic experiences of the non-Jewish population. At the same time they bring attention to the silence surrounding the Holocaust and commemorate their personal and national loss through a narrative silence.

In the combined stance of eyewitness, participant, and historian, they seek to reenter language and collective memory. In the memoirists' desire to reach an audience and assert narrative authority, they unmask their own marginalization in the descriptions of and reflections on their exchanges with Austrians concerning the National Socialist years. By highlighting the linguistic divide between themselves and non-Jewish Austrians, the memoirists draw attention to the constructed nature of reality through language and question the validity of Austrian collective memory. They demand a reassessment of the mainstream narratives and the behavior of the general population, and they seek to open up Austrian narratives to more stories.

As part of their effort to convince their audience and reclaim their past, the memoir writers simultaneously document their memories and construct their memories as documents, insisting in both cases on the truth value of the memories. They reconstitute themselves as "speaking" subjects whose identity is based on the suffering of others as well as their own experiences and memories. In struggling for a place in collective memory, the memoirists show themselves as a repository for the memories of many who did not survive to tell their stories.

ᴂ 3 ᴓ

Mapping Trauma and Mourning

In *Shanghai Passage*, Franziska Tausig poignantly captures one of the challenges of articulating extreme emotional loss in the description of her reaction to her husband's death in exile. "Then I jumped up and began to howl. I howled like an animal. I howled at God who had inflicted this upon me. The howling didn't want to stop, but then it did grow fainter so that only I could still hear it. I still hear it thirty years later" (1987, 94).[1] Tausig's experience of the trauma of her husband's death seems to defy language. Although not "a frightening event outside of ordinary human experience" (van der Kolk and van der Hart 1995, 172), the death of her husband contributed to Tausig's perception of exile as a traumatic experience. Her sense of profound loss finds voice in a pre-language. As trauma researchers Bessel A. van der Kolk and Onno van der Hart maintain, "[t]he experience [of trauma] cannot be organized on a linguistic level." Tausig captures not only the pre-linguistic character of trauma, but also the possible lasting effects of such an emotional wound. After Tausig's open expression of grief ceases, the howl appears to take on a life of its own, separating itself from her but still ever present within her. The howl of grief remains audible to no one but her, suggesting that on one level she is able to function normally, but on another level, the pain of this loss will never disappear.

In addition to trauma's resistance to verbal expression and its persistence in traumatic memories, the memoirists are faced with further challenges that point to the cultural context within which remembering and telling take place. Not only do the writers grapple with turning the "howl" into words, they struggle with capturing the severity of the pain in a way their audience can hear. Hans Thalberg addresses the dilemma of telling to those who have no basis for understanding. After learning about the murder of his father and receiving news that his mother in Auschwitz is doing very poorly, he seeks out a Swiss lawyer in the hope of gaining contact with American relatives: "In the lawyer's office I was received in a friendly fashion and asked about my concern. But it was totally impossible for me to express what was in my heart. How can one speak about Auschwitz, war, and resistance in a totally bourgeois, expensively furnished library of a friendly, but totally uncomprehending, smiling lawyer from Zurich" (1984, 119–20).[2] The impossibility of telling his parents' story to those who have no frame of reference parallels the challenges facing the memoir writers in telling their stories to an Austrian audience. As I argued in chapter 2, the memoirists must relate their own traumatic experiences and those of Jewish Austrians within a society that has long held on to its victim status and made its experiences of the trauma of war part of an exclusionary collective identity.

The search for the words to convey the processes of trauma and mourning is further complicated by the writers' knowledge of the suffering and genocide of those in the concentration camps. The memoirists usually situate their own suffering and loss of *Heimat* in relation to those who suffered or were murdered in the concentration camps. For example, Ernst Lothar comments on the difficulty of finding the right balance of emotion in his life story in the face of the horrors of the concentration and internment camps. "Perhaps it all sounds too rosy, perhaps the gray, howling misery is not present that was present and darkened every bright spot. However, I do not want to try to show off with suffering that pales in comparison to that of those in Dachau or Belsen, Mauthausen, and Gurs" (1961, 137).[3] In situating himself in relationship to those who were persecuted in the concentration camps and internment camps, Lothar suggests that he tones down the emotion in his narrative in order not to diminish the suffering of those in the camps while at the same time he recalls the pre-linguistic nature of his pain. Like Lothar, most of the memoir writers make reference to concentration camps, stating that their experiences could never have been as bad as the experiences of those in the camps. But by the same token, they also intimate that their experiences were much worse than words could ever express and point to the poverty of language.

Faced with the challenges of putting words to extreme emotions, while seeking to reach a largely non-Jewish Austrian audience and honoring the murders of friends and family, the writers express their loss and healing in manifold ways. If we consider specific representations of the trauma and mourning of the loss of *Heimat*, two related constellations emerge: the body and Austria are recurrent "sites" onto which the memoirists inscribe the complex processes of trauma and mourning. They suggest the importance of body and spatial memories for accessing traumatic memories as well as finding a means to express the inexpressible.

Because being Jewish in post-1938 Austria had physically dangerous if not fatal consequences, it is not surprising that the reémigrés remember their psychological trauma through their corporeality. The writers use the body, as the potential or actual receiver of blows, literally and figuratively to represent their emotional wounds. They illustrate the complexity of memory and challenge any facile distinction between physical and psychological trauma. Furthermore, by depicting the impact of the political constellations on their bodies, the memoir writers purposely blur the borders between public and private experiences. The consequences of the profound loss of *Heimat* are most immediately conveyed through the corporealization of traumatic memory and mourning.[4]

Because the memoirists' sense of spatial identity is tied to Austria, Austrian cityscapes and landscapes also play a central role in representations of trauma and mourning; the healed self is mapped to specific Austrian locations of personal significance to the individual writers. If the corporealization of trauma and mourning provides a means to express how the racism of National Socialism affected individuals, the projections of trauma and mourning onto specific Austrian cityscapes and landscapes allow the writers to externalize these psychological processes. Their injured bodies become symbolic of the impact of the nation's trauma on individuals. The nation's body in the form of its cityscapes and landscapes embodies the exiles' personal trauma and mourning.

The Corporeality of Trauma and Mourning

Drawing on the original meaning of the Greek word *trauma*—"wound"—the majority of the writers effectively convey their extreme emotional injury by using the body both literally and figuratively. With the *Anschluss* in March 1938, the bodies of people who perceived themselves as having multiple identities were reduced to specifically "Jewish" "alien" bodies (*Fremdkörper*). As such, they found themselves in mortal danger within the borders of the expanded Germany. The memoir writers describe physical humiliations they and other Jewish Austrians were subjected to, threatened with, or witnessed after the

Anschluss. Although Minna Lachs and Hilde Spiel make references to pre-*Anschluss* attacks on Jewish students and Lachs and Thalberg write about open anti-Semitism before 1938, these physical and verbal attacks and social snubs pale in comparison to what followed the *Anschluss*. Reflecting on the days immediately following the *Anschluss*, Elisabeth Freundlich writes: "One is more than aware of the images of what would have awaited us, if. . . . The old people, crawling on their knees, scouring away the *Kruckenkreuze* [crosslike symbols of the Austro-Fascists] with toothbrushes and soapy water, amid gleeful looks and catcalls from passers-by" (1999, 56).[5] Lachs's description of one scene where she witnessed a group of Jews being rounded up only to find out later that they were driven into the Danube Canal is typical of the brutality of those days. "Only very good swimmers could save themselves" (1986, 201).[6] Tausig, whose husband was arrested during the November Pogrom, or *Kristallnacht,* was thrown down a flight of steps in her efforts to secure her husband's freedom (1987, 28). At a time when they were most strongly aware of their bodies, it would have been desirable to be invisible, to lose one's corporeality and disappear into thin air. "To be nowhere, that was our motto" (Tausig 1987, 31).[7] In the face of such almost unimaginable—yet horribly real—persecution, many chose death. "A wave of suicides had set in" (Lachs 1986, 188).[8]

If the memoir writers were not conscious of their physical features and physicality before the *Anschluss,* this changed radically in the days following it. Those who looked "Jewish" were particularly endangered. Tausig relates the story of how a group of Austrian Jews were rounded up during one of the SS actions, humiliated, and forced to do exercises until they collapsed. Because she did not look Jewish, she was separated from the group in order not to destroy the picture (1987, 39–40). Thalberg writes of his sister: "*Marietta* seemed particularly endangered because she had inherited dark hair and eyes from Father and looked 'Jewish.' I myself felt safer, I had light eyes and hair" (1984, 63).[9] Marietta was indeed in danger. After saying good-bye to her brother when he left on the train for Yugoslavia, she was picked up by the Nazis, never to return. Both Tausig and Thalberg underscore the absurdity of the notion of an essential Jewish body. Tausig shows that she did not fit the stereotype and thus was spared, at least in that instance, bodily harm. Thalberg illustrates that he could move around unscathed.

However, escaping their familiar surroundings—now turned into a death trap—does not ensure the memoirists' bodily safety. All stations of exile are shown as impacting on the exiles' bodies. Thalberg describes the conditions of an internment camp in France: "Naturally, they were not death camps and every comparison with the Nazi camps has to be ruled out. Nonetheless, especially those people from well-ordered bourgeois households suffered a severe shock right away; the degradation and humiliation, the physical strain were overwhelming" (88).[10] What was particularly ironic for many of those in the internment camps was the fact that they were treated like "German" bodies by the native population. "We left Colombes in big buses; a yelling and threatening mob of French women awaited us in front of the stadium, spit on us, threw stones at us; they thought we were Nazis" (89).[11] With this, Thalberg again dispels the racist ideology of the Nazis. The bodies of the exiles are floating signifiers that take on different meaning according to the situation and location.

Lachs provides several examples of how women's bodies are more vulnerable or threatened not only because they are Jewish bodies, but also because they are female bodies. Lachs relates a humiliating body search at the border. The female border guard orders Lachs to strip and accuses her of "Jewish tricks" when she sees the sanitary napkin Lachs is wearing after the difficult birth of her son. Suspecting Lachs is hiding jewels, the guard forces her to remove it and as a result Lachs bleeds onto the floor (1986, 211). Lachs also tells of precautions taken on the boat to the United States to protect the young women from rape (264).

Both Tausig and Lachs describe their journeys by boat to their country of exile as harrowing experiences. For Tausig, traveling on a ship under the control of the Germans meant that she and the other German and Austrian Jews on board were not safe until they reached China. Besides the miserable conditions on the boat, the passengers were in danger of being murdered at sea if the ship had had to turn around before arriving in Shanghai. In the chapter entitled "The Concentration Camp Catches Up to Us," Lachs describes the deplorable conditions on board the *Navemar,* so bad they led to the arrest of the entire crew upon arrival in New York. The ship was overcrowded and had inadequate air circulation, insufficient sanitary facilities, and unacceptable medical staff. During the trip from Spain to the United States, a typhoid epidemic broke out and many of the passengers did not survive.

Once they reached their destinations, the exiles' physical hardships did not cease. In England, Klein-Löw first worked as a domestic servant under extremely physically demanding conditions. Moreover, her first employer delighted in showing off her maid with a Ph.D. Initially Lachs's husband labored all day in a factory and attended night school. Spiel laments the fact that her father was interned on the Isle of Man and he was never able to reestablish himself professionally. Of all the memoirists and their family members who escaped, Tausig suffered the most long-term physical degradation. Living in Shanghai, culturally and climatically very different from Austria, she was faced with extreme living conditions and abject poverty.[12] Moreover, in 1943 when Shanghai was under Japanese control, the majority of the Jewish exile population was confined to the section of town known as Hong Kew, which they could leave only with special permission. Tausig's life in Shanghai proved both emotionally and physically taxing. "The years in Shanghai were bitter years. They were like a cup filled to the brim with a terrible fate that I had to drink to the last drop" (1987, 66).[13] However, for someone who had no formal education, from a well-to-do family used to domestic servants, Tausig proved extremely resourceful and resilient. She had to support herself and her sick husband, which she did largely with domestic and strenuous service jobs, including running a café, doing laundry, and working as a private cook. Understandably, the hard years in Shanghai took their toll on her. Before she began her last job in the kitchen of a hospital, she commented, "[h]unger and deprivation had cost me much strength. When I finally had tied the white apron around my waist and put on the white cap—my future uniform for several years—I had no strength left" (100).[14] Her body becomes a barometer of the strains of exile.

However, the body is used not only to represent real physical hard-ship; it is the embodiment of the pre-linguistic aspect of trauma as well as the corporealization of emotion. Both Thalberg and Lachs provide examples of episodes where the magnitude of events overwhelms their bodies. After hearing about the death of his father and receiving news of his mother in Auschwitz, Thalberg breaks down in an internment camp in Switzerland and loses memory of the days that follow:

> At that point the tremendous emotional breakdown followed. I do not know anymore how many days and nights I could not get up from my straw bed. A few camp comrades, among them a very hard-boiled fellow, took care of me in a touching fashion. When I woke up from my feverish dreams, I had only one desire—to get in touch with my relatives who had saved themselves to the safety and prosperity of the USA in order somehow still to organize help as soon as possible. (1984, 119)[15]

What Thalberg calls an "emotional breakdown" is inseparable from his physical collapse. His father's death and the likelihood of his mother's death along with his own helplessness cannot be processed and can be dealt with only by shutting down temporarily. The loss is too over-whelming to face on a conscious level.

Lachs similarly shows that the traumatic events manifested them-selves in her body. In the days before her escape from Austria, she witnessed a group of fellow Jewish Austrians being brutally abused. Her body reacted to the emotional stress. "During the night I suddenly had terrible pains" (1986, 201).[16] Because she can easily imagine herself in their place, her body is only narrowly removed from their fate. However, still being free, she does imagine how she can exert some control over her body and the situation. Six months pregnant, she finds herself caught in the unthinkable dilemma of carrying her baby to term or protecting it from the world by self-aborting. "For me these were critical hours and days. It also appeared that it was left up to me whether I would carry this growing new life to term or whether I should protect it from entrance into this horrible world through gymnastics" (202).[17] The traumatic experience "threatens" Lachs's subjectivity. However, within the narrow confines of the situation, Lachs exerts limited control over her body and opts for her child.[18]

By focusing on their corporeality at particular historical junctures, the writers provide snapshots of traumatic moments and of their bodies in peril. In contrast, in order to consider the long-term effects of the trauma of loss of *Heimat* and its consequences, the writers use the body as metaphor. They interpret its present state in light of past events or they figuratively "read" the body, plotting changes in it over time. Thalberg depicts the result of the trauma as an irreparable injury. He views and palpably feels the life that he left behind in Vienna like an amputated leg. His connections to the past had been brutally severed with the murder of his parents, sister, and numerous other relatives. "I built up a new existence, a new family, a new life. But the old life that came to an end at that time in 1938 is like an amputated leg that hurts incessantly although it was cut off long ago" (1984, 73).[19] After the defeat of the National Socialist regime, Thalberg was able to establish a new life for himself. He married a non-Jewish Austrian woman whom he had met in Switzerland, and they had a child of their own. He had a very successful career as a diplomat. Nonetheless, the loss of his family and the loss of "Jewish" life in Vienna are a constant wound, perceived like the phantom pain of a lost limb.

Although this is not a particularly original metaphor, it conveys the intense sense of loss and lasting pain.[20] At the same time, Thalberg's body imagery confirms psychiatrist Henry Krystal's observations among elderly Holocaust survivors. Krystal notes that "there is a limitation to how much an individual can absorb through grieving and achieve integrity and good-natured acceptance of the past" (1995, 84). When Thalberg says "I," his inner picture is of someone who has had part of himself brutally cut off. Like Tausig, who alone perceives her howl of pain years after her husband's death, Thalberg alone feels the phantom pain of his amputated life.

The metaphor of amputation, echoed throughout Thalberg's book in anecdotes and marginal comments, is amplified by the very structure of the book. Thalberg explains in the introduction that the first part of the book, entitled "The Amputated Life," is an attempt to acquaint the reader with the author's background and early influences as well as to introduce a side of Vienna that no longer exists. Within the first section is a subsection also labeled "The Amputated Life" (70–73). Here, Thalberg relates his last days in Vienna before exile, the future fates of his parents and sister, and his visit after 1945 to his parents' last apartment before they were deported. By juxtaposing the time frames and depicting the postwar non-Jewish occupant in his parents' apartment, the break caused by the Holocaust is magnified. In addition, Thalberg makes marginal comments that convey his profound loss and recall the phantom pain.

The way in which Thalberg has organized the book sets up a split between Thalberg's past and present selves. The first section of the book ("The Amputated Life") follows his early life up to his return to Vienna and his decision to work for the Austrian foreign service. The remainder and largest part of the book—between two-thirds and three-quarters of the text—spans his career as a diplomat and rarely brings in memories from his "amputated life." Thalberg separates the rest of the book not only with the section divider, but with a series of pictures. Included are three family photos from the period before 1938, a picture of Thalberg and his young daughter, a photo of the internment camp in Switzerland, a series of photographs of Thalberg in the foreign service, and a final family photo of him, his wife, and a relative from the United States in Vienna. The photographs act as a physical and visual divider between his two lives, underscoring the great divide between the period before and after the Jewish genocide.

Ernst Lothar develops an elaborate body metaphor revolving around his own exile experiences and his observations of others in exile. Constructing an explicit pathology of exile, the writer plots exile as a progressive disease, using himself and other exiles to prognosticate. The "emotional death" (*seelischer Tod*) that he and his daughter suffer while preparing to flee marks the onset of his disease. With flight comes shame (1961, 115), and in the new country loss of confidence accompanies displacement (168). As Judith Lewis Herman argues, "[s]hame is a response to helplessness, the violation of bodily integrity, and the indignity suffered in the eyes of another person" (1992, 53). Lothar found himself in a situation where he could not protect his daughter, where he was publicly humiliated, and where his professional accomplishments meant nothing. For a man from a traditional patriarchal society, this must have been particularly emasculating. Lothar, like Améry, observes that exile is a "progressive disease" that leads to homesickness (*Heimweh*):

> Homesickness is an overlooked disease. Whoever suffers from it is not likely to talk about it. It occurs in bouts when one least expects it. A smell can set it off, a song, a bend in the road, a dream, a face, a bird song, a bell ringing. In that very second everything breaks down, the realization of futility emerges as stifling. Every bout resembles the feeling after the death of a loved one, time after time someone dies. With time the bouts become less frequent, never weaker; on the contrary, they increase in vehemence. It is an unresearched disease and for this reason it does not count as one. However, some people die from it. (209–10)[21]

Lothar's pathology of exile is reminiscent of a much earlier discussion by an Alsatian doctor of the seventeenth century. In an article on nostalgic and critical memory within the Jewish émigré community in Bolivia, historian Leo Spitzer outlines the main points of this older study:

> Literally translated, the German word *Heimweh* means "home hurt" or "home ache," and its sense is closest to the English term "homesickness." Few persons nowadays, perhaps, would think of the feelings associated with homesickness—"missing home," or "the desire to return to one's native land"—as a medical problem. But that is exactly how they were considered for almost two centuries after Johannes Hofer, an Alsatian, first coined the term "nostalgia" in a 1688 Swiss medical thesis. His intent was to translate *Heimweh*, the familiar emotional phenomenon primarily associated at the time with exiles and displaced soldiers languishing for home, into a medical condition. Through its formal identification as a disease, "nostalgia" (from the Greek *nostos,* to return home, and *algia,* a painful feeling) could thus be opened to rational inquiry and possible cure. As such, learned physicians would soon observe that the "melancholic," "debilitating," "sometimes fatal" symptoms of nostalgia could be triggered in its victims through the associations of memory—by sounds, tastes, smells, and sights that might remind individuals of the homes and the environments that they had left behind. A "homecoming" and return to the familiar and local, however, could also be restorative, ending the problem and curing the affliction. (1999, 89–90)[22]

As in the seventeenth-century study, Lothar shows homesickness as inextricably linked to memory. Sounds, smells, or sights might trigger a memory that reminds one of home. The memories provide no comfort; they are painful reminders of loss. Although more recent studies such as

Grinberg and Grinberg 1989 suggest the problematic nature of return, Lothar argues like Hofer that return is a potential cure for homesickness. Lothar, who returned and perhaps felt compelled to justify this return, painted a rather grim, one-sided picture for those who could not or chose not to return.

If return is not an option, Lothar considers two possible outcomes: death or a lifetime of pining over the lost *Heimat*. Lothar provides numerous examples of those who died from exile, including the well-known writer Stefan Zweig and the stage director Max Reinhardt. In his description of Reinhardt's death, he maintains that exile attacks the soul. "He, too, died of the fatal disease emigration, then call it what you will, heart attack or suicide, the hearts of those far from home that suddenly cease to beat, the souls of those who tired of foreign lands decided to die, were mortally used up" (1961, 311).[23] The premature death of exiles becomes a sad alternative whether willed or done with one's own hand. Lothar's discussion of the pathology of exile echoes Hofer's treatise from 1688 and prefigures Améry's discussion of his "insidious disease" in 1966, from which he is freed by his suicide in 1978.

For Lothar, the alternative to dying of homesickness is being caught in an endless cycle of grieving. Those who do not die or are unable to return present a rather pitiable picture for him. He recalls meeting a group of exile Austrians in England after the war who speak English among themselves, pretending they have fully adapted to life in England. However, their eyes light up when he speaks to them in German of Salzburg and of Austria (372). According to Lothar, since they lack the strength or money to return, the thought of return can only be an illusion. Nonetheless, they demonstrate their undying love for Austria by founding the Hofmannsthal Society. Lothar views this skeptically as a sad attempt to re-create their lost *Heimat*. "Those destroyed built themselves houses in the land of homesickness" (373).[24] Rather than interpreting this as a means of dealing with exile constructively, Lothar "diagnoses" this as yet another sign of the effects of the devastating disease, "exile." In his discussion of the lively cultural activities of the Austrian exile community in Bolivia, Spitzer interprets similar efforts in part as what he labels "nostalgic memory" or "a creative tool of adjustment, helping to ease their cultural uprootedness and sense of alienation" (1999, 92). In many ways their "reconstructed version of Viennese bourgeois culture" was a way of using the past to live with the present (94). As Spitzer recognizes, in exile communities all over the world "nostalgic memory" was "a reassertion of rightful belonging within a body politic and cultural tradition from which the Nazis had attempted to sever them" (89).

Lothar himself is ostensibly saved from the disease of exile and suicide—which according to him he had contemplated (282). For him the cure comes in doses. The war appears to be the first possible "salvation" opening up the possibility of return (212). After he does return to Austria, Lothar does not immediately find the desired peace of mind. Initially, he suffers from a sense of divided loyalties. Having become a citizen of the United States, he feels indebted to the nation that saved him and gave him a new home, but he also feels dishonest because of his continued strong emotional attachment to his *Heimat,* even though he had been expelled from it. Relinquishing his American citizenship, he resettles permanently in Austria, which he paints as the only possible place for him to recover from his "disease." Ironically, he re-creates a *Heimat* in the *Heimat* through very selective perceptions and "nostalgic memory" in ways similar to those of the exile communities he criticized.

Spiel, too, classifies exile as a disease and develops her own pathology of exile. On the occasion of an international symposium on Austrian exile from 1934 to 1945 held in June 1975 in Vienna, Spiel was invited to give a talk on the psychology of exile. She defined exile as "a disease, an emotional disorder, a mental disease, yes, even a physical disease" (1977, xxii).[25] Cautioning against making generalities about exile, she draws the audience's attention to different motives behind exile. Nonetheless, she does pinpoint commonalities among exiles, which lead to the same painful experiences: "Homesickness, the feeling of being rejected, of being misunderstood, the irreconcilable barriers of language, tradition, education, custom, familial relations that separate the emigrant from those among whom he has found asylum" (xxv).[26] She then highlights three specific aspects of exile in England for Austrians, in addition to the basic struggle for survival, that shaped the pathology of exile—divided loyalties, fear, and homesickness (xxxiii). Austrian (and German) exiles found themselves in the difficult position of welcoming the war, but at the same time not wanting the death and destruction it would bring to their fellow citizens "at home." Those who had experienced or witnessed the brutality of the National Socialists after the *Anschluss* particularly feared the deadly consequences of a possible German victory. Concomitantly, they were subjected to air raids like the rest of the population. Lastly, the Austrian exiles who had a strong emotional attachment to Austrian geography suffered when "visions" of home appeared before them.

This triad of divided loyalties, fear, and homesickness is also significant for Spiel's self-diagnosed "schizophrenia," a theme she develops in her memoirs. An incident she briefly relates in the talk and describes in greater detail in her memoirs can be seen as an illustration of her own personal position vis-à-vis this interrelated constellation and key to an understanding of her self-alienation. Having left Austria in 1936, she cannot claim the same traumatic memories of those who had experienced the concentration camps or the *Anschluss* and its aftermath. Consequently, she invests a childhood incident of alienation with particular significance. During a summer in Denmark, she hears two children speaking Viennese German and she feels estranged from herself. In light of her experience of exile, she interprets this as a prescient moment of "future terror":

> In front of me two children are cowering on a bench, they are hardly older than I am and are whispering with one another in an idiom that I hear but don't understand. Suddenly a cold chill runs down my spine when I realize they're speaking Viennese German. They're speaking like my classmates in Heiligenstadt, yet I'm not one of them anymore. I can express myself in Danish and Friesian; the elemental sounds of my people are foreign to me.
> Premonition of future terror. (1989b, 33)[27]

The very fact that she includes this anecdote in both her talk and her memoirs marks it as a key experience in her interpretation of her own self-alienation or "schizophrenia." Her estrangement from imagined classmates in Heiligenstadt, due to her facility in Danish and Friesian and her distance to Viennese German, suggests that in some ways her own ability to adapt is part of the source of her self-alienation. Feeling alienated from children who speak as people do from a section of the city with which she so strongly identifies prefigures her sense of loss when she returns in 1946.

After the *Anschluss*, Spiel made a concerted effort to become fully integrated into English life. She made the linguistic leap from German to English in both her professional and personal life. She was relatively successful in her effort to publish in English. In addition, she gained British citizenship during the war. Part of her self-diagnosed "schizophrenia" appears to lie in the very fact that she adapted so well, since one's ability to adapt, as Spiel finds, does not necessarily bring with it unqualified acceptance.[28] Reminders that she was an outsider in both worlds compound her "schizophrenia."

The first time Spiel explicitly writes of her "schizophrenia" is when describing her return to Vienna in 1946 in British uniform. The return to Vienna in the uniform of her adopted country makes her all the more aware of her position between two worlds. "Only in a telegraph style can my schizophrenic emotional state of these weeks be imparted, on the arrival at Schwechat, on the dampness, the mud, and the black snow, on the drive past the four cemeteries, this metropolis of spirits in a city possessed by death" (1986b, 226).[29] Her trip to Vienna gives rise to conflicting emotions. In the context of her discussion of Spiel's relationship to exile and language, Germanist Konstanze Fliedl points out, "[t]he émigré, this symbol of a 'schizophrenic age' . . . is characterized by the stigma of a split personality. Paradoxically, this form of emotional and mental affliction . . . was exacerbated even after the collapse of the National Socialist regime" (1995, 83). Consequently, "Hilde Spiel felt that her whole existence had been shaped by a form of 'schizophrenia.'" Return brings back memories that made her acutely aware of aspects of herself she had had to suppress to survive emotionally. Spiel is faced with a sense of estrangement from a place with which she simultaneously strongly identifies. For Spiel, who derives her identity from her rootedness in specific places in Austria and Austrian culture, return was bound to prove alienating. As a Jewish Austrian, she is reminded of her connection to Austria—but also reminded of Austrian anti-Semitism. As a British-Austrian in Austria, she is forced to reflect on the validity of her membership within a British "we."

Spiel experiences this feeling of "schizophrenia" again at a friend's funeral in England after William Blake's "Jerusalem" was sung:

> It's amazing just how much we're shaped by songs! I can follow all the phases of my life with their help. The Viennese songs from the Krems collection that I sang as a small child in the Wollzeile. The Brecht-Eisler songs that strengthened us in our solidarity with the poor, and our rebellion against the threatening National Socialist regime. The extremely naive and sometimes puzzling nursery rhymes that we learned along with our own children. The old folk songs of the islands, from Ireland and often Scotland. What moves me more? "Greensleeves," with its echoes of the Elizabethans, of Shakespeare's poetry? Or the simple wine garden song, "An Old Nut Tree Stands in Heiligenstadt"? In this doubt the schizophrenia of my existence is captured. (1990, 285–86)[30]

The *Heimat* songs Spiel associates with Vienna tie her to particular places within Vienna. They remind her either of places dear to her where she sang such songs or they conjure up beloved moments in the songs themselves. These songs and the British songs allow Spiel to reflect on her rootedness to both cultures. However, they do not appear to lead to an inner reconciliation. Indeed, the melodies seem to bring forth cacophonous or "schizophrenic" strains rather than inner harmony. Spiel's "schizophrenic" moments underline her inability to resolve the question she poses with title of her second memoir, *Welche Welt ist meine Welt?*

Spiel is most reminded of her "split personality" when she feels the pull between two cultures. At the same time, she appears unable to synthesize her experiences of the cultures internally.[31] However, if we consider the house "a magnification of the body" and "simultaneously a miniaturization of the world" (Scarry 1985, 38), then there is a domestic space where Spiel integrates her Austrian and British identities. She does this after return in the house in Sankt Wolfgang she acquired after the war. She closes the second volume of her memoirs with the chapter entitled, "Three Folk Chests. Farewell," in which she describes her new home. In this house she creates a homey space for herself and family by combining objects that bring together multiple worlds. She relates the story of the discovery and purchase of three antique chests from 1794, 1828, and 1841. Then she goes on to explain their placement in the house:

> Then the three [chests] came to the house on the stream, still in half-empty rooms; however, they soon received company. For the clock chest the finest of all was intended. Two chairs in the style of Louis XVI, not genuine, but imitations probably from the previous century, because here, too, the gold border had peeled off or paled in many places, found in the Viennese auction house the Dorotheum. A sofa with almost the same pattern and the same fluted arm rests and legs had been waiting for a buyer in a display window of a junk shop in Chepstow Road for a long time; its shipping cost more than it did. Reupholstered by the upholsterer Rechberger in Sankt Wolfgang uniformly with green and white striped silk damask from London. The furniture looked as if it belonged together, and the clock chest did not need to be embarrassed because of them. A baroque chandelier on a Turkish turned stem was added from Salzburg, and on the walls of the small salon hung copper engravings by Hogarth next to the many small London landscapes from the same period. (1990, 306–7)[32]

Spiel creates a space that becomes both an extension of herself and a refuge from the world. It offers her and her family a place of certainty in the world. "Then, whenever we doubted where we belonged or preferred to belong, whether it was London or Vienna, here we—my children and I—felt at home in any case" (316).[33]

In his discussion of *Heimat,* Améry argues the importance, particularly for his generation, of "living with things that tell us stories" (1980, 57).[34] Spiel surrounds herself with objects rich in history from different eras. With her interior decorating, Spiel creates stories within which she can live. She combines objects from Austria and England as well as other countries, synthesizing her attachment to her two homes and to the rest of Europe.

Unlike Spiel, who professes to be unable to integrate her experiences of two cultures into one body, Klein-Löw accomplishes this first by illustrating the combined physical and mental dangers for her as a Jewish Austrian in the loss of *Heimat* and second by using the body literally and figuratively to map the possibilities for healing. If we follow Klein-Löw from 1938 to her return, we see the transformation from attacked body to intact body. Initially, Klein-Löw is "paralyzed" by the *Anschluss*:

> If the years under the Austro-Fascists from 1934 to 1938 had awakened feelings of indignation, anger, contempt, sorrow for something lost and led to protest, to the recognition that one has to fight for lost freedom, then 1938–1939 lamed me because I recognized my own helplessness. I was afraid and ashamed of myself because of it, fearful not just for my own life, much more: there was the fear, not to be able to stand up to the horrors, to become disloyal to one's own self and one's own friends who one could pull into one's own distress and hopelessness. The concentration camps, the Gestapo, the brown house on Morzinplatz [location of the headquarters of the Gestapo in Vienna]. (1980, 93–94)[35]

Klein-Löw experiences shame and fear. Her fear, directly connected to the threat to her body by the institutions of terror of the National Socialists, robs her of the possibility of control. She is afraid she will not be able to stand up to torture. Her fear of being trapped manifests itself in the body on both conscious and subconscious levels. "Everything was over: personal happiness, security of home, love of *Heimat,* the feeling of belonging—my entire life. What remained was panic-driven fear, choking breathlessness, black despair" (94).[36] Nonetheless, she continues her work in the Jewish high school, motivated by her concern for her Jewish students. However, her ability to act is severely restricted, and exile appears her only alternative. Her fears of being trapped plague her even in her sleep. "A door slams shut, shut for good. There is no way out. I'm shut in, I fight for air. . . . I want to get away. Where is the key? It doesn't fit—I wake up moaning, feeling only one thing: I have to get away!" (93).[37]

Klein-Löw blurs the distinctions between the literal and the metaphorical reactions of her body to unresolved emotions resulting from the *Anschluss,* her flight from Austria, and her arrival in England. She experiences her flight from Austria as "an incomprehensible pain" (101). She depicts her arrival in England as a multiple estrangement:

The first few days—the people around me, the many trips of a foreigner to official offices in the new land of residence—that was all so alarming and shadowy, so unaccustomed and tiring that I moved my limbs, spoke, acted like an automaton. I was not there where I was. I was somewhere in between, in a land with no distinguishing features. I lost myself in the process. One thing was clear: this was "*the* strange or foreign place" about which the poets spoke. . . . I discovered that I could neither speak nor understand the language, that I could not understand the behavior of the people, could not comprehend their attitude, could not understand their living customs and—as I thought at the time—would never adopt them. (125)[38]

Like Améry, Klein-Löw has no semiotic competency for reading her new surroundings. The alienation she experiences as a result is expressed on a physical level. She remembers these days as a type of out-of-body experience, perceiving herself as both an automaton and separate from herself.

Klein-Löw slowly begins to recover. "Somehow, I gradually found my way back to 'myself.' I liked to work and decided to use my free time . . . in order to obtain an M.A. from either Cambridge or Oxford" (134).[39] She accumulates new experiences and she reflects on her metamorphosis, anchoring it in her corporeal experiences:

I had become a new Stella in these two years. I had experienced the fate of the proletariat on my own body. . . . Hands that are torn and sore from work speak another language than regularly manicured fingers and polished nails. I learned some new things. Above all, I now spoke British English. I had become more tolerant, firm in my convictions, but ready to respect those of others and understand them. I had been "internationalized," had remained an Austrian, but was more open. The horrible days of the Nazi regime had disappeared from my dreams. The shock had been lifted, my behavior proved that—my calmness and concern for others during the "Blitz" and later. This Stella was now placed in a pedagogical and professional position in which she would and wanted to prove herself. (159–60)[40]

She reaches a new sense of self through the integration of body memories. On numerous occasions, Klein-Löw traces both the loss and recovery of self using the body to signify her transformation. She interprets the exile experience as ultimately positive because of her forward-moving metamorphosis.

As someone who had taken numerous courses in psychology and had seriously considered a career in the field, Klein-Löw has the vocabulary to describe and reflect on psychological processes.[41] She portrays the experience of trauma as an integral part of her life, which can be overcome and actually contribute to the formation of a new, stronger "I." She demonstrates that traumas precipitated either by purely personal losses (such as the suicide of her first husband) or by historical events (her reaction to July 1927, February 1934, March 1938) result in a diminished sense of self. However, in each instance, she shows herself capable of full recovery. By talking about her traumatic experience, by ridding herself of guilt, and by finding herself through work, Klein-Löw recovers from the mental wound or shock that expresses itself in the body as a sense of lameness or diminished sense of self. Each healing cycle frees her productive and creative energies.

The transformations appear almost too facile at times. Klein-Löw herself even obliquely casts doubt on the efficiency of her method of dealing with trauma. She writes of memories she has kept under lock and key, and at times a traumatic event she has supposedly dealt with continues to haunt her. Her model cures for trauma must be understood within both a Socialist context and the postwar Austrian context. The words of Socialist leader Otto Bauer, written to her after her first husband's suicide in 1933, seem to encapsulate her lessons from earlier traumatic experiences and serve as a motto for future trauma. "Mourning and sorrow are here for the purpose so that one can build new things, living things, elevating things on them" (70).[42] Perhaps Otto Bauer provided her then with a lesson for her future life or perhaps she interpreted it retrospectively; this is the model of working through trauma she offers to her readers. Her formula is an implicit invitation to Austrians to talk about traumatic events of the past, to deal with possible guilt, and to create a foundation for a productive future.

The body imagery and metaphors the writers employ convey not only the real physical danger the exiles faced, but also the seriousness of the trauma or wound inflicted by the loss of *Heimat*. The loss of "we" brought on by exile forced the writers to rethink what it meant to say "I." Severed from their past, they were at least temporarily without orientation. Thalberg shows the injury as an irrevocable loss. His reconstituted "I" permanently suffers. With Lothar's pathology of exile he claims the precariousness of existence and the difficulty of regaining a full sense of self in exile. Return appears the only means of recovery for him even if it is done within limited space, as we will see. If Lothar is able to find himself through return and ostensibly appears to deal with his divided loyalties, Spiel is made even more aware of her split or "schizophrenic" self after returning. Her exile continues even after the defeat of National Socialism as a sense of emotional loss in momentary bouts of "schizophrenia." In contrast,

Klein-Löw uses the body to plot her trauma and illustrate her growth and development to a new "I." Her body—that is, her body's ability to work and adapt—becomes the means to her recovery of "I." By describing body memories, the writers access memories that have long defied language. Moreover, they demonstrate almost without exception that exile was experienced as an injury that permanently changed them. In all cases, the corporealization of trauma and mourning creates a palpable immediacy between reader and narrator. The figurative and literal body images offer the writers the opportunity to draw in readers, activating their emotions and creating possibilities for identification.

Topographies of Trauma and Mourning

With the realization of impending loss of place, Minna Lachs tries to "internalize" a Viennese cityscape as she and her husband take an evening walk through the city in 1937:

> As my husband and I walked home arm in arm in the cold winter air, we looked lovingly and sadly at the silhouettes of the buildings so familiar to us in the center of the city and the city's dreamy squares. I felt as if I had to caress every house and every tree with my eyes. I had just realized that we would have to say good-bye to this beautiful and much-loved city soon, very soon. My husband sensed what I was feeling and pressed my arm firmly. (1986, 183)[43]

Lachs commits the city to memory by "touching" it visually. Like Lachs, the other memoir writers carry "memory maps" with them in exile that demonstrate their strong attachment to place.[44] This attachment to place no doubt contributed to their profound sense of loss and was a strong motivating factor in return. Elisabeth Freundlich correlates the pull of the physical surroundings of Vienna with her desire to return and confirms its importance for her sense of well-being after return:

> In fact the chasm between those who had stayed—this term also encompasses those who supposedly had clear consciences—and those who had been chased away never closed completely. But still, as in song, the lilacs burst into bloom on the Heldenplatz as they had since time immemorial; they did not know what had gone on there. On the main promenade of the Prater, the chestnut trees perfumed the air with their white and red blossoms. All of this, which I had been longing for for years, made me defenseless against many other things. (1999, 98–99)[45]

Vienna exerts a strong emotional pull over Freundlich. During her years in exile, images of Vienna in spring had been the source of intense longing. Once back in Vienna, they become a renewed source of identification with the city and an antidote to memories of past and present injustices. By separating Vienna's aesthetic attraction from the political events, Freundlich is able to deal with many of the unpleasantnesses brought about by return. Her sense of well-being in Vienna is based on a vision of a landscape without people. Her recovered spatial identity is rooted in her relationship to her surroundings removed from history.

The sense of one's self within a specific environment and its impact on sense of self are key aspects of one's spatial identity. As discussed in chapter 1, Améry considers the ability to read one's surroundings and identification with one's surroundings as the sine qua non of possessing *Heimat*. If Freundlich were typical of the exiles, it would appear that spatial identity within *Heimat* could easily be reestablished by return alone. However, as we will see, spatial identity is also influenced by spatial memories. Sketching the (traumatic) memories associated with specific places, the memoirists create a multilayered emotional topography and suggest that the original relationship to space cannot easily be reconstituted by return.

In his essay on grieving for place, sociologist Marc Fried investigates the importance of spatial identity for personal well-being. In his study on citizens dislocated from the west end of Boston, he argues:

> [A] sense of spatial identity is fundamental to human functioning. It represents a phenomenal or ideational integration of important experiences concerning environmental arrangements and contacts in relation to the individual's conception of his own body in space. It is based on spatial memories, spatial imagery, the spatial framework of current activity, and the implicit spatial components of ideals and aspirations. (1963, 156)

In relating their life stories, the memoir writers' concepts of themselves as bodies within an Austrian landscape, their spatial memories, and the "spatial framework of their current activity" intersect and they create emotional topographies of varying sophistication. The exiles project their sense of belonging as well as their feelings of loss and longing onto specific places within Austria.[46] Memories of specific Austrian locales convey a full palette of emotions, ranging from positive nostalgia to an engulfing sense of profound loss.

The memoir writers' relationship to Vienna as a space changes because of the historical circumstances that severed their bonds to

Heimat. Consequently, the memoir writers sketch Vienna as a traumatic landscape, both describing specific sites and providing a general
picture of humiliation and persecution. Locations associated with extreme emotions include the South and West Station, where many of
the exiles said good-bye to family members (Thalberg, Tausig, Klein-
Löw, Freundlich); the University of Vienna, where Jewish students were
beaten and forced out by other students (Lachs, Spiel); the second
district Leopoldstadt, where Jews were forced into the Danube Canal
(Lachs), the location of the Jewish high school (Klein-Löw), and the area
where the greatest destruction against Jewish property occurred during
the November Pogrom of 1938 (Klein-Löw). The memoir writers also
depict general scenes of humiliation wherein Jews were forced to scrub
the sidewalks and scenes of desperation in which hopeful exiles stood in
line at embassies and travel agencies.

The memoir writers invest specific locations in Austria with emotional meaning, which among other things conveys to the reader the
importance of place in memory and remembering. They design topographies of emotion that impart the impact of the loss of spatial identity
on one's sense of self and allow them to explore the possibilities of
recovering part of *Heimat* through reconnecting to place. Furthermore,
by associating specific events and emotions with real places, they create
"memory maps" for readers. Reminiscent of the mnemonic devices created by the Greeks, these "maps" help "memory by arousing emotional
affects through . . . striking and unusual images" (Yates 1974, 10). The
"striking and unusual images" in the memoirs, however, are not based
on an imaginary mnemonic, but derived from life experiences.

Just as Thalberg, Spiel, Klein-Löw, and Lothar inscribe psychological blows and healing onto the body, they map out a topography of
trauma and mourning using Austrian locales, showing the (im)possibil-
ities of mourning within postwar Austria. Like the memory maps of the
Greeks, they preserve memory; however, they also create memory for
the reader by associating particular memories with specific locations in
present-day Austria.

The Vienna of Thalberg's childhood, so important for his sense of
Austrian identity, changes permanently after 1938. Thalberg not only
depicts Vienna as a death trap after 1938, he shows that the people have
changed as well. Moreover, the city is experienced in radically different
ways by Jewish and non-Jewish Austrians:

> People of Jewish heritage disappeared overnight from daily life, from
> offices, from the coffeehouses, from the cityscape; everyone knew what
> happened to the Jewish businessman across the street, to the Jewish

doctor, to the Jewish neighbor. It was quite official in all the gazettes and could be observed by everyone on the streets and squares. Our neighbors, acquaintances, colleagues, and business partners continued to go to work, to their offices, to coffeehouses and the theater, attended church, went on vacation, as if nothing had happened. (1984, 66–67)[47]

Because his sense of spatial identity is inextricably bound to his interpersonal relationships, Thalberg cannot divorce his perception of the city from its history and its people. After March 1938, Vienna becomes a different city for him. What shocks and disappoints him is his perception that his non-Jewish compatriots carried on as if nothing had happened. For non-Jewish Austrians, the city had and had not changed. For Thalberg, in contrast, the changes irreversibly affect his identification with the city.

Thalberg defines the city as an entity created by people and bound to them. Consequently, his emotional connection to Vienna as *Heimat* is very much bound to his pre-1938 life in Vienna and its destruction. Thus, when he returns to Vienna in 1945, he perceives the city as a metaphorical cemetery:

What is a city? A landscape of stone buildings, streets, and some green areas created by human hand. Cities only gain life when they are connected with people. Otherwise, they become dead piles of stone that smell like a grave. This is how Vienna appeared to me in 1945. All the people whom I had known and loved, with whom I had been bound either by blood or friendship, had disappeared: emigrated or been gassed. Every street corner, every park bench, every part of Vienna in which I had lived and which I now sought out, spoke to me of the horrors of the past. (152)[48]

The profound absence of relatives and friends underlines the graveyard quality of Vienna for Thalberg.

The city functions as a lasting reminder of loss. As a diplomat, Thalberg spent little time in Vienna after the war. However, when assigned to Vienna in the mid-fifties, he again found himself both drawn and repelled by certain locations in Vienna: "Every corner, every little square breathed of memories, spoke of the past, of another world that I and only I as the last survivor of my first family had known. Exploratory trips through Vienna exercised a great nostalgic pull over me, but they were so infinitely painful that I usually had to break them off in the middle" (213–14).[49] As the only survivor in his family, Thalberg can only map out a topography of perpetual mourning. Similar to his metaphor of the past as an amputated leg, his forays through Vienna embody loss. The memories prove too painful, perhaps, because they would force him to consider that he has constructed his postwar life and identity on an illusion.

As a diplomat, he has been able to identify with Austria, but he did not reside there during much of his professional career. Thalberg's Austria is constructed from memories. "From my personal perspective, that postwar era in Austria, the subject of my report which reached its culmination in the *Kreisky* era, represents the conclusion of a historical era that had already found its horrible end on March 11, 1938. The light of the star had long gone out" (17).[50] Like his metaphor of the amputated leg or Vienna as a cemetery, the metaphor of the light from a dead star captures a sense of loss of *Heimat*. Thalberg devoted his life to an ideal that no longer existed.

In contrast to Thalberg, who creates a general emotional topography, Spiel maps her emotional topography by naming specific places in Vienna important for her sense of self. She captures the ambivalent nature of memories of Vienna for both exiles in general and herself in particular: [T]he *Heimat* that we had worked so hard to repress broke forth again and again. I dreamed of Heiligenstadt, of walks in the Prater with our dog Diemo, who had died a long time ago, of the contours of the Salesian Church on Rennweg, and of the nightmare of waking up in Vienna, foreign among enemies, with English money in my pocket, fair game for anyone" (1989b, 194).[51] While in England she tries to repress her memories of Austria—in vain. Specific places of emotional importance force their way to her in her dreams. As a part of memory and identity, *Heimat* cannot easily be shaken off. Because specific places are associated with the loss of a happier past, they are not viewed as unambiguously positive, and they haunt Spiel.

As we have seen in chapter 1, Heiligenstadt and Pfarrplatz in particular stand at the center of Spiel's emotional topography. Her ambivalent feelings concerning her return to Vienna are expressed in multiple renderings of the memory of her first visit to Heiligenstadt after the war in 1946. The memory is very much a corporeal one: here she breaks down (1990, 8). In her calendar/diary from 1946 she writes: "Heiligenstadt unchanged. Walked in sinking light. Heartbreak beyond words" (1999, 82). In *Rückkehr nach Wien,* she pinpoints Heiligenstadt as the origin of her sense of identity. "In the fading light I stand on Pfarrplatz. Here my soul lies buried. During the past ten years of my absence, whenever I was homesick, it was for this square" (1968, 54).[52] In *Die hellen und die finsteren Zeiten,* Spiel quotes from a letter to her husband relating her feelings: "Saturday afternoon, I walked around Heiligenstadt in the melting snow around 4:30 P.M., at dusk, and it was one hundred times more heart-wrenching than I had ever expected. I went into the little chapel and simply wept" (1989b, 231–32).[53] In her memoirs, she even avoids a detailed description of her first visit to Vienna after the war, referring her readers to *Rückkehr nach Wien*: "I do not want to conjure up yet again in great detail those places of the past that were sought out in the following days down to the exact topographical source of my unity with Vienna, Pfarrplatz in Heiligenstadt—these memories, too, hurt after all the time that has passed since then" (1989b, 226).[54] Recalling in detail appears too painful. Spiel's spatial identity is very much bound to the image of her past self in this part of town and the security she felt as part of this world. The contrast between the beloved place and knowledge of persecution, her confrontations with those who did not leave, and the realization of her emotional connections to Vienna bring to life the knowledge of the unbearable. Returning to Heiligenstadt, to the place of her unity with Vienna, precipitates feelings of "schizophrenia." She feels caught between two cultures, belonging to neither. As such, her first return visit to Heiligenstadt remains a lasting wound.

Unlike the picture Freundlich paints, return alone cannot restore a former sense of spatial identity for Thalberg and Spiel. Since Thalberg cannot divorce a city from its inhabitants, when in Vienna he is constantly reminded of the murder of his family. Nonetheless, the memories of pre-*Anschluss* Vienna remain a constituent of his professional identity. Spiel uses specific locations and landmarks to infuse place with multiple historical significances. Heiligenstadt, perhaps best known for its illustrious inhabitant Beethoven and his *Heiligenstädter Testament,* also becomes the site to mark her estrangement from place and self and the loss precipitated by expulsion.

Only Klein-Löw and Lothar map out a more complete mourning process and suggest the possibility of using their confrontations with place to reconstitute an Austrian identity. Klein-Löw localizes her "catharsis" to a specific district in Vienna and ties her metamorphosis very much to her work in the Socialist Party. In contrast, Lothar maps his emotional processes of trauma and mourning onto a variety of Austrian locales from western Austria to Vienna.

Klein-Löw's location of her transformation is not only a place of personal trauma, but also a major site of National Socialist brutality against Vienna's Jewish population. She devotes an entire chapter to Leopoldstadt, a Jewish section with the heaviest concentration of Galician, or eastern European, Jews (Rozenblit 1983, 96). This district, which had played an important role in her life before exile, was the locus of ambivalent feelings for Klein-Löw. She describes the transformation of Leopoldstadt for her emotionally. "What had been a dream in my

Pfarrplatz in 1911 (courtesy of Bildarchiv/ÖNB Wien)

childhood would later turn into a nightmare" (1980, 188).[55] It is a world of contrasts, contrasts between the amusement park of the Prater and the proletarian underworld, between conservative orthodoxy and liberal assimilation, and between Jews and virulent anti-Semitism. As a student she tutored there and later she taught at a Jewish secondary school. She comes to associate Leopoldstadt with bad smells, which she connects indirectly with eastern European Jewry and directly with the anti-Semitism that culminated in the November Pogrom of 1938. "Many of my friends had lived and worked there. What had happened during the ill-fated time of Jewish persecution, I could not and did not want to forget or forgive" (189–90).[56] Projecting her trauma onto Leopoldstadt, she had vowed never to set foot there again (189).

After her return to Vienna, she avoids Leopoldstadt, suggesting that the emotions she associates with the district frighten her. She finally returns for the first time in 1949, three years after her return to Vienna, to give a talk at a function sponsored by the Socialists. She recalls a physical and psychological reaction marking her emotional dislike for this section of town (189). However, after her speech she reflects on the confrontation with the district and decides to work in Leopoldstadt.

Through her work in Leopoldstadt, which Klein-Löw describes in detail, she experiences a transformation that frees her from past fears and allows her to function to her fullest. Her work there appears to precipitate a full emotional recovery from the psychological wounds of the thirties. "In Leopoldstadt, I was freed from inhibitions that had prevented me from writing. Here I threw off my reluctance to relive the past through memories" (198).[57] At this point one might expect Klein-Löw to relate how she dealt with her tremendous sense of loss or was able to forgive. Rather she writes of feeling cleansed of personal guilt:

> I was freed of prejudices, of guilt feelings, repressed memories came to light. Once coaxed out of their hiding place, they did not oppress me any longer.
>
> I changed my attitude toward people. All discriminatory thoughts disappeared. Only a great sense of astonishment remained that I had ever distinguished between people who spoke Yiddish and people who spoke polished German, between people from Orthodox families and people from assimilated families. (198)[58]

Her catharsis is somewhat unexpected because of her initial determination not to forget or forgive and because of her position as a Jewish exile. Upon close examination, the cathartic experience reveals itself as one that has to do with her personal guilt as a survivor and her past prejudice toward eastern European Jews.

Klein-Löw's transformation eclipses her resolve neither to forgive nor forget. Indeed, a discussion of forgiveness is completely missing in her memoirs. She shifts attention from the past destruction of Austria to her personal guilt, addressing her own prejudice, which was emblematic of the very real prejudice of the assimilated Jewish community toward eastern European Jews. If the expression of guilt is unexpected, so, too, is Klein-Löw's self-labeling as *Zugereiste*—a sometimes pejorative term used for newcomers to Vienna (198). In her work for the Socialist Party in the second district, she is happy that as a *Zugereiste,* she was so accepted there. Her use of the term appears very odd for a person who was raised in Vienna and who fled at age thirty-five. She could be using this somewhat tongue in cheek as someone from another district in Vienna working in the second district, or she could be underscoring her acceptance as a bourgeois intellectual working with members of the working class.

But Klein-Löw's puzzling choice of expression can perhaps best be understood as an indication of her sometimes conflicting subject positions. As a Socialist in postwar Austria, she has been part of an organization that has done little either to challenge Austria's victim status before the eighties or to question anti-Semitism within the party. As a Jewish Austrian, she had witnessed extreme brutality, been in mortal danger, and felt obliged to remember those who had perished. As a pedagogue conversant in psychology, aware of the importance of dealing with loss brought about by traumatic events, she uses herself as a nonjudgmental model. Just as she has used her corporeal reflections to signal her personal and political growth, her experience of place appears personally and politically transformational. By returning to the site of her trauma, by letting reason win out over emotion, she can realize her full personal potential and free herself of her own prejudice.

In contrast to Klein-Löw's focus on Leopoldstadt for the locus of her ultimate catharsis, Lothar extends his emotional topographical map from western Austria to Vienna. More than any of the memoirists, Lothar extensively uses geographical locations to map out a topography of trauma and mourning. As he and his daughter leave Austria, Lothar employs pathetic fallacy to underscore his emotional state and the impending danger. "We drove into the valley on the magnificent Arlberg highway; it was not magnificent. The ice cracked, the snow dirty, the beloved landscape threatening" (1961, 122).[59] The landscape (in German a feminine noun) appears sullied—it is as if it had been raped and was now assuming a threatening pose.[60] As Lothar crosses the Arlberg Pass when leaving Austria, he reflects on his identification with his country and all that he has done to defend it out of love. He first describes his connection as falling apart and then he sees himself performing an operation on himself: "Reflecting about this when I was almost at the border, I felt that connectedness dismembered piece by piece for every part of the highway we passed. Everything, or so it seemed to me, had been a deception. The magnificence was a backdrop for baseness, the sweetness a cover-up for the contemptible. An observer at an operation, I looked at myself as I tore the love of my life out of my body piece by piece" (122).[61] With this scene, Lothar combines the body and topographical metaphors, illustrating the interrelated nature of body and place to spatial identity. Not only does Lothar remove his "love" for Austria, a central part of his identity, but he observes himself performing the operation. Even if this is only a temporary reaction— in the next sentence he is somewhat appeased by an encounter with a humane Austrian official—the imagery is powerful. His connection to Austria, an integral part of his identity, is transformed into something that becomes potentially malignant and has to be removed. At the same time his encounter with the humane Austrian official does not allow him to make a clean emotional break from Austria.

While in exile, his memories of his beloved landscape are the catalyst for numerous bouts of *Heimweh*. During a trip to the Rockies to the "Garden of the Gods," he cannot help but compare the landscape to his *Heimat*. "Under the silent flight of the peacock blue birds, in the totally unspoiled solitude, at the most inappropriate moment at the most inappropriate place, I was overcome by an attack of longing for the modest majesty of Untersberg, the mountain where the little church in Morz with its green church tower stands at its foot" (209).[62]

Although Lothar develops an elaborate pathology of exile and, like the Alsatian doctor Johannes Hofer, views return as the only hope of recovery, return does not bring with it an immediate cure. When he returns to Austria after World War II, Lothar associates landscapes with both the humiliation of his flight from Austria into exile and earlier happy memories: "St. Anton, where they had surprised us. Landeck, from where the SA man had come. Again and again an indelible memory slipped in between the longed-for sights. In Kitzbühel, where Mary, the children, and I had spent three happy summer vacations, I recognized several people standing in front of the train station who had been aligned with the Nazis during Schuschnigg's time" (287).[63] The use of a specific locus to connect two or more levels of time and memory occurs often in the memoirs. As the memoir writers relate their life stories chronologically, they often interrupt their descriptions of the years before 1938 with the memory of events in the unhappy future past. The writers signal the tragedy to come and they convey the ways in which these tragic memories overshadow other, happier memories. In Lothar's case it is both the happier past and the tragic past he maps out onto the mountains of Austria as he returns. He shows the ways in which the past persists, suggesting the richness of the memories associated with place.

As Lothar continues further east into the Austrian interior, the idyllic images replace or elide the events of the past. Lothar's arrival in Salzburg transports him for a short time into "paradise," which seems to rejuvenate him:

> When we rolled in, the mountains Gaisberg and Untersberg, the fortress Hohensalzburg, the towers and the cupolas of the churches stood out clear and marvelous against the sky. The conflicting emotions disappeared abruptly, it did not matter what held itself up against the desired reunion— the miracle of having returned and survived happened even more won-

derfully than I had believed. In the gently grayed light it stood out, the proud-modest mountain Untersberg, more glorious than the Garden of the Gods; the wooded mountain Gaisberg, ridiculously unprepossessing compared to the wooded mountains of Maine, yet more magical than those without secrets; unthreatening Hohensalzburg, the loveliest of all fortresses, rose up; church clocks struck nine and bells rang with a harmony that existed nowhere else because it was Mozart. That banners filled with words of hate hung here, they rang that fact away. (288)[64]

The traumatic memories fade in the light of the physical beauty of Salzburg, and Lothar feels a newfound sense of well-being in familiar and beloved surroundings.

Lothar characterizes his initial reunion with Salzburg as one of the best experiences of his life. He likens it to an emotional renewal or a type of redemption. Here, he learns how to love again:

I had been aware how false the assertion is that the expected never measures up to expectations. . . . In this hour, in any case, one of the best, perhaps the best of my life, the expected had surpassed my expectation because I had expected to be moved by that which I had long gone without but not by my love of it. Only life teaches truths. The truth of the reunion is dependent on the truth of the ability to be able to love again. That I could love again made me happier than that which awaited us. (289)[65]

Lothar's ability to love again is wholly dependent on his identification with the physical beauty of Austria and is not connected with people in a landscape.

Lothar likens this experience to a "moment in paradise," noting that "the 'moment in paradise' is more paradisiacal for those who came too close to hell" (288–89).[66] With this pseudo-religious experience, Lothar can convince readers of his devotion to and identification with Austria. He also suggests that through his traumatic experiences, he has a better appreciation of Austria than those who were not expelled, for Lothar, who lost his *Heimat,* is more aware of its beauty. At the same time, he also perceives the transitoriness of the return to paradise: "a *moment* in paradise."

Lothar's reactions to specific geographical locations continue to act as an emotional barometer of his renewed relationship to Austria. His arrival in Vienna is marked by a type of stocktaking—noting the division of Vienna into different Allied zones and the bombed-out buildings. This signals a certain emotional detachment, or perhaps a fear of becoming too attached to Vienna since his future is still uncertain.

Only after he returns to Vienna permanently do the specific Viennese locations take on an almost magical, mystical character. Upon Lothar's second return to Vienna, he is greeted by a rainbow, which brings him to a new emotional recognition. "To quarrel with fate is futile. An everyday phenomenon brought this home to me too late. Fate is a natural occurrence." (425).[67] By convincing himself that the historical events were acts of fate, he frees himself from some of the past bitterness.

In mapping out a "new" spatial identity for himself within postwar Austria, Lothar appears to be drawing on "nostalgic memory," which Spitzer (1998; 1999) noted among Austrian refugees in Bolivia and which Lothar saw as a lamentable characteristic of exile communities. If we use Spitzer's definition, the major difference is that the exiles turn to the past to strengthen their "sense of cultural and historical continuity" in the absence of *Heimat* (1998, 150). In contrast, Lothar revisits specific locations in Vienna associated with Austrian cultural icons of the nineteenth century in order to affirm his sense of self in post-Holocaust Austria. He selectively appropriates parts of Austria's more illustrious past. He dates his return to Vienna to the day he goes by the Schubert house: "When I arrived in Vienna, where I should be staying from now on, at the beginning of September at the Franz Josef Station, I felt the first passionate feelings of a reunion in the face of the run-down, shabby Nussdorf Street. I stopped in front of the Schubert house, entered, and had, with a delay of three months, finally arrived" (325).[68] After he is rewarded Austrian citizenship, he makes a "pilgrimage" to the monument of the Austrian playwright Franz Grillparzer in the Volksgarten. "After the decision I went to the Vienna Volksgarten to the monument of a great Austrian" (435).[69] Lothar identifies with Grillparzer, the Austrian Goethe, unappreciated writer, and misunderstood civil servant, who he views as "a great Austrian" bound to the Austrian people despite their lack of appreciation.

Anyone familiar with Austria cannot deny the power of the landscape, from the romantic city of Salzburg, to the splendor of the Alps, to the magnificence of the nation's capital. Nonetheless, Lothar's emotional hymns to specific Austrian cityscapes and landscapes can appear overly sentimental. They are best understood in the context of the Austro-Fascist images of the thirties. In the early thirties, the Austro-Fascists had drawn on Austrian cityscapes and landscapes to create an emotional identification with Austria as a bulwark against German National Socialism (Seeber-Weyrer 1997, 131). Indeed, Lothar's attachment to the Austrian landscape is reminiscent of the pronouncements of writer-politician Guido Zernatto. Zernatto had been an Austro-Fascist cabinet minister and general secretary of the Patriotic Front before he

Franz Grillparzer Monument in the Volksgarten, 1938 (courtesy of
Bildarchiv/ÖNB Wien)

fled Austria in 1938. As a high government official for the Austro-
Fascists, Zernatto was clearly in danger. His flight took him first to
France and then to New York, where he died on February 8, 1942. In
his book *Die Wahrheit über Österreich* (The truth about austria), written
in 1939 from exile, Zernatto compares the Austrian and the National
Socialist. "The philosophy of the Austrian is unthinkable without his
country. The philosophy of the National Socialist is imaginable without
a country. . . . For the National Socialist the law of blood rules, for the
Austrian the law of the landscape" (19).[70]

Among exile groups, the loss of *Heimat* has been noted to lead
to the idealization and sentimentalization of the home country (Seeber-
Weyrer 1997, 132; Spitzer 1998, 143–52). Common to Lothar's ideal-
ized topographical memory maps is the absence of people. Lothar even
insists to exiles in New York, when defending his decision to reemigrate,

that he is not returning to people, but to a landscape that is essential for his survival. Quoting himself, he recalls, " 'And what's more, I'm not returning to people, but rather, you'll forgive the pompous expression, to a landscape that I need in order to live' " (409).[71] Lothar's relationship to the Austrian landscape brings to mind both Guido Zernatto in 1939 and Johannes Hofer in 1688. Lothar can recover his sense of self to a satisfactory degree only by returning home. However, Lothar's topographies are not singularly positive. Only when he can block out people from the landscape does the landscape have its healing effects. Seen as a whole, his emotional topography conveys loss as well as the possibility of recovering himself through returning to familiar surroundings. His memories of return appear as maps that combine nostalgic memory and critical memory. The memoirs assert a "rightful belonging" and incorporate "what was negative and bitter from the immediate past" (Spitzer 1999, 89; 1998, 153).

Thalberg, Spiel, Klein-Löw, and Lothar inscribe parts of their life stories onto their maps of Austria, creating multilayered memory maps. By infusing history into well-known Austrian cityscapes and landscapes, their confrontations with specific locations afforded them the possibility of mourning but also underline the enormity of their loss. For Thalberg, Spiel, Klein-Löw, and Lothar, specific locations serve not only as mnemonics of past injuries and as emotional barometers, but also as indicators of the ways in which the writers construct a sense of spatial identity and constitute their (Austrian) sense of self. They also remap *Heimat* by infusing geographical locations with multiple layers of emotion and history.

Conclusion

The memoirists use body memory both to access traumatic memories and to express the pre-linguistic nature of trauma through these memories. Their body memories are in turn related to the memoirists' metaphorical use of body and Austrian cityscapes and landscapes, which allow the writers to plot trauma and mourning while at the same time countering and undermining the "blood and soil" philosophy taken to the extreme by the National Socialists. Such configurations illustrate the connection of memory and spatial identity to their perceptions of themselves in Austria. For example, Thalberg's extreme emotional pain over the loss of his family is expressed in the phantom pain of a lost limb and a Vienna filled with phantoms from his past. Spiel and Lothar plot their emotional losses as an illness or disease with varying prognoses.

Spiel, caught between two worlds and unable to reconcile her Austrian and British selves, describes her incurable personal "schizophrenia," which is exacerbated when she revisits emotionally charged places from the past. By weaving representations of body memory in her descriptions of encounters with specific experiences and geographical locations, Klein-Löw creates a model for dealing with trauma and extreme loss. By claiming the subjectivity of her attacked body and facing her own prejudice, she shows herself emerging a stronger person. The memoirists recapture body memories, draw on body metaphors, and inscribe bodies, cityscapes, and landscapes with trauma and mourning to construct their bodies and Austrian surroundings as historical entities that express both the uniqueness and commonality of their experiences.

Just as the memoir writers externalize their emotional experiences, so, too, do they seek to transform readers' perceptions of Austria and consequently their spatial identity, adding layers to their own memories of specific locations. Pfarrplatz in Heiligenstadt becomes more than just a quaint square reminiscent of the Biedermeier era; Leopoldstadt is more than a district with a high percentage of foreigners; and the train stations mark more than just one's personal trips. The compelling nature of the memoirists' body memories and memory maps concretizes painful memories and recasts the Austrian landscape.

✂ 4 ✂

Reclaiming the Past

For Jean Améry, identity and "ownership of the past" were inseparable. His coupling of memory and identity echoes the work of researchers from a variety of disciplines who have asserted that one's understanding and assessment of the past are integral parts of one's sense of self and one's individual and group identity.[1] As philosopher Mary Warnock writes, "[m]y present cannot be divorced from my past, neither can my concept of self be separated from my awareness of what I was in the past" (1987, 63), and as historian David Lowenthal maintains, "[a]wareness of history likewise enhances communal and national identity, legitimating a people in their own eyes" (1985, 44). Reflecting on his diminished sense of self in exile, Améry lamented, "I was no longer an I and did not live within a We. I had no passport, and no past, and no money, and no history" (1980, 44).[2] Améry's memories neither enhanced nor legitimized his identity as an Austrian; they remained only sore reminders of his loss.

Unlike Améry, the memoirists restore a sense of self and an Austrian identity by revisiting and reclaiming their past. In the Austrian context, reclaiming the past takes on multiple meanings and is both a personal and a public act. If being "Jewish" resulted in being eliminated from an Austrian "we" in 1938 and marginalized in a national "we" after 1945, then the memoirists' assertion of their connection to Austria and its past can be seen as an attempt to legitimize themselves *in Austria as Austrians by reconstituting an Austrian self.*

Warnock argues that through narration or interpretation of the past, humans have the capacity to use the past as a tool for shaping the future:

> In the case of humans, . . . since they reflect on what they are, there is room for them to determine what they will be, in accordance with the interpretation they place upon what has happened to them. The past becomes "their" past precisely because it is the subject of reflection. Although I cannot change the past, I can change my view of it, and the use I put it to. It is like a tool made in a certain shape, but flexible, and thus able to be adapted to new circumstances. (62)

Although they cannot change their past, the memoirists share the belief that they can make their past their own through their interpretations of it. They use the past as a tool to root themselves in Austrian society and determine for themselves the meaning of a Jewish identity. They simultaneously strive to reconfigure Austrian collective memory and identity. The major focus of this chapter will be a distilled view of select ways in which the writers use the past to construct and reconcile Jewish and Austrian identities. Born into families that had distanced themselves from Judaism and their Jewish past in the desire to become fully integrated into Austrian society, the memoirists can more easily articulate what it means to be Austrian than Jewish. As Beller argues, "[t]he denial of the past, a precondition of assimilation, now produced not a group of people, but only a 'sum of individuals,' dependent solely on their own resources and their education, not their heritage" (1989, 214). For their parents' generation, a Jewish family past seemed more a liability than an asset. One strategy of integrating was to "invest" in the future, be it through involvement in the Social Democratic movement, or in progressive education, or in culture (See Beller, 207–37). To become integrated into Austrian society, it seemed imperative to efface one's Jewish roots. The families of the memoirists were part of "a particularly Jewish phenomenon," that is, "the whole process of overcoming one's Jewishness" (210). If their parents believed in the promise of assimilation and hoped their children or grandchildren would not have to experience anti-Semitism, the memoir writers certainly did not have this luxury. This realization no doubt complicated their understanding of themselves as Austrians and forced them to deliberate on the meaning of a Jewish identity.

The memoirists plot their connections to a Jewish Austrian "we" spatially, temporally, and relationally through familial, professional, political, and cultural histories. As Sander Gilman contends:

The complexities of the models for Jewish identity and historiography rest in part on the link between knowing who you are (identity) and knowing how you came to be who you are (history). The linkage between questions of identity/identification and history/historiography rests on the construction of organizational categories by the authors and readers of texts. We inscribe who we believe ourselves to be and where we believe ourselves to have come from in these texts we call "history." Identity is what you imagine yourself and the Other to be; history/historiography is the writing of the narratives of that difference. (1999, 2)

The memoirists construct identities that respond to racist definitions of Jewishness and the position of Jews in mainstream narratives. Taken as a whole, the iterations of Jewish Austrian identities reveal the complex and conflicting nature of weaving their stories into an Austrian story.[3]

Reclaiming Jewish Austrian Identities in Family Histories

When they introduce themselves to the reader, Elisabeth Freundlich, Hilde Spiel, and Hans Thalberg explicitly anchor themselves and their families in a specific Austrian context and illustrate the ways in which their families were rooted in Austrian society. The spatial, temporal, and social coordinates of their early life provide them with the opportunity to reflect on the "we"s into which they were born. Born in 1906, 1911, and 1916 respectively, they demonstrate that by the time of their birth, their families were firmly anchored in Austria. Then they turn to family histories to legitimize further their position in Austrian society. Indicating that they had a very distanced or nonexistent relationship to Judaism growing up, they establish an intellectual connection to a Jewish cultural heritage through their family histories: each a story of successful Jewish integration.[4] They reclaim—or rather claim—a place for themselves in an Austrian story and in Austrian history, drawing on family memory.

Freundlich uses the occasion of her birth to tie herself and family temporally, spatially, and culturally to Vienna. She first situates her parents' position in time and her own position within the family: "My parents must have led a truly bohemian life in the early years of their marriage. At the time, just after the turn of the century, barely a decade separated us from the outbreak of the First World War. They had married in 1905; in 1906 I came into the world and would remain their only child" (1999, 7).[5] Freundlich then describes her parents' nightly peregrinations in Vienna at the time of her birth. "Wherever their evening had begun, it was dead certain to end (or so, at least, I have been told) at the Café Central, which even then had long been legendary" (7).[6] A photograph of this famous coffeehouse (patronized by Trotsky) is sandwiched between the introductory passage and the description of Freundlich's parents' visits; thus they are tied to an institution and a past that is seen as emblematically "Viennese" by Austrians.

Freundlich goes on to anchor her parents more concretely within specific Austrian cultural traditions at a specific historical juncture in which Jewish Austrians played prominent roles in Austrian society:

> After those late nights long before the outbreak of the First World War, Father adhered strictly to his eight-o'clock breakfast time despite his chronic sleep deficit, while Mother was allowed to indulge her need for slumber. Thus Father ate his breakfast alone and buried himself in his beloved *Arbeiter-Zeitung* (in addition he also received the *Neue Freie Presse*, just so that mother could get upset over the—in her opinion—completely uninformed music criticism by X and Y, and also because it was, after all, a major newspaper, whose influence reached to the furthest corners of the Empire and beyond; in short, because it was considered indispensable). (9)[7]

The *Arbeiter-Zeitung* (The Workers' Newspaper), the newspaper of the Socialist Party, situates the father within an Austrian Social Democratic political tradition that attracted large numbers of the Jewish intelligentsia (Wistrich 1987, 114). Indeed, he served as a lawyer for the Socialists.[8] The *Neue Freie Presse* (New Free Press), with its Jewish editor Moritz Benedikt, also locates the family within an Austrian liberal bourgeois cultural tradition.

Whereas Freundlich ties her parents (and herself) immediately to an urban Vienna, Spiel locates her beginnings in an unmistakably rural milieu on the outskirts of Vienna in "INTROIT: A Child in Vienna," the short preliminary chapter in the first of her two-volume memoirs:

> In the outskirts of the city—not too long ago villages—the last years of the great peace lay nestled like they themselves in the furthest hollows of the Vienna Woods. Pötzleinsdorf was the beginning, viewed when the eyes first opened, but not perceived. Sievering, recognized and immediately forgotten, with the second year already disappeared; Heiligenstadt with its Pfarrplatz, a house and a garden in the Probusgasse, the already unforgettable landscape of a childhood into which the war broke before the third year had passed. (1989b, 7)[9]

The three Viennese suburbs, Pötzleinsdorf, Sievering, and Heiligenstadt—predominantly non-Jewish areas located on the outskirts of the

Café Central (courtesy of
Bildarchiv/ÖNB Wien)

city—situate her socially in a well-to-do family.[10] Spiel situates her beginnings within a geography rich with associations, particularly of the
Vienna Woods with Beethoven and his *Heiligenstädter Testament* with
the Biedermeier tradition. Like Freundlich, she makes reference to the
proximity of her birth to World War I, suggesting its impact as an early
caesura.

In "Childhood and Parental House," a short section at the beginning of his memoirs, Hans Thalberg plots the geographical, temporal,
and social coordinates at his birth, immediately anchoring himself and
his family in a lost or sunken Austrian past: "When I was born, *Emperor
Franz Josef* ruled in Vienna and *Czar Nikolaus II* in Petersburg. From
my earliest childhood I believed I remembered my nursemaid Zita taking
me in the baby carriage to the changing of the guard at the inner
courtyard of the imperial residence. It was a solemn occasion that took
place at noon every day and during which the emperor appeared at the
window" (1984, 21).[11] Thalberg situates himself and his family among
the cultured haute bourgeoisie loyal to Emperor Franz Josef. Thalberg,
like the other memoirists, was born into an Imperial Austria, and his
family, like the majority of Austrian Jewry, was loyal to the Habsburg
monarchy.[12]

In their brief introductory passages, Freundlich, Spiel, and Thalberg portray an almost idyllic world and an unquestioned sense of belonging to this world. This connection to Vienna, which they took for granted in their childhood, was preceded by the story of erasing traces of a Jewish past and of their families distancing themselves from a religious Jewish identity. As the daughter of a Social Democrat, religion was of little importance to Freundlich. Although she participated in Jewish religious instruction at school, this was the first time she heard the term "Mosaic Confession" (1999, 25). Spiel pinpoints the final turn away from Judaism in her parents' generation: "No one in my family as far as I experienced it was openly religious. That my ancestors' religion was not my own was unknown to me as a child. My father had become a Catholic, perhaps already as a student. My mother, whose two uncles had already converted, followed him without giving much thought to the matter" (1989b, 32).[13] Spiel grew up celebrating the Christian holidays like the other children in her elementary school. A memory that she can understand only in retrospect suggests the quick integration of the family and the erasure of a Jewish past: Spiel's grandmother was disturbed that Spiel crossed herself whenever she passed a church.

As with Freundlich and Spiel, Thalberg's family's connection to Judaism seemed to be a thing of the past by the time of his birth, although the matter was less straightforward in his family. Thalberg pinpoints his family at a transition along the path toward assimilation. On numerous occasions he explicitly expresses his family's identification with Christian Austria rather than the ethnic traditions of Judaism:

> We celebrated the Austrian Christian holidays, lived and behaved like other citizens. We were consciously Austrian, had shared joy and sorrow with this country, had served in the war and lost a fortune through war bonds like all other Austrians. . . . Our Jewish heritage was something that still lived in memory, something about which we seldom thought, which in all probability would disappear into nothing in the course of the next generation. And yet . . . (33–34)[14]

Assimilation, which appears uncomplicated in the memoirs of Freundlich and Spiel, is doomed because of racial anti-Semitism.

Although being Jewish had little emotional meaning for the young Thalberg growing up, he was nonetheless acutely aware of his status as an outsider. The remarks of others (35) and the role that being Jewish played in major decisions concerning education and profession (46) showed that being Jewish remained "a threatening reminder, an element of eternal uncertainty" (46).[15] His parents' attempts to protect Thalberg from the "mark" of being Jewish by having him baptized Protestant ultimately only marginalized him more.

This very desire of assimilated Jews to distance themselves from Judaism or their claims of its irrelevancy to the family "implies . . . that at a deeper and wider level there was a considerable consciousness of the problem of being Jewish" (Beller 1989, 74). However, in a country where the Jewish population had gone from 201,513 at the time of the official census in 1923 to 11,000 shortly after World War II, the "Jewish problem" is somewhat different.[16] For the writers, it is not a matter of effacing Jewish traits, but (re)discovering family histories and determining for themselves what it means to be Jewish and Austrian and remembering a world destroyed by Jewish genocide.

Unlike their parents, who wished to distance themselves from their Jewish roots, Freundlich, Spiel, and Thalberg use their family histories to define themselves as Austrians and simultaneously find meaning in a Jewish identity. They draw on individual and collective family memories, often enhanced by research and photographs, to show the extent to which their families were rooted in an Austrian story. Yet they find or disclose little information about a Jewish past, only the erasing of this past.

With their family histories, these three memoirists attempt to illustrate the ways that "Jewish" and "Austrian" are not mutually exclusive categories. They seek a positive Austrian identity through the story of their family's integration. The various ways in which they present their family stories uncovers their family's and their own ambivalent feelings toward a Jewish heritage and their acute awareness of continued anti-Semitism. Simultaneously, the efforts highlight their commitment to recovering Jewish contributions to Austrian society.

While Freundlich does not deny her Jewish background, she places her family within recognized Austrian histories and cultural traditions, drawing parallels between her family's history and that of non-Jewish Austrians and showing the enormous progress they made in one short generation. In "Family News," the second chapter of her memoirs, Freundlich traces her family's history back as far as her mothers' parents, both orphans from Jewish communities in Moravia. She connects her family's history to the stories of migration in the multicultural empire and depicts Vienna in particular as a melting pot.[17] In the late nineteenth and early twentieth centuries, approximately one-third of the population in Vienna was from Bohemia or Moravia. The majority of the men from Bohemia and Moravia were employed as workers or engaged as apprentices and the majority of the women as domestic help (John and Lichtblau 1990, 19). Like them, Freundlich's maternal grandparents came to Vienna from Moravia during this time. In this generation Freundlich's mother's family settled in Vienna and made considerable social and economic advances. After being orphaned, Freundlich's maternal grandmother, Rosa Herlinger, moved in with relatives in Vienna, where she worked as a domestic servant for a more well-to-do branch of the family. Freundlich's maternal grandfather, Ernst Lanzer, settled in Vienna after having served twelve years in the Imperial Army. In Vienna he worked his way up to become a buyer for a meat firm. The author shows her grandfather as viewing himself as very much a beneficiary of the diversity of the Habsburg empire. From family stories, she learns that her grandfather believed the army helped him advance in society and supported an ethnic mix (English 18–19, German 24–25).

Freundlich fictionalized the story of her maternal grandparents and her mother in her novel *Der Seelenvogel* (The soulbird, written in exile, published in 1986). In contrast to the ways in which she underplays her family's self-consciousness as Jews striving to integrate in the memoirs, in the novel she highlights aspects of Jewish identity and an acute awareness of wanting to erase traces of being Jewish. In the introduction alone, she repeatedly notes incidents where the elders in her family admonished those who gesticulated, thus acting Jewish, or behaved wildly, as if in a "Jewish school."

The author views her novel as a soulbird, a symbolic carving of a bird used to bring home the souls of Jews who died away from their *Heimat*: "Nothing is left for me to do, but erect the soulbird between these white pages; to try to tear all of your lives from oblivion, to capture it in these pages, so that you will find rest and my soul will also be more peaceful. May I have the strength to pull you into these pages and give you life once again so that you're not just a handful among the six million" (1986, 10).[18] She provides a fictionalized social history of Vienna at the turn of the century and highlights her family's effort to distance themselves from a Jewish identity and assimilate.

Her memoir is also a way of giving life to her family. However, the shift of emphasis opens different possibilities for identification. In the memoir, she highlights the parallels between her family and her non-Jewish Austrian readers, striving to create a stronger sense of identification.

Like Freundlich, Spiel devotes an entire chapter to family histories. For Spiel, her family history offers proof of her legitimacy as an Austrian and the key to a Jewish identity for her as a "non-Jewish" Jew. The first full chapter, "Aura and Origin," is a brief family chronicle complete with family photographs. She describes what she views as a typical Jewish family with deep Austrian roots well on its way to integration. "My mother's birth name was Marie Gutfeld. She belonged to a family who had already completed its entry into the Viennese social structure. Their rise to an educated class from a Jewish background was exemplary" (1989b, 16).[19] This opening gives her the opportunity to explore the genealogical history of her mother's family and locate their Viennese roots.

Spiel traces her mother's family's roots in the Austrian empire back to the eighteenth century, to her earliest known relative, Markus Benedict (1753–1829), a well-respected rabbi. She traces her family's Viennese ties to Benedict's son, who moved to Vienna after his father's death and became a businessman. The family's move to Vienna is paralleled, at least in the narrative, by the family's distancing itself from Judaism. Within five generations, the family's identification as Jewish had totally disappeared. Spiel follows the disappearance of identity as religious Jews from a distinguished rabbi; to a great-uncle, who converted to Catholicism and married a Christian; to her parents, who both converted; to herself, who was unaware of her Jewish heritage growing up.

This family story, particularly the episode of Markus Benedict, takes on multiple meanings. Made into a Jew by the Nazis, Spiel sets out to find who these Jewish ancestors were. By highlighting this branch of the family, she develops a particular strategy of claiming legitimacy and demanding respect. She constructs a Jewish heritage with which she can identify.

Spiel had already begun historical research on her mother's family's past in 1941 in England as part of a book project in an earlier attempt to recover her stolen past. In her memoir, her search for her family's past also becomes a search for a Jewish identity. She carefully selects and underscores certain facts of Markus Benedict's life and presents them in such a manner as to underline his progressive tendencies, providing her with points of identification. His work on a Hebrew grammar, his interest in Moses Mendelssohn (the famous Jewish representative of Enlightenment thought), and his insistence on speaking and writing correct German, all align him with her as an intellectual. She quotes historian Hugo Gold's study of Benedict to give her understanding of the past further legitimacy (1989b, 17). By including a letter about Benedict from her great-uncle, who had long ago converted to Catholicism but still respected the learned ancestor, she provides a model of identification for herself.

Spiel combines photography and text to insert her family simultaneously into an Austrian story and into a Jewish story. The photographs visually anchor Spiel's family in an Austrian story. In her introduction, Spiel includes a picture of her parents with two other couples. The men, all officers, appear in uniform, and the caption indicates that the three couples are celebrating the emperor's birthday in Olmütz in 1916.[20] In the first full chapter she includes a total of seven family photographs: of a maternal great-uncle, her maternal grandmother Melanie with the Alps in the background, her mother, her father as a student and in military uniform, her paternal great-grandfather, and her paternal grandparents with her father's sister. In the photographs, her family members are shown as successful and respectable and captured in poses or activities typical of the Viennese upper class. The accompanying text complements the pictures and squarely locates Spiel's family members as part of the Austrian scene.

In her discussion of the rise of family photography in the late nineteenth century and its significance, Marianne Hirsch has commented that "photography quickly became the family's primary instrument of self-knowledge and representation—the means by which family memory would be continued and perpetuated, by which the family's story would henceforth be told" (1997, 6–7). The photographs serve as a means for Spiel to retrieve knowledge and document her family's past, to plot the family's story as an Austrian story, and to highlight gaps in her family memory.

With the texts, photographs, and textual pictures, Spiel stylizes family members as figures reminiscent of those found in the literature of famous fin-de-siècle Jewish Austrian writer Arthur Schnitzler (1862–1931), thereby adding layers to the specific Jewish Austrian story. Schnitzler was a well-respected Austrian Jew who addressed questions of Jewish Austrian identity and Austrian anti-Semitism in works such as the novel *Der Weg ins Freie* (1907) and the play *Professor Bernhardi* (1912).[21] "Unflinchingly he acknowledged the sociopsychological fact of anti-Semitism, but he insisted on living out his life as a Jew in Vienna, the city he regarded as his emotional home" (Schwarz 1994, 61). In his personal stance and in his writings, he offers a wide range of Jewish identities. He remained skeptical of Jews who believed in the success of assimilation and portrayed the richness of Viennese and Jewish life before 1938.

Spiel's mother, who longs to return to Vienna during trips away from home, is both explicitly and implicitly compared to Schnitzler's female figures:

> My mother, a beautiful dark girl, remained untouched by such turmoil of the soul and the time. From her ancestors she had inherited a good sense of humor, good taste, musicality, and a certain dreamy casualness that sometimes, but not in her case, is accompanied by or preceded by a

Hilde Spiel's parents (middle) with two other couples in Olmütz celebrating the kaiser's birthday, 1916 (courtesy of Österreichisches Literaturarchiv/ÖNB Wien)

contemplative introspection. In contrast to her brother, she was easygoing as long as she remained unscathed by fate. She clung to Vienna fervently and longed to return to her city during all trips, all holidays. She had a delicate nose, a delicate mouth. Her girlfriends called her Mizzi; the Schnitzlerian name reflected her temperament. (1989b, 25)[22]

Not only does the name Mizzi immediately bring to mind Schnitzler's *Comtesse Mizzi*, but Spiel's description makes the identification overt. The photograph complements Spiel's description and captures her mother's grace and that dreamy quality associated with the characters of the classic Austrian playwright.

Spiel's textual portrait of her father and the accompanying photographs clearly align him with Austrian history and Schnitzler's turn-of-the-century characters. Spiel describes her father as a devotee of Wagner, Schubert, and Mahler, and by extension of mainstream German and Austrian culture. She portrays him in the mold of the classic turn-of-the-century Austrian hero, as a passionate man who belonged to a

Hilde Spiel's grandmother in
Gastein, 1908 (courtesy of
Österreichisches
Literaturarchiv/ÖNB Wien)

dueling fraternity (wherein he had acquired the requisite scars) and who supposedly had once fought a duel to defend the honor of a woman. She includes photographs of him as a student in his fraternity uniform, in which he proudly displays his scars, and as an officer in a uniform "that fits him like a glove" (1989b, 27). With this composite picture, he almost appears to have stepped out of the pages of a work of Schnitzler.

The dueling scars constitute "badges" connecting her father to the "we" of upper-class German nationalist circles in Austria. The marks on a duelist's face indicated "his integration into German culture" (Gilman 1991, 181) or in this case, Austrian culture. As Sander Gilman explains: "Students [in German fraternities] challenged each other to duels as a matter of course, without any real need for insults to be exchanged. Being challenged was a process of social selection." The duelists had their eyes and throat protected, but their faces were purposely exposed to the blade of the saber. When a cut was made, there were guidelines as to how to repair it to maximize the resulting scar. The scars were proof that one was *satisfaktionsfähig*: deemed "worthy" of a duel. Such scars must have taken on additional significance after the Waidhofen Resolution of 1896, mentioned in Schnitzler's *Der Weg ins Freie*, "which

Hilde Spiel's mother
(courtesy of Österreichisches
Literaturarchiv/ÖNB Wien)

forbade German students to 'give satisfaction' to Jews as members of an 'inferior race' " (Wistrich 1989, 613).

Although according to historian Keith H. Pickus, the *Corps* was a nonpolitical, religiously neutral student dueling organization, the dueling scars nonetheless were perceived by others as associated with anti-Jewish German nationalistic student organizations.[23] Indeed, after 1938 the scars on Spiel's father's face "protected him from unearned humiliation" (1989b, 27).[24] However, the currency of these painfully earned scars as a sign of membership in an exclusive Austrian German "we" was short-lived. "He was subjected to the humiliation of his descent when people began to differentiate some Viennese from other Viennese" (27).[25] All of his efforts to be Austrian were undone by anti-

Hilde Spiel's father as a
Corps student (courtesy of
Österreichisches
Literaturarchiv/ÖNB Wien)

Semitism. The infliction of wounds did not guarantee membership in an Austrian "we," and the scars were painful reminders of a failed effort.

Spiel's inclusion of a picture of her great-uncle rounds out the stylization of her family in a Schnitzlerian mode. Shown seated in a tie and jacket, her great-uncle Gustav Singer, a doctor at Vienna's renowned Rudolfspital, who had been bestowed the honorary title "*Hofrat*" (court councilor) appears the epitome of success and could easily be a figure out of Schnitzler's drama *Professor Bernhardi*. Singer distinguished himself as the director of a hospital in Vienna and as the

Hilde Spiel's father as an officer (courtesy of Österreichisches Literaturarchiv/ÖNB Wien)

personal doctor of the prelate-chancellor Ignaz Seipel. In this one man's story, we see the ways in which Jewish Austrians were an integral part of Viennese society. By 1880, more than half the doctors in Vienna were Jewish, although many had converted to Catholicism, including Singer (Beller 1989, 37–38).

In contrast to her extensive exposition of her mother's side of the family and her parents' attachment to Vienna, Spiel claims near ignorance when she discusses her father's family. "Where did they come from, the Spiels, what had their bourgeois existence been founded upon? I do not know. . . . Presumably, this branch of the family had also been living in Vienna for some time" (29).[26] By noting their presumed longtime residence in Vienna, she implies her family's Viennese roots go back as far or further than those of many non-Jewish Austrians.

The pictures of her paternal relatives serve not to jog her memory and prompt family stories but as traces of a past she knows little about because it has not been a part of family memory. "Three photographs from the estate of Aunt Lonny . . . give meager information" (27, 29).[27]

These photographs allow Spiel to speculate on her father's ambivalent feelings toward his mother's eastern European roots. His desire not to talk about this indicates the hierarchy among Austrian Jews themselves and the common prejudices toward eastern European Jews. Just as there are no family stories about this side of the family's eastern European past, there are no traces of this past in the photographs. The photographs are a way for the family to remember and reproduce itself, inventing itself in such a way as to erase traces of an unwanted past. The pictures, as well as the paternal grandmother's family name change from the Sephardic "Pereira" to the German "Birnbaum," are evidence of the desire to integrate into the Austrian mainstream and erase traces of a Jewish heritage.[28] However, at the same time Spiel highlights her family's efforts to erase the part of the past, she constructs a very specific Jewish identity.

Spiel does not go into any detail in her memoirs speculating about how her Sephardic ancestors could have reached Vienna from Spain. However, she nonetheless brings attention to the family's desire to forget its past and connects her family to a specific Jewish tradition, which in other sources she has privileged over a Hassidic tradition. For example, in her biography *Fanny von Arnstein*, Spiel discusses the Sephardic tradition and characterizes the Sephardim as "imaginative Jewish nobility" (1991, 125) and "the natural nobility of the Jews" (179).

Spiel only mentions the picture of a great-uncle who "was a doctor, he was homosexual, and he committed suicide" (1989b, 32)[29], providing us with no reason for the suicide nor an explanation for her exclusion of the picture itself. Nonetheless, the "textual picture"[30] she creates is significant in the context of her construction of Jewish Austrian identities: "In the picture he is sitting with a cheerful expression, reading the newspaper in a café. Those characteristics that are supposedly typical for people of his background are not to be discovered on him; he could be a department head in the Ministry of Transportation reading a report of the opening of a new railroad line in the crown land Croatia" (32).[31] By describing someone with no external "Jewish" markers, she rejects theories of essential racial characteristics. She situates him in an unmistakably Viennese milieu possibly as a bureaucrat, a domain into which Jews hardly made inroads. Ironically, she chooses a branch of Austrian bureaucracy with a higher representation of Jews than other branches. As Rozenblit summarizes, Jews "rarely worked for the prestigious ministries or services. Some worked for the Finance Ministry, but most pursued careers in the less prestigious Railroad and Post Office Ministries" (1983, 50).

Spiel appears to hold on nostalgically to the promise of assimilation. However, her portrayal of her family is much more than a naive belief in a multicultural society predicated on successful assimilation. Underlying Spiel's story of her family is a claim to an Austrian past and a desire to see Jews as once again integral parts of Austrian society, not victims. Nonetheless, it remains a very selective view of Jewish life in Vienna, one that privileges assimilated Jews.

In her biography of Spiel, journalist Sandra Wiesinger-Stock writes that Spiel never felt Jewish and that she herself claimed that her interest in Jewish contributions to Austrian culture was not based on any sense of being personally affected by anti-Semitism, but arose purely from objective interest (1996, 51–52). Wiesinger-Stock suggests that Spiel refused to identify with Jewish victims because of her unrelenting individualism (53). However, the ways in which Spiel constructs her family story in her memoirs and her publications on the contributions of Jewish intellectuals to Austrian culture go beyond mere objective interest and are an expression of a Jewish identity that she determined herself.[32]

The story of Jewish assimilation allows Spiel to highlight the contributions of Austrians of Jewish heritage to a culture with which she fiercely identifies. Simultaneously, she can highlight an emotional attachment to Vienna shared by many Austrians of Jewish heritage. In her book *Vienna's Golden Autumn, 1866–1938* she explicitly describes the valuable and varied contributions of Austrians of Jewish heritage to Austrian culture. She regrets having to state specifically which artists, poets, and musicians were of Jewish heritage, but feels it necessary to draw attention to their accomplishments and to their contributions to Austrian culture then and now. But she also abhors the continued anti-Semitism in Austria (1987, 236). She further remarks that the Second Republic has indeed profited from the marketing of this turn-of-the-century Vienna.

Spiel holds up this very selective view of Jewish life in Vienna as a mirror in which postwar Austria can look at itself and consider its continued anti-Semitism and xenophobia. However, missing from her picture are questions concerning the failure of assimilation as a viable model and the need of a society to accept difference.

Thalberg devotes much more space to the history of his family and the history of Jews in Austria than do any of the other memoir writers. In contrast to Freundlich and Spiel, who discuss their family's past primarily in the preliminary chapters and rarely comment on it later, he intertwines his family's story with the nation's story throughout the first section of his book. To illustrate that just as the history of Austrian Jews is inextricably bound with the history of Austria and the history of Austria incomplete without the history of its Jews, Thalberg combines a narrative of himself and his family with an academic discourse on the history of Jews and anti-Semitism in Austria. He devotes two of the chapter sections exclusively to the historical background: 1.6, "Concerning the Question of Anti-Semitism in Austria" and 1.13, "Vienna and Its Jews, Observations of the Violent End of a Historical Epoch." He includes a brief history of anti-Semitism in Austria, a discussion of Zionism versus assimilation, his view on the political rivalries in the Second Republic, and a brief overview of the rich contributions Jewish Austrians have made to Austrian culture. In the other chapter sections, he uses his family to illustrate the intersection between a family's history, the history of Austrian Jewry, and the nation's history. For example, his great-grandfather was a Freemason and a member of the citizen's militia during the revolution of 1848.

His depiction of the contributions of Austrian Jewry to Austrian culture before 1938 not only counters a binary categorization of Austrian and Jewish identity, but also points the reader toward an even stronger conclusion. To be Austrian and Jewish is not a contradiction in terms, rather to be anti-Semitic is to be anti-Austrian:

> The contribution of Jews to the development of an independent Austrian culture cannot be underestimated. So close was the connection of Jews with Austrian intellectual life, so deeply rooted in their country that an independent Austrian culture has become unthinkable without their contribution. Thus, it is in no way surprising that exactly those who opposed the existence of an independent Austria and the thought of an Austrian nation were simultaneously the most rabid anti-Semites. For National Socialists, the physical destruction of Austria's Jewry stood for the disappearance of an independent Austria altogether. (1984, 43–44)[33]

On the one hand, Thalberg sets out to show that Austrian culture was unthinkable without Jewish contributions. On the other hand, he points to the tenuous position Jews actually held in Austrian society with his own and his family's story. Only by distancing itself from Judaism does his family see advancement as possible.

Thalberg employs strategies similar to those of Freundlich and Spiel in writing himself into Austrian history. Like Spiel, Thalberg engages in a genealogical history. He traces his paternal grandfather's Viennese roots back to the late eighteenth century and his paternal grandmother's roots to a patriotic Hungarian family background (27). He then provides information about his mother's Moravian family, rooting his family both spatially and temporally even more firmly in an Austrian past (32–33).

Like Freundlich and Spiel, Thalberg also frames the story of his family in terms of other stories of Jewish Austrian integration. In contrast to theirs, his story is decidedly focused on the paternal connections to Austria. In his portrayal of his grandfather and father, he captures the typical generational conflict between successful liberal Jewish businessmen and their sons who are more interested in the arts. More generically, this is the tale of numerous turn-of-the-century male artists and writers.[34] Thalberg describes his grandfather, Josef Thalberg, as a "typical man of the Founding Years, a patriarch in his large family, a Renaissance man who wanted to reshape the world, his Austrian world, in a time of technical and scientific upheaval" (25).[35] According to Thalberg, his grandfather considered himself a true representative of Austrian liberalism (26). Typical of that generation of businessmen, the grandfather supported the arts but did not approve of his son's pursuit of music (26–27). (The son studied law only to please his father.)

Like Spiel, Thalberg uses family photographs to underline his family's relationship to Austria. However, the arrangement and selection equally highlight Thalberg's great personal loss. Whereas Spiel scatters photographs throughout her memoirs, Thalberg includes thirty-four consecutive photographs between pages 159 and 160 in a book of 517 pages. The photographs create a physical divider between the first and second sections and a symbolic divider between his life before and after 1945.

Only six of the thirty-four photographs are personal and only three of these date from pre-1938 Vienna. Two pictures of Thalberg with each of his parents and one of his paternal grandfather alone create a haunting triptych. The pictures with his parents evoke a physical and emotional closeness. One shows a beautiful, young, apparently well-to-do mother gracefully and lovingly holding her baby up to her cheek. The picture with his father shows father and son in Styrian suits, a type of Austrian regional costume Jews were forbidden to wear after the *Anschluss*. Father and son assume the same pose, holding walking sticks, playfully mirroring one another. Thalberg's grandfather is pictured with his medals. With these few pictures, Thalberg ties his family to an Austrian past and an assimilated Jewish Austrian "we."

Thirty-four years separate the photograph of father and son (1923) from the next picture, a snapshot of Thalberg with his young daughter on his shoulders (1957). Much had happened in these thirty-four years. The rich Jewish Austrian culture of pre-*Anschluss* Vienna had been destroyed. But perhaps most devastating for Thalberg, his parents had been murdered in a concentration camp and his sister had disappeared, never to be seen again. The pictures of Thalberg's first and second family are separated not just by years, but by worlds. Thalberg is the only bridge

Hans J. Thalberg with his
mother in 1917 (courtesy of
Böhlau Verlag)

between them; however, he offers no commentary on the "ghostly
revenants," as Marianne Hirsch labels such photographs (1997, 22).

As remnants of a lost past full of personal and symbolic meaning,
the photographs raise more questions than they answer. Why does
Thalberg include only these pictures? Are these all he has left of his
first family or are they selected? How did he manage to save them?
What are his feelings when he looks at these pictures? For this reader,
the dearth of family pictures, the absence of a picture of his sister or
any other family members from such a large extended family magnifies
the sense of loss. The lack of commentary and their isolated position in
Thalberg's memoirs transform the pictures into symbolic gravestones
for this side of the family. Silence surrounds the pictures.

Hilde Spiel and Hans Thalberg tie Austrian identity to loss and
mourn the absence of a rich Jewish cultural heritage, whereas Elisabeth
Freundlich parallels her family's story of integration with that of other
immigrants from Moravia. The family histories and photographs complement each other to serve as a means of constructing identity and

Hans J. Thalberg with his father in the park of the Villa Vetsera, Küb bei Payerbach, around 1923 (courtesy of Böhlau Verlag)

self-knowledge.[36] They are as much a way to access memory as a proof of connection and loss. They are stories of a double loss: of their Jewish identity in the generations before their birth and of their whole world, destroyed after 1938.

Complementary Identities

For Stella Klein-Löw and Minna Lachs, identification with the Austrian Socialist Party was coterminous with their Austrian identity when they returned to Austria after 1945. As with many other political reémigrés, the party gave them a feeling of continuity with their pre-1938 selves and a sense of *Heimat* (Embacher 1995, 120). The

Hans J. Thalberg's
grandfather, Josef Thalberg
(courtesy of Böhlau Verlag)

Austrian Social Democratic Movement offered Klein-Löw and Lachs a
community through which they believed they could realize their goals
for a better Austrian society. However, being part of a movement that
did little to question Austria's victim status after the war posed potential
problems for the negotiation of Jewish Austrian identities. Likewise, the
experiences of exile and the events of the Holocaust made it impossible
for them to ignore the meaning of their Jewish identity.

Klein-Löw and Lachs construct their Jewish and Austrian (Socialist) identities as complementary. However, the space they devote
to the construction of their Jewish identity is in inverse proportion to
the amount they devote to their Austrian identities. In her memoirs,
Klein-Löw traces her "adoption" in the Socialist "family" as a bourgeois
intellectual. She focuses on her commitment to Socialist ideals and
the party. In contrast, she minimizes the importance of her Jewish
identity, barely discussing it. On the other hand, Lachs devotes little
time to her identity as an Austrian Socialist. As a Polish-speaking eastern
European Jew, Lachs struggles in Vienna to find a *Heimat* for herself.
Consequently, she focuses on the ways in which her turn toward religion
and Zionism helps her find a *Heimat* in anti-Semitic Vienna and shows
how her involvement in a Socialist Zionist youth group allowed her to
embrace Austrian Socialism.

Klein-Löw's and Lachs's introductions of themselves are key to understanding the interplay between Jewish and Austrian identities and their invention of self. They develop distinct strategies for constructing their stories as a move from the periphery of society to its center. Both start from outsider positions and narrate themselves into an Austrian story that culminates with their involvement in Austrian Socialism.

Klein-Löw introduces herself with the description of a photograph of herself as a four-year-old:

> I clearly remember the atelier and the photographer, my own indignation during the preparations, and the procedure itself. Compromises had to be made. The beautifully curled locks—with the exception of one— disappeared under my hat as a result of my unrelenting demands. My parents had to bribe me to get me to put on white shoes and socks: the cane, borrowed from a friend, I held in my hand as if I were fending something off.
>
> The poor photographer was in despair. I did not smile like he wanted me to; despite his pleas I did not lean my head to the left in order to hide my scar; and my chin remained impertinently stuck out. (1980, 11)[37]

Although this textual picture appears to offer little information about the ways in which she will identify herself as an Austrian and Jew, it is emblematic of the author's invention of self. Using the description of the picture and the picture-taking session, Klein-Löw presents a personality trait that appears to be integral and lasting. She constructs herself as a strong-willed person who even at the age of four had an enormous say in the representation of herself. Likewise, she implies that her self-portrait is also born out of compromise and is not solely of her own making. So it is with her memoirs.

Equally significant is Klein-Löw's unwillingness to hide the scar on her nose, a scar to which she devotes a short digression (15–16). The origin of the scar is surrounded by mystery. It is the fault of either the midwife or her maternal grandmother. Aware of it only after she was taken to a doctor to see if it could be removed, she became obsessed by it. "I was different from the others. I was ashamed" (16).[38] This shame, however, turned to protest. She insisted that her parents note the fact that she had a scar in school papers. " 'The scar has to go in so that they know right from the start!' That was the moment of release from a nightmare!" (16).[39] Immediately afterward, she gives her father credit for leading her out of this emotional impasse. However, she offers no further explanation. Was it her open and defiant recognition of the scar or her father's undisclosed explanations that freed her from her obsession? Or both?

135

The discussion of the scar, to which she devotes more space than to a discussion of her Jewish identity, can be read as a metaphor for her "Jewishness." Like the scar, her Jewishness is something she has inherited without explanation and that has little personal meaning. The family's assimilation involved "overcoming Jewishness," and this often meant abandoning traditions from which one could construct a Jewish identity. The initial shame she felt because of her scar is parallel to the situation facing a nonreligious Jew in Austria. Being Jewish appeared to have little personal relevance; however, in anti-Semitic Austria, it marked her as an outsider.

As in the digression concerning the scar, Klein-Löw rationalizes her Jewishness with an authoritative explanation and simultaneously defiantly reclaims it as a badge representing solidarity with the oppressed. She recalls a conversation with her grandfather: dissatisfied with his explanation that they are Jewish because his father, grandfather, and great-grandfather were Jewish, the young Klein-Löw protests. The grandfather then offers the future Socialist a much more satisfactory explanation. " 'The Jews are persecuted, hated by many. Stelli, do you think that we should abandon them and their religion? Wouldn't that be cowardly?' " (13).[40] Klein-Löw adopts a Jewish identity that complements her rebel stance, her desire to determine her own identity within certain constraints, and her need for a logical explanation.

Klein-Löw traces her move toward "membership" in an Austrian Socialist "we" from the position of outsider as the daughter of a bourgeois Jew. In the process, she discloses surprisingly little about her family's history. We learn that her grandfather was a banker, her father the director of a ship company, and her maternal grandmother the owner of an estate. We also learn that her family lost most of its wealth in World War I. The personal information she does divulge allows her to anchor herself more easily in a Socialist Austrian "we" and cast her ethnic heritage as a badge of solidarity with outcasts. By revealing the wealth into which she was born, she can take an oppositional stance to it and construct herself as someone who was always sensitive to those less fortunate than herself. By mentioning the loss of her family's wealth, she can underline her own self-sufficiency as a wage earner.

However, just as revealing is the omission of information included in most of the other memoirs. At no point does Klein-Löw explain how long her family had been in Vienna nor where she was born. It is not her biological family, but her "adopted" Socialist family that connects her to Austria. By omitting her birthplace in Przemysl, she can distance herself from her eastern European roots and seem her own creation.

Klein-Löw plots her entrance into a Socialist "we" from her concern as a child for the socially weak to her full-fledged acceptance in the party as an adult. As a child, she hated going to her maternal grandmother's estate, where she was confronted with crass social differences. "My disapproval, my fury were so great that from the time I was six, I pretended to be sick so that I wouldn't have to go to the village" (12).[41] She then follows her developing political conscience, interpreting her student position as a type of homeroom representative as a stepping stone in her development toward a Socialist identity.

Klein-Löw clearly distinguishes between her acceptance in a Socialist "we" and her perception of herself as a Socialist. She pinpoints her feeling of belonging to a "we" to a very specific incident. At her first Austrian Socialist Youth (SAJ) meeting, she remembers, "I felt out of place. . . . They tried to draw me into the conversation. The people didn't speak my language and I didn't speak theirs. They formed a tightly knit circle. I stood outside, I was an outsider" (32).[42] As someone from a bourgeois background with different educational aspirations from the majority present, Klein-Löw no doubt did speak a different language from the rest of the group. In a city in which dialect identifies one's social standing, she would have easily been spotted as an outsider. However, her perception of herself as such changes dramatically during the meeting: "Then a woman entered, simply dressed, homely. 'Mundl,' the representative, stood up. We also stood up. We were met with the loud greeting 'friendship.' We (by then I had come to consider myself a member of the group) returned the greeting. What was it that changed me from one moment to the next from an outsider to a 'member?' I don't know" (32).[43] Klein-Löw offers readers and herself no explanation for this sudden feeling of belonging. She miraculously became part of a "we" devoted to working toward social change. However, she does suggest the importance that the speaker, whom she identifies as comrade Fleischner, played in her life as a Socialist. Fleischner accompanied her home, making her feel more a part of the group, and later she invited her to her home, lending her books formative to her intellectual development as a Socialist.

It may seem contradictory that Klein-Löw did not feel that she had become a Socialist at the same time that she became a part of the Socialist "we" on that first evening with the Socialist Youth. Being part of the "we" appears to have been based on an emotional sense of belonging to a group and a desire to shed her bourgeois identification and be accepted by a group oppressed by bourgeois capital. *Being* a Socialist for Klein-Löw is connected to an inner intellectual transformation brought about after an accumulation of knowledge and experience. By the time she leaves the SAJ, she considers herself a true Socialist. She marks this intellectual transformation by becoming a party member at the age of eighteen. She is able to realize her Socialist identity and strengthen the feeling of belonging through her involvement in the university student Socialist group. In the twenties and thirties, Klein-Löw became increasingly involved in the Socialist movement until she fled in 1938.

If her Austrian *Heimat* and her Socialist *Heimat* were not necessarily synonymous before 1938, they certainly were after 1945. After the *Anschluss*, Klein-Löw lost both her Socialist *Heimat* and Austrian *Heimat* (94). Once the war was over, she returned to Austria as quickly as possible. Klein-Löw attributed her ability to return home to her identity as an Austrian Socialist, contrasting the privilege with those who could not return. "Perhaps it was different for me because I had had a second home in the party, because Socialism created strong familial bonds" (166).[44] However, Klein-Löw's ability to remain in Austria was contingent on her acceptance by the postwar Austrian Socialist community. Klein-Löw considered the return home complete only after she delivered a talk before a group of Socialists in Vienna and received a warm reception. She told her audience, "[t]onight, you have given me my *Heimat* in Vienna, in Austria, in the Socialist Party, anew" (171–72).[45]

Reflecting on her first days in exile, Klein-Löw writes, "I was without a home and a *Heimat*. At the beginning of this new period of my life, I only had one goal before me—to forget the past, to live in the present, and to form a worthwhile future" (125).[46] If she wanted to sever emotional ties and forget her Austrian past in 1938, Klein-Löw uses her pre-*Anschluss* past to insert herself into a history of Austrian Socialism. She not only recovers her own past by recalling her journey to an Austrian Socialist "we," but she uncovers a past for Austrian Socialists. Part of this past is the participation of Jewish Socialists and Socialist Jews in the party. She highlights the contributions of numerous leaders of Jewish heritage. She devotes a short chapter to Otto Bauer, an important Austro-Marxist theoretician, onetime editor of the *Arbeiter-Zeitung*, and the leader of the party in the interwar period. The author also describes the Socialist Jewish members of the rank and file she counseled before 1938. "Many of my members were Jews, some of them were pious Jews . . . all aware of class difference, all poor devils, proletarian and Jews—two burdens that they had to bear. Then there was anti-Semitism" (42).[47] By mentioning the anti-Semitism of the twenties and thirties but not of the Second Republic, she implies the disappearance of anti-Semitism after 1945. However, it is not anti-Semitism that has disappeared, but Austrian Jews. Most of the Jewish leadership had either died or emigrated. Most of the Socialist exiles, whether they were Jewish or not, did not return, as Klein-Löw herself notes (43). Certainly, Jews in the rank and file were virtually nonexistent.

Klein-Löw conjures up images of her initial self-portrait and brings her story full circle when she closes her memoirs with the question "Am I still a rebel?" (210).[48] The answer would have to be yes and no. She provides numerous examples wherein she acted independently from the mainstream. However, she ultimately does not rebel against the party's role in perpetuating Austria's victim narrative.

In contrast to Klein-Löw's memoirs, Lachs's memoirs do not share the same teleological movement toward her membership in the Austrian Socialist Party. Her connection to an Austrian Socialist *Heimat* results from a combination of coincidence, her pedagogical convictions, and the Socialist aspects of her Zionist youth group. Her story is not that of a "Jewish Socialist" nor a "Socialist Jew," but a young Austrian Zionist who opted for Austria in the late twenties.[49]

From the perspectives of an Austrian Socialist and an eastern European Jew, Lachs embeds her story in the story of discrimination within Austria and the story of extreme loss. Moreover, she invests the place and date of her birth with extreme meaning, tying her struggle for identity and her search for *Heimat* to her position as an eastern European Jew: "I was born on July 10, 1907, in Trembowla. Time and place are in my case significant: the time because I as a two-month premature baby would probably have had no chance of survival during a cooler time of year, and the place because the east Galician town in the northeastern tip of the Austro-Hungarian monarchy shaped my earliest childhood and with that gave direction to my entire development" (1986, 9).[50] The intersection of time and place is essential for Lachs's desire to show the ways in which her individual life is tied up with a larger web of events. Highlighting the place of her birth sets the stage for exploring personal memories of larger historical events.

Lachs's personal memories are like a spider's web, with countless threads bound to the place of origin. Within her narrow family circle in Trembowla, she witnesses the animosities between ethnic groups in the disputes of her family's Polish and Ukrainian domestic help. She is present in August 1914 when the mayor of Trembowla reads the emperor's declaration of war, which is the beginning of the end for the empire and for eastern European Jewry. Sheltered by community and wealth, Lachs finds that her sense of security comes to a swift end. Like many other Jewish families, Lachs's family fled the advancing Russian army at the beginning of World War I and sought refuge in Vienna.

Only after she arrives in Vienna in 1914 does she perceive herself as a sometimes unwelcome outsider. Lachs's identity as a Polish-speaking eastern European Jewish refugee from Galicia marks her as a linguistic and ethnic outsider. Although her family had every intention of moving back to Galicia after the war, her father opted for Austria and Austrian citizenship after the breakup of the Austro-Hungarian monarchy. For him, settling in Vienna was the dream of a lifetime. For his oldest daughter, it brought both inner conflict and insight into the problems of other eastern European Jews.

More than any of the other memoirists, Minna Lachs chronicles her search for personal identity and her search for a "we" in Vienna. Her exploration of her personal development coincides with her search for a *Heimat* in anti-Semitic Austria. From her dual consciousness as eastern European Jew and Austrian, Lachs has the opportunity to follow her own development and to sketch the position of eastern European Jews in Vienna in general. "They [the Viennese] did not see them [eastern European Jews] as fellow citizens of the monarchy, but foreigners, from whom the majority of Austrians differed in dress, language, and customs. They were 'Zuagraste' [newcomers] and they found as little sympathy then in Vienna and Austria as they do today" (1986, 47).[51] By highlighting the continuing antipathy of the Viennese toward outsiders, Lachs embeds her story in a tradition of Austrian discrimination.

At the same time, Lachs reveals her perceptions of identity to be situational and often independent of her own sense of self. If in Galicia her family was viewed with suspicion by the Polish population as representatives of German culture and Austrian patriots, in Vienna they were greeted with prejudice as eastern European Jews:

> First I was the nice, well-behaved refugee child who had come from so far away and had had to leave her *Heimat*. People were universally friendly to me, people caressed me, made me a present of this and that. When the number of eastern European refugees grew, as one of them I became a "Polack." Finally, because the overwhelming number of eastern European refugees were Jewish, I was degraded to "Jew" and as such cursed at as a "bloody Jew." (48)[52]

As an obvious outsider, Lachs had to learn to be Viennese before she could hope to be accepted by a Viennese "we." Not only did she have to learn German, but Viennese German. Although she did master the intricacies of Viennese dialect, she nonetheless long retained the feeling of an outsider. She quickly learns the lesson that the meaning of "I" and "we" is not determined solely by the speaker but must be endowed by societal consensus.

In the chapter "In Search of My Own Identity," she first reflects on her Jewish roots and the sense of homelessness she feels because she is Jewish. As she says good-bye to a Jewish school friend returning to what had become part of Poland after the war, she hears her own thoughts expressed in the lines of a song. "Where do I belong, who am I, why are we Jews so different from the others?" (111).[53] Still suffering from the loss of her Galician *Heimat*, she has not yet found a home in Vienna. The search for a "we" seemed to be satisfied at least temporarily when she became a member of a Zionist Socialist youth group (the Schomer). "This first year in the Schomer was a happy one for me. The torturous identity crisis was overcome" (131).[54] In the youth group and through her religion class in school, Lachs becomes familiar with Jewish customs. Although her father had been raised in an Orthodox household, she did not attend synagogue until she was ten, when her religion class went to temple after the emperor's death. The youth group provided her with a group of like-minded idealists in search of a home in anti-Semitic Vienna and with a model for dealing with conflict. "We in the Schomer knew that an unscathed world without conflict does not exist and one has to learn to steer one's own future and the future of the world in new directions" (135).[55] In addition, the Schomer fostered leadership qualities and her pedagogical talents.

Lachs's self-criticism of her arrogant attitude toward non-Zionists marks a turning point in her commitment to Austria. Lachs does not, as originally planned, join her boyfriend in Palestine. Years later in writing her memoirs, she considers her choice not to emigrate to Palestine a moral failing, but at the same time, she realizes she would never have been happy there. Lachs's personal abandonment of Zionism is not a rejection of Judaism, but rather an affirmation of her identification with Austria. The Socialist ideals she finds attractive in the Schomer overlap with those of a Socialist student group she joins. Moreover, the emotional bonds created in the group provide her with a *Heimat* in anti-Semitic Austria.

Although Lachs mentions her husband only later in her narrative, he no doubt played an important role in her identification with and her desire to return to Austria. While in the student group, she meets her husband-to-be, a very open-minded (western) Jewish Socialist from an Austrian family. One of the few exiles invited back, Ernst Lachs returned to Vienna after the war to work in municipal government. Lachs joins him as soon as possible and resumes her work as a teacher, working in a public high school.

In her description of her life before 1938, Lachs underlines the relationship between Jewish Austrians and non-Jewish Austrians, which she plots as both complementary and conflicting. With this strategy, she inserts the stories of Jewish Austrians into Austria's history and seeks to reshape Austrian stories of the past. With her early childhood memories, she points to a heterogenous Jewish population in Galicia.[56] Her early memories of Vienna highlight the tensions between Jewish populations as well as the blatant discrimination against eastern European Jews. As a student, she searches for a Jewish past that will help her construct a sense of belonging to Austria's history and demonstrate the cultural importance of eastern European Jewry for Austria as well. In her dissertation, "Die deutsche Ghettogeschichte" (1931; The German ghetto story), she compares the eastern Jewish and western Jewish mentality as manifested in German-language ghetto prose (158). She later returns to Galicia to gather material for the foreword to the complete works of writer Karl Emil Franzos (1848–1904).[57]

After the war, Lachs is instrumental in integrating the study of the persecution of Austrian Jewry into the educational system by setting up exhibits and other educational programs dealing with the Nazi era. However, this appears to take on a different status from her literary and historical studies before 1938. If her research before 1938 was to establish a connection for herself between a Jewish heritage and Austria, her work after World War II is to inform a largely ignorant non-Jewish student population of the persecution of Jews.

In their initial political involvement, Klein-Löw and Lachs participated in what Beller describes as a pariah strategy. "Jews looked to the other outsiders, the workers, for help. Socialism was, after all, the last major political theory after liberalism's demise in which Jews could hope to be seen as equals" (1989, 208–9). After the war, membership in the Socialist Party did not have the same meaning. The Socialists were no longer the outsiders or the revolutionary force they had been at the turn of the century or in the interwar period. Yet the Austrian Socialist community represented the "other" Austria and Socialism held the possibility of fulfilling their political goals in an Austrian *Heimat*. Consequently, Klein-Löw and Lachs plot their Jewish identities as complementing their Socialist identities, albeit in very different ways. Klein-Löw turns being Jewish into a statement of solidarity with the oppressed that has nothing to do with a set of religious beliefs, rituals, or cultural identity. Lachs finds overlaps in the Zionist and Socialist ideologies, allowing her to find a home in anti-Semitic Austria.[58] However, other than a few educational initiatives, she offers us little insight into her life in postwar Austria, suggesting that it was difficult for her to reconcile her identities in a postwar context.

Irreconcilable Identities

With the words "My first memories are fixed bayonets and a theater performance" (1961, 9) Lothar introduces his life story.[59] In the fixed bayonets memory, the Czech population in Brünn, the capital of Moravia (then still a part of the monarchy), is demanding more political rights. In the second memory, Lothar experiences the magic of the theater and its ability to lift him out of everyday reality for the first time. He relates the personal significance of these memories. "Whenever I think back, these two initial memories, before which lies an absolute void, appear characteristic for my life. It began with bayonets and the theater. It ended almost the same way" (10).[60] Lothar views the turbulent historical events in Austria and his love of the theater, particularly the Austrian theater, as the two major forces in his life. They shape his interpretation of his life and the construction of his Austrian identity. Indeed, Lothar views his life as an odyssey that parallels Austrian history. Near the end of his memoirs, he summarizes his life's journey:

> It [my existence] all began with anti-Austrian demonstrations in Brünn, the city of my birth; the breakup of Austria was my youth, Austria's rape and damage done middle age, anger and anguish because of Austria, the hope in and desire for Austria were the time of emigration, return to Austria was old age. Everything else remained secondary. Profession, perhaps even calling, adventure, success, unrealized and used possibilities, disappointment, being effective with my works—all secondary. It was founded on Austria or based upon it, on one single country, whether better or worse than the others remained immaterial. (438)[61]

His life story is organized around what he claims as his inescapable identification with Austria.

By reviewing his past and tying himself to Austria at every station of his adult life, Lothar shows not only his personal and professional connections to Austria but also his dedication to Austria and the idea of Austria. In all his professional endeavors, he sought to promote Austrian culture and identity. As a bureaucrat during Ignaz Seipel's government, he tried to work with Austrian artists to fight government censorship (70–73). Once a theater director, he specialized in producing plays by Franz Grillparzer, a nineteenth-century Austrian playwright. In exile, he lectured against the world's identification of Austria with Germany and defended Austria's victim status (179). After return, he continued to promote Austrian theater, and his literature reflects his deep love for Austria.

Born in 1890, the oldest of the memoirists discussed here, Lothar experienced World War I and the breakup of the monarchy as an adult. For him, the dissolution of the monarchy and Austria's subsequent loss of identity were traumatic. To help him deal with the trauma, he sought advice from Austria's renowned Dr. Sigmund Freud, a fellow Moravian. Freud proposed a strategy to deal with the loss that combined nostalgic memory with a heavy dose of denial. Lothar recalls a meeting in which Freud drew an analogy between his (Lothar's) mother and *Heimat,* contending that just as his dead mother lives on in memory, so can the Austro-Hungarian monarchy. He then suggests the virtues of denial. "Austria-Hungary exists no longer. I do not want to live anywhere else. Emigration is not something I would ever consider. I will live with the torso and imagine that it is whole" (39).[62] For Freud, living with the memory of an unscathed Austria seemed most appropriate given the situation. Although Lothar finds it supremely ironic that Freud, who so loved his *Heimat,* should die in England in exile, he comments on the helpfulness of this conversation for him at the time.

However, the significance of Lothar's meeting with Freud goes well beyond its usefulness or its irony. The combined model of selective memory and active denial Freud proposed is emblematic of Lothar's strategy of integrating the trauma of exile into his life and reintegrating himself into postwar Austria. As someone who totally identified with Austria, but who had been rejected by it, Lothar reconciles his love of Austria and ejection from an Austrian "we" by creating an imaginary Austria with which he can identify.

As discussed in chapter 3, Grillparzer played a significant role in Lothar's ability to return to Austria. His identification with the dead playwright tied him to an Austrian past far removed from the tragedies of the twentieth century. The nineteenth-century bureaucrat/writer was someone who, like Lothar, recognized Austria's "Janus-headedness." "Austria's secret—Grillparzer had known it and disclosed it bluntly in his autobiography—lies in its demonic Janus-headedness: here one reaches goals via detours, the absolute through the conditional. Nonetheless, the abyss over which one traverses in order to reach Hellbrunn is a thousand times more preferable to the desert that one crosses to reach Hollywood" (399).[63] Like Grillparzer, Lothar recognizes a darker side to Austria, yet he cannot resist Austria's pull. Here, too, his attraction to Grillparzer's work can be seen as an explanation for his behavior. "The time that surrounded him was a void. But with the country, to which he belonged, with the indestructible essence of its people, with the weaving of great destinies—to all this he knew he was bound (435).[64] By identifying with pre-*Anschluss* Austrian culture, particularly the work of nineteenth-century playwright Grillparzer, Lothar created a world for himself that lived on in words and that he could re-create on stage.

However, this backward look to the distant past is of no help in defining his Jewish identity. Certainly, Lothar struggled with the dilemma expressed in the title of Jean Améry's essay: "Über den Zwang und Unmöglichkeit, Jude zu sein" ("On the necessity and impossibility of being a Jew"). Like Améry, he cannot become someone or identify with something that does not exist for him in memory (English 84, German 134). But like Améry, Lothar was made into a Jew by the Nazis and most particularly by the genocide of six million Jews, including his brother. So he must respond. He embraces an essentialist identity and turns himself into "a living reproach" (George Steiner 150), defiantly re-claiming the identity assigned to him by the Nazis as a moral imperative.

In contrast to Spiel, Freundlich, Thalberg, Klein-Löw, and Lachs, he does not mention his Jewish heritage until he tells of being forced to flee Austria. He includes no incidents or discussion of his family's Jewish roots. It is not until Lothar applies for United States citizenship that he directly acknowledges his Jewish heritage. During his formal interview he is asked if he is Jewish and replies, "[b]y heritage, but Catholic by religion" (241).[65] This circumscribed self-identification radically changes when he returns to Austria. He relates several instances in which he openly identifies himself as Jewish after someone makes an anti-Semitic remark. He comments on the moral imperative of declaring oneself openly as a Jew. Appalled by an Austrian Jewish journalist who denies Jewish traits in light of the resurgence of anti-Semitism in Austria, Lothar contends that "non-Jewish Jews" must not deny their past, as they have six million murdered Jews standing behind them (333–34).

Lothar's strategy for negotiating conflicting ethnic and national identities lies in conceiving them as tied to blood and therefore un-avoidable. Indeed, he describes both race and nationality as accidents of birth. "The conditions that make a person are geography, nationality, and race. From these three a person receives his talents and his vices. He can shake them off only externally. . . . *Heimat* cannot be taken off like a shirt, even less so nationality, and least of all race" (333).[66] Later, when justifying his return to Jewish Austrian émigrés in New York, he again embraces an openly essentialist view of race. "Baptismal water does not wash off the mixture of blood" (410).[67] By viewing both nationality and ethnicity as based in blood and indisputable, he can reconcile these apparently irreconcilable identities. Lothar seeks to construct an Austrian identity based on a rich nineteenth- and twentieth-century conservative Austrian cultural tradition. Because of Jewish genocide and continued anti-Semitism in Austria, he feels morally bound to identify himself as Jewish.

Heimat: A Family Affair

Originally entitled "Shanghai ohne Retourbillett: Die Lebens-geschichte einer unbedeutenden Person in einer bedeutenden Zeit" (One-way ticket to Shanghai: the life story of an insignificant woman in a significant time), Franziska Tausig's memoirs focus on the intrusion of the outside world into her domestic sphere. As someone who was not involved in professional life in Austria and who strongly identified with her family, this memoirist does not feel the need to go to great lengths to root herself in an Austrian tradition or consider her position as part of an Austrian "we." She gains her sense of self from her relationship to others in her family—as daughter, wife, and mother.

Tausig's very personal connections to *Heimat* offer a point of comparison that will provide additional insight into the strategies of claiming a place within an Austrian "we" for the other memoirists. Tausig does not search for her family's Austrian roots or plot her quest for personal identification within Austrian history. She nonetheless sit-uates herself temporally, spatially, and socially using her birth in her opening chapter, "The 'Carefree' Time." She was born "on the most beautiful morning in May of the year 1895"[68] (1987, 1) without com-plication at the home of her mother's parents in Temeswar, which at the time was in the Hungarian part of the Austro-Hungarian monarchy. In the opening scene, her mother's father, brother, and brother-in-law—all doctors—are playing cards and seem not to be taking too much notice of Tausig's birth. The very private, familial scene of Tausig's birth sets the stage for the parameters within which she defines herself.

In the first chapter, which spans the period from Tausig's birth to the birth of her son in 1922, she devotes only seven pages to the first nineteen years of her life. In abbreviated fashion, she describes her childhood, her coming out, and her short courtship with her husband. Tausig narrates most extensively when the larger historical events in-terrupt her otherwise quiet family life. After relating her adventures in World War I, she ends chapter 1 with three terse sentences: "We had to begin all over again, my husband in a new profession. In 1922 I had a son, a true Viennese. The next twenty years we lived a productive and successful life in Vienna" (19).[69] Her narrative resumes with the *Anschluss.* The second chapter is devoted to escape, her third chapter to life in Shanghai and reunion with her son in Vienna.

Tausig constructs her connection to Austria through her father, husband, and son, thereby illustrating how the men in her life were rooted in Austrian society and to what extent they were part of an Austrian "we." She sketches how grave the impact of the "larger" historical events on their lives was. Since these men defined themselves in large part through their public personas, they were deeply affected when the circumstances of their public lives changed. In contrast, Tausig continued to be daughter, wife, and mother—even if under radically different conditions.

Although we learn relatively little about Tausig's father, she notes that he went from rags to riches and back to rags in his long life. A poor orphan who became a well-to-do businessman (his business was "Aryanized" in 1938), he later died in a concentration camp. Tausig contrasts her father's appreciation of art and theater and his success as a businessman with his humiliation during and after the *Anschluss*.

Before 1918 and the breakup of the Austro-Hungarian monarchy, Tausig's husband had been an officer in the Royal and Imperial Army and practiced law in Temeswar. After 1918, they return not to Temeswar but to Vienna, where Tausig's husband worked for her father. Tausig describes her husband's losses in particularly compelling terms: "He completed everything 'with distinction': his two doctorates, his obligations as the business manager of my father, his position as an officer and person. He deserved honors for all his actions, and very special recognition as a person. He received them for his two degrees; as a person fate denied him almost everything" (26).[70] One could easily replace "person" with "Austrian" to illustrate the blows he received as a Jewish Austrian. Tausig's husband suffered a loss of dignity as a traditional man who could not protect his family, let alone feed them, after 1938.

We learn the least about Tausig's son, Otto Tausig, who was to become a well-known stage and film star. However, she does describe him as identifying with Vienna very strongly already at age sixteen: "My son had believed for sixteen years that no power on earth could get him to leave Vienna. However, there was a diabolical superpower. One day he came home early in the morning shaking all over. He had been thrown out of school. Not because of poor academic achievement or bad behavior. His religious affiliation proved to be unacceptable in the eyes of the new powers-to-be" (20).[71]

As a result of the *Anschluss*, Tausig became a more public person and part of a larger Jewish "we." In this context, she recalls collective memories of those who sought to escape Austria. She then continues with her story and that of others persecuted until she returns to Austria.

In China, the loss of her immediate family and the common hardships create a sense of community for her. "We had borne hard times together, and misery had welded us together. Poverty had made brothers and sisters as thick as thieves out of us" (129).[72]

Tausig returns to Vienna to be with her son, who so strongly identified himself as an Austrian. Thus, for Tausig, family translates into Austrian *Heimat*. "I would have had to die of suffocation if I had gone to Australia, America, or anywhere else, because my son returned to Vienna. I would surely have succumbed to eternal homesickness" (112–13).[73] The other memoirists return to a political family or become involved in professional life. Tausig returns to Austria solely as a private person, a mother reuniting with her son. She relates the moving reunion after almost ten years of separation. At the West Station, after a long wait, she is approached by a young man who asks her (using the formal "you") if she is his mother. "My son's question drew my emigration to a close and marked the beginning of a new phase of life in the *Heimat*" (154).[74]

As someone who defined *Heimat* primarily through family ties, Tausig did not feel the need to legitimize her own position within an Austrian "we." However, she uses the past to illustrate how the events of World War I and 1938 and exile disrupted her "insignificant" life. She also demonstrates the impact of these events on three generations of men who considered themselves bound to an Austrian *Heimat*. Her father was murdered in a concentration camp, her husband died a broken man in exile, and her son spent difficult years in England before returning to Austria after the war. After she is reunited with her son, she is reunited with her *Heimat*. As a mother, she does not need to discuss or justify any further her place in Austria, and her narrative ends.

Conclusion

By reclaiming the past, the memoirists demand ownership of that past and an Austrian identity of their own making. At least symbolically, the memoir writers strive to repair the temporal link severed by the original loss. Yet the memoirists' Austria is a remembered community bound by loss. Freundlich, Spiel, and Thalberg look to family histories to uncover the loss of memory of the place of Jews in turn-of-the-century Austria. Klein-Löw points to the loss of a rich Socialist community in the interwar period, shaped in great part by Jewish leadership. Lachs reveals the struggles, absent from collective memory, of eastern European Jews in Vienna. For Lothar, his Austria after 1945 exists as an imagined community. Returning to a landscape and not a people, he views Austrian theater as his home. Franziska Tausig, who suffered the loss of her parents, siblings, and husband, finds her Austria alone in her son and his family.

The memoir writers use the past as a tool to demonstrate the ways in which they and their families are part of an Austrian story. Through their family histories, Elisabeth Freundlich, Hilde Spiel, and Hans Thalberg use their family's past to legitimize themselves as Jewish Austrians. Writing for a Socialist and supposedly open audience, Stella Klein-Löw and Minna Lachs show unique ways their Jewish identity complements their Austrian identity. As someone from a well-to-do family, Klein-Löw plays down this part of her family's past and uses it as a means to support her place within a Socialist "we"—as a Jewish exile, she has experienced many of the same hardships as working-class members of the party. After years of searching, Lachs finds a home in Austria through her engagement in the party. However, she offers little insight into her life after return. Her identity as a Socialist and Jew no longer mesh in post-Holocaust Austria. Lothar's entire life as mapped out in his memoirs can be seen as evidence of his undying love for Austria. Tausig, who was the least involved in public life and has the least invested in a public identification, does not display the same need as the others to legitimize her place within an Austrian "we."

Although the memoirists explore the past, their stories are ultimately forward-looking, in that they seek to reshape Austrian collective memory and identity. There is no single Austrian past, no one single Austrian story, no one single Austrian identity.

CONCLUSION: REINVENTING *HEIMAT*

If we return to Améry's definition of *Heimat* and the linguistic, spatial, and temporal links and apply them as a yardstick to determine whether the memoirists were able to reconnect to an Austrian "we" and repair the traumatized self, we would have to answer the question with yes and no. Throughout the memoirs, a tension between the memoirists' desire to reconnect to an Austrian "we" and the memories of their experiences as part of a persecuted Jewish "we" and an "imagined" Jewish community after 1945 can be observed. The pull of their multiple subject positions over time and the unique Austrian context invariably shaped their narratives.

The memoir writers uncover the divide separating them from non-Jewish Austrians and suggest the struggle in reaching across this divide, which has also manifested itself in language. The memoir writers challenge their marginalization in language and standard uses of language to describe the experiences of most non-Jewish Austrians concerning the National Socialist past. Concomitantly, the memoirists are faced with the divide between language and their own traumatic experiences that defy language. Language is inadequate to express their experiences, yet it is the material with which they have to work.

The memoirists salvage traumatic memories through body memories and emotional associations with place to convey a sense of loss, which has remained with them. Consequently, their experiences and their memories of these experiences permanently change their spatial identity and their relationship to their Austrian surroundings. Because being thrown out of an Austrian "we" transformed their spatial semiotic competency, they experience emotionally "saturated" places with a sense of temporal simultaneity. Such locations hold multiple memories of the past. They use their altered perceptions of familiar locations to plot memory maps that reconfigure and historicize *Heimat* for their readers. Austria is much more than the Austria of the present or the Austria of the glorious Habsburg past or an Austria of unpopulated natural grandeur.

The temporal link to a pre-*Anschluss* history appears the easiest to reestablish. Yet even these configurations of their past illustrate the tension between various subject positions. If they could not totally reconnect to a contemporary Austria, they could to its past. The tentativeness of the links or connections confirms the conclusions of sociologist Christoph Reinprecht (1992), who argued in Améry's terms that return was the real "existential misunderstanding." The experiential "gap" or "rift" between the memoirists and many of their contemporaries was unbridgeable.

By extending his study of Jewish Austrian reémigrés to include their children and grandchildren, Reinprecht uncovers different strategies among and between generations for reconciling their Jewish and Austrian identities. For those who were children at the time of exile or born in exile, Austria played a much different role in their sense of self. Although it may have been a major point of identification within the family, as Leo Spitzer illustrates (1998), firsthand knowledge of Austria did not exist until return. Moreover, many of them felt more connected to their new home than to Austria. Reinprecht notes that this generation was more reluctant to be interviewed. More than the other generations, they seem to be caught between worlds. Their perceptions of Vienna after 1945 are no doubt very different from those of their parents.

Although the generational comparison goes beyond the scope of this study, different relationships to Austria across generations is suggested in the memoirs. In the case of the memoirists studied here, Lothar and Tausig had children sixteen or older at the time of exile, Lachs had an infant, and Spiel bore two children in exile. Thalberg's only child was born after 1945. Lothar's daughter died in exile. Tausig's son, who was sixteen at the time of his departure from Austria, returned home before his mother and actually encouraged her to join him. For Otto Tausig, his emotional connection to Austria, the German language, and his work with political exiles no doubt made return not only possible but desirable. In many respects, his profile fits that of some of the memoirists. In contrast, the younger children born shortly before exile or in exile undoubtedly were very much acculturated to their non-Austrian home and therefore found return challenging in ways very different from their parents. For example, Lachs notes that on their return journey to Austria, her young son wanted to go home, meaning Arlington, Virginia (1992, 177). Spiel returned permanently to Austria after her children were grown. Her daughter, the older of her two children, chose to remain in England while her son settled in Vienna.

With the third generation (the second postwar generation), Reinprecht uncovers a relationship to Austria that he characterizes as critical, distanced, and ambivalent (129). His findings are echoed by filmmaker Ruth Beckermann in a series of essays entitled *Unzugehörig* (1989; Not belonging). As the title of her book suggests, this generation felt defined by their feeling of not belonging. Born in Vienna after the war of a Jewish Viennese mother who had spent exile in Palestine and a father from Czernowitz who had served in the Red Army, Beckermann positions her generation in a very different place from her parents:

> The Austrian diplomat Hans Thalberg writes in his memoirs that it is more likely that he shares the same perspective concerning the Nazi period with a Dutchman or a Yugoslav than with an Austrian. According to him, an intellectual and emotional divide separated him from the country and people to whom he felt a part of growing up. We were born in this divide. Into families for whom nothing was like it had once been. (10)[1]

She creates a particularly vivid image of her generation's dilemma by referring to the spatial metaphor in Thalberg's memoirs. Her generation can neither relate to the ways in which their parents identify with Austria nor can they construct a sense of authentic identity by identifying with postwar Austria. Growing up in post-Holocaust Austria in decimated families in a country that had constructed itself as the first victim of National Socialism, they were faced with a different set of challenges than their parents.

If the members of the oldest reémigré generation defined themselves as Austrians first and Jews second, members of the second postwar generation rarely do. In three separate studies—one by a sociologist (Reinprecht 1992), one by an anthropologist (Matti Bunzl 1996), and one by a Germanist (Konzett 1998)—the investigators suggest that representatives of generations born after the war construct themselves consciously as Jews living in Austria. The studies suggest that the Jewish genocide is a defining moment in their constructions of self that permanently altered the meaning of being Jewish in Austria. Their generation could not suffer the illusory promise of the success of assimilation. Thus, regardless of religious beliefs, this generation tends to define themselves as Jewish and claims a Jewish identity that often puts them at odds with mainstream Austria. Nonetheless, the "assimilation" of turn-of-the-century culture is often central in new configurations of Jewish identity. If many of the older generation viewed themselves and their families as part of an assimilated Austrian culture, their children and grandchildren reframe the phenomenon of Jewish participation in turn-of-the-century culture, claiming it as a Jewish phenomenon rather than evidence of successful Jewish integration.

With their life stories, Ernst Lothar, Stella Klein-Löw, Hans Thalberg, Minna Lachs, Franziska Tausig, Hilde Spiel, and Elisabeth Freundlich have shown that the " 'truth' of the past . . . is not to be found unambiguously deposited in some objective social record or archive, nor yet as infinitely malleable in the service of the present" (Middleton and Edwards 1990, 9). Their life stories are a bridge to a marginalized past for those willing to listen. With their life stories and their explorations of their relationship to language, space, and time within an Austrian context, the memoirists reinvent *Heimat*. They use their past as a tool to root themselves in an Austrian story and to define for themselves what it means to be Austrian and Jewish. They seek to change readers' perceptions of Austrian history and transform Austrian stories about the past. However, just as their stories have emerged from an implied dialogue, the integration of these stories into Austrian collective consciousness rests with Austrian interlocutors.

NOTES

INTRODUCTION

1. All state-recognized religions in Austria keep membership rolls for tax purposes.

2. Some who were not particularly religious registered with the Jewish Community Organization out of a sense of solidarity. Others registered in order to be eligible to receive relief packages. Consequently, their registration was interpreted as opportunism and they were often pejoratively labeled "package Jews" (*Paketjuden*) by others in the Jewish community (Embacher 1995, 49).

3. The figures in Bruce F. Pauley's two studies are contradictory. In his 1992 study, Pauley states, "[o]nly 4,500 Jewish émigrés ever returned to their former homeland; the remainder had no desire to return to the scene of so many painful memories" (301). In his later study, he maintains that "[a]t most only 12,000 to 15,000 Jewish émigrés ever permanently returned to their former homeland, although another 18,000 to 22,000 returned for long stays; the remainder had no desire to return to the scene of so many painful memories" (1996, 493). In light of numbers noted by the other scholars, 12,000 to 15,000 appears high, but since the lower figures are based on the registration rolls of the Jewish Community Organization, they have to be seen as low estimates.

4. See Beller 1989; Berkley 1988; Freidenreich 1991; McCagg 1989; Rozenblit 1983; and Wistrich 1989.

5. Rozenblit notes that "[m]ost Viennese Jews who wrote memoirs came from assimilated backgrounds" (1983, 6).

6. By contrast, I leave out the memoir of Willy Verkauf-Verlon (1983), who emigrated to Palestine in 1933, because his sense of self was not as bound to his identification with Austria.

7. Because of the extent to which Bruno Kreisky's memoirs (1986) were based on extensive interviews, I excluded them from this study. They nonetheless exhibit many of the same qualities as the memoirs discussed here. In excluding those who experienced the *Anschluss* and exile as children, I eliminated Deutsch 1993. Because I wanted to study the ways in which writing from a marginalized

position shaped the narratives, I did not include autobiographies and memoirs by Austrians who did not return permanently. Thus I do not discuss Clare 1981, Schwarz 1979, Foster 1989, Troller 1988, Lambert 1992, Leichter 1995, or Zaloscer 1988. By excluding memoirs that did not span from childhood in Austria to exile and return, I omit Rattner 1989, which focuses only on return. Because I am interested in the rhetorical use of the memoir form, I do not include Drach's autobiographical novel (1966), which focuses on exile. I do not include Wander 1996 because he experienced both exile and concentration camps. Because I only focus on Jewish Austrians who returned, I do not deal with Gessner 1985. Gessner, Ernst Lothar's wife, was an "Aryan" and thus was not in the same life-threatening situation as Jewish Austrians, nor had she been suddenly excluded from an Austrian "we."

8. New memoirs appearing by Austrians interned in concentration camps include those by Jewish Austrian Begov (1983), Socialist resistance fighter Bruha (1984), and conservative Catholic politician Maleta (1981). Most works on the topic appeared in the mid-eighties.

9. One of the first works of fiction on Austria's National Socialist past to appear in the eighties was Kerschbaumer 1980. Filmmaker Susanne Zanke produced a television film on the book in 1981. Oral histories appearing in the eighties include: Sichrovsky 1985, Berger et al. 1985 and idem 1987. The most recent volumes of oral history that have focused on Jewish life in Vienna and Austrian exiles include *Jüdische Schicksale* (1993) and Wimmer 1993.

10. Notable exceptions are Weinzierl 1969 and Aichinger 1948. Aichinger's novel was one of the few works of Austrian prose dealing with this period to gain critical acclaim in the early postwar period.

11. In the immediate postwar years, numerous personal narratives written by Austrians who had been interned in concentration camps or in prison were published in Austria. For a listing of these writers and a brief discussion, see Vansant 1994a. The majority of the writers sought to enlighten fellow Austrians about the true character of National Socialism. They also wanted to portray the fate of the particular group with which they identified most and pay tribute to the murdered. One of the few concentration camp testimonials by an Austrian to have gained recognition is Frankl 1946.

12. For further discussion on anti-Semitism in Austria, see Pauley 1992, Bunzl and Marin 1983, and Bunzl 1987.

13. The most disturbing incident in the sixties was the controversy surrounding the university professor Taras Borodajkewycz, who gave vent to overtly anti-Semitic and German nationalistic views. There were demonstrations both for and against him, during which an elderly Communist was beaten to death by a neo-Nazi student (Pauley 1992, 303). In 1966 Borodajkewycz was forced to retire.

14. Compare with the situation of Willy Brandt in Germany. Because he had been in exile as a Socialist, his alliance to Germany was cast in doubt by his opponent Strauss.

15. See Secher 1993; 1994. See van Amerongen 1977 specifically on

Kreisky's attacks on Simon Wiesenthal during the controversy surrounding Kreisky's cabinet appointments.

16. Austrian writers individually and collectively criticized their country's leader, producing among other things Haslinger 1987 and the essay collection *Die Leiche im Keller* (1988). Filmmaker Ruth Beckermann integrated the protest activities into her autobiographical film *Die papierene Brücke* (1987), which explores Jewish-Austrian identity in post-Holocaust Austria. During these years, lectures concerning these topics were regularly announced in the major Austrian newspapers. Exhibitions included *Wien: 1945 davor/danach* (1985), *Der November Pogrom 1938* (1988), and *Vertreibung der Vernunft* (1995). Excellent catalogues were printed to accompany each exhibition. Other publications include Safrian and Witek 1988 and Talos, Hanisch, and Neugebauer 1988. See Lorenz 1992b for the most extensive bibliography of German-language primary literature and films on this topic.

17. Greenspan 1998 notes a long delay in the United States between the end of the war and interest in Holocaust narratives. Immediately after the war there was a flurry of publications, then a hiatus until the late seventies. In the case of the United States, he attributes the resurgence of interest to changes within the American Jewish Community, the political climate in Israel, America's changed perceptions after Vietnam, and a growing interest in survival stories in general (40–47). In Austria, published autobiographical accounts of concentration camps and exile lagged behind those published in nonperpetrator countries. A comparison with bibliographies of major studies on Holocaust narratives (Des Pres 1976; Heinemann 1986; Young 1988) as well as the exile narratives (Lixl-Purcell 1988) illustrates this point. The researchers list numerous examples of memoirs written by Jews published outside Austria in the sixties and seventies well before similar personal narratives by Jewish Austrians were published for an Austrian audience.

18. Scholes and Kellogg 1966 define a narrative as being characterized by "[t]he presence of a story and a story-teller" (4). They refer strictly to literary works. I apply the definition to oral as well as written "texts" and label oral and written narratives in which the non-Jewish Austrian population and the Austrian state claim victimhood "mainstream victim narratives." Other groups, such as Romanies, homosexuals, and political and religious opponents of National Socialism, were also largely absent from public discourse concerning the years under Nazi rule. In no way do I wish to diminish their suffering when I do not mention them.

19. Compare Lixl-Purcell 1988, 4. See also Epstein 1979, in which she describes difficulties children of concentration camp survivors have in dealing with their parents' fate and the cloak of silence surrounding the past.

20. All translations are mine unless a published translation exists. "Die Auseinandersetzung mit der Vernichtung der Juden geschah damals in sehr abstrakter und verschämter Weise. Jeder wusste irgend etwas, jeder hatte etwas Komisches an seinen Verwandten bemerkt, doch keiner kannte eine zusammenhängende Familiengeschichte. Alles, was mit der Zeit der Verfolgung zu

tun hatte, war mit grosser Angst und Scham verbunden. Es war eine Wunde, die man nicht berühren wollte, die man verdeckte und versteckte."

21. In Whiteman 1993, one of the first major studies to focus on the emotional repercussions of escape, the psychologist author addresses a major reason for the long silence among this group. European Jews who escaped National Socialism often felt that "nothing" had happened to them in comparison to those who experienced the death camps and that their stories were not worth telling.

22. There has been very little work done on the memoirs. For the most extensive work on autobiographies of exile writers, see Critchfield 1984; 1994. The memoirs of Ernst Lothar, Hilde Spiel, and Elisabeth Freundlich, all professional writers, have received the most scholarly attention. See Daviau and Johns 1989 for an in-depth biographical article on Lothar. Articles on Spiel with particular focus on her experience of exile include Fliedl 1995; Howells 1994; Pabisch 1985; and Strickhausen 1995; 1996. For articles on Freundlich, see Alge 1992 and Hertling 1992; 1997. See Liessmann 1998 for a discussion of Améry's essay, Spiel's memoirs, and the autobiographical essays of Günther Anders, Freundlich's husband. See also Reitani 1992 for an overview of Jews returning to Austria in the context of literature in general.

CHAPTER 1

1. In the chapter title I retain the German word *Heimat* to capture the sense of its untranslatability. Similarly, the *Heimat* the memoirists seek to reclaim cannot be totally rendered through language.

2. "Wer das Exil kennt, hat manche Lebensantworten erlernt, und noch mehr Lebensfragen. Zu den Antworten gehört die zunächst triviale Erkenntnis, dass es keine Rückkehr gibt, weil niemals der Wiedereintritt in einen Raum auch ein Wiedergewinn der verlorenen Zeit ist" (1966, 72).

3. For an outline of Améry's life and an overview of name variations of Hanns Maier and the more radical change to Jean Améry, see Pfäfflin 1988.

4. See Remmler 1994b, for the effect torture had on Améry's self-image and his name change.

5. For an in-depth discussion of *Heimat,* see Applegate 1990. In the context of Austrian *Heimat* films, see Gertraud Steiner 1987.

6. See Sebald 1988 for an insightful biographical essay on the essayist and his understanding of *Heimat.*

7. "Heimat ist Sicherheit, sage ich. In der Heimat beherrschen wir souverän die Dialektik von Kennen-Erkennen, von Trauen-Vertrauen: Da wir sie kennen, erkennen wir sie und getrauen uns zu sprechen und zu handeln, weil wir in unsere Kenntnis-Erkenntnis begründetes Vertrauen haben dürfen. Das ganze Feld der verwandten Wörter treu, trauen, Zutrauen, anvertrauen, vertraulich, zutraulich gehört in den weiteren psychologischen Bereich des Sich-sicher-Fühlens" (1966, 80).

8. "Ich war ein Mensch, der nicht mehr 'wir' sagen konnte und darum nur noch gewohnheitsmäßig, aber nicht im Gefühl vollen Selbstbesitzes 'ich' sagte" (75).

9. "Um dieser oder jener zu sein, brauchen wir das Einverständnis der Gesellschaft. Wenn aber die Gesellschaft widerruft, dass wir es jemals waren, sind wir es auch nie gewesen" (100).

10. "Wir waren aus der deutschen Realität ausgesperrt und darum auch aus der deutschen Sprache" (88).

11. "Täglich las ich trotz äußersten Widerwillens die 'Brüsseler Zeitung', das Organ der deutschen Besatzungsmacht im Westen. Es hat meine Sprache nicht verdorben, hat ihr aber auch nicht fortgeholfen, denn ich war ausgeschlossen aus dem Schicksal der deutschen Gemeinschaft und damit auch aus der Sprache. . . . Der Sinngehalt jedes deutschen Wortes verwandelte sich für uns, und schließlich wurde, wir mochten uns dagegen wehren oder nicht, die Muttersprache ebenso feinselig wie die, welche sie um uns redeten" (88–89).

12. See the discussion on language and reality in Berger and Luckmann 1966, 64–68. Compare Améry with George Steiner 1998. Several of the themes discussed here—such as language and reality, language and the unspeakable, and Jewish identity—are similarly examined in Steiner's work.

13. "So wie man die Muttersprache erlernt, ohne ihre Grammatik zu kennen, so erfährt man die heimische Umwelt. Muttersprache und Heimatwelt wachsen mit uns, wachsen in uns hinein und werden so zur Vertrautheit, die uns Sicherheit verbürgt" (81).

14. "Gesichter, Gesten, Kleider, Häuser, Worte (auch wenn ich sie halbwegs verstand) waren Sinneswirklichkeit, aber keine deutbaren Zeichen. . . . Ich wankte durch eine Welt, deren Zeichen mir so uneinsichtig blieben wie die etruskische Schrift" (79–80).

15. George Steiner also writes of the cultural dimension of language and suggests that one might become proficient in a language and still not understand all its cultural nuances (1998, 125).

16. "Ich war kein Ich mehr und lebte nicht in einem Wir. Ich hatte keinen Pass und keine Vergangenheit und kein Geld und keine Geschichte" (75).

17. "Wir aber hatten nicht das Land verloren, sondern mussten erkennen, dass es niemals unser Besitz gewesen war. Für uns war, was mit diesem Land und seinen Menschen zusammenhing, ein Lebensmissverständnis" (84).

18. See Spitzer 1998; 1999 for in-depth discussions of homesickness as a disease. See also Lowenthal's discussion of nostalgia (1985). Both draw on the 1688 medical treatise of Johannes Hofer on *Heimweh*, or nostalgia.

19. "[U]nser Heimweh war Selbstentfremdung. Die Vergangenheit war urplötzlich verschüttet, und man wusste nicht mehr, wer man war" (74).

20. "Das echte Heimweh war nicht Selbstmitleid, sondern Selbstzerstörung. Es bestand in der stückweisen Demontierung unserer Vergangenheit, was nicht abgehen konnte ohne Selbstverachtung und Hass gegen das verlorene Ich" (86).

21. Although their analysis is based on Freudian concepts that have little relevance to my discussion, the Grinbergs (1989) are among the first researchers to look at migration and exile in terms of potentially cumulative traumas.

22. "Erinnern. Das Stichwort ist gefallen, und unsere Reflexionen schwingen von selbst zurück zu ihrem Hauptgegenstand: dem Heimatverlust dessen, den das Dritte Reich vertrieb. Er ist gealtert, und er hat in einer Zeitspanne, die nun schon nach Jahrzehnten zählt, lernen müssen, dass ihm nicht eine Wunde geschlagen wurde, die mit dem Ticken der Zeit vernarbt, sondern dass er an einer schleichenden Krankheit laboriert, die mit den Jahren schlimmer wird" (95).

23. Joseph Buttinger and Otto Leichter were both Socialists who tried unsuccessfully to reestablish themselves in Austria. Rather than being accepted into the Socialist "we," they were perceived as rivals. Bruno Kreisky, who along with other reémigrés had been recruited into the foreign service was, at least in the early postwar years, eliminated as a political rival (Embacher 1995, 123).

24. "Das Heimweh hat mehrere Dimensionen, vor allem eine sentimentale (Kindheits- und Jugenderinnerungen) und eine politisch-kulturelle."

25. "Warum wollten wir, obwohl wir von Not und Kälte, Hunger und Unfreiheit in Österreich wussten, England verlassen?

Wir wollten als österreichische *Sozialisten* in Österreich, dem besetzten Österreich, leben und arbeiten: persönlich, beruflich, politisch. Wir wollten das durch die Emigration unterbrochene Leben den neuen Gegebenheiten anpassen, alte Freundschaften wieder aufleben lassen, bestehende Bindungen vertiefen. Das Abenteuer 'Neues Österreich—alte Heimat' reizte und lockte uns. Auch hätten wir uns geschämt, gerade jetzt Österreich, Wien, den Sozialismus im Stich zu lassen und auf bessere Zeiten zu warten."

26. Both Elisabeth Freundlich (1992, 135) and Hilde Spiel (1989b, 227) recall meetings with Matejka.

27. "Durch den Opferstatus konnte man offiziell jegliche Schuld oder Mitverantwortung, die über individuelle Verbrechen hinausgeht, abschieben, die neuen Identitätsbestrebungen bewirkten und bewirken einen neuen Nationalismus. Ein solcher verstärkter Nationalismus schaffte auch neue Grenzen, die die Aufteilung der (kognitiven) Welt in eine entsprechende 'Ingroup' and 'Outgroup', in 'wir' und die 'anderen' ermöglichten."

28. See Bischof 1997 for a discussion of the literature on Austrian identity and a brief examination of the major constituents of postwar Austrian identity. See also Bruckmüller 1998 for an excellent overview of the situation after 1945. Bruckmüller provides a more detailed discussion of the reactions of the individual parties to the question of Austrian identity.

29. See Koebner and Rotermund 1990. In a discussion on German writers who returned to the two Germanies and Austria after 1945, it is clear that they faced similar problems. See particularly Klaus Müller-Salget's essay on Alfred Döblin and Erwin Rotermund's essay on Leonard Frank. See also *Exilforschung* (1991), dedicated to exile and reemigration.

30. For an excellent historical overview of the various countries' responses

to the Holocaust, see Wyman 1996. For a discussion of German responses and the Jewish returnees' position, see Borneman's introduction in Borneman and Peck 1995.

31. "Der Westbahnhof in Wien: Lärm und Bewegung, Baracken, Unordnung, Chaos. Die Strassen: alle bekannt—alle fremd."

32. "Neue, unbekannte Menschen—bei denen man im übrigen nie sicher sein konnte, wie sie an die Stelle der früheren Menschen getreten waren—begegneten mir tielnahmslos an den altvertrauten Plätzen."

33. "Zunächst ließen wir uns durch die Stadt treiben, sie war mir völlig fremd geworden" (1992, 133).

34. "Nun muss ich alles von neuem lernen. Ich lerne wieder den kalten, muffigen Steingeruch der Wiener Häuser, die porösen abgetretenen Treppen aus Granit, die dürftigen Stiegenhäuser mit den Kritzeleien auf dem abblättern-den Anstrich. Ich lerne den starren Blick der Hausmeister, die Neugier der alten Frauen im Kopftuch, und jenes misstrauische, unfreundliche Lächeln, das vor den Nazis dagewesen ist und immer da sein wird."

35. "Es gibt auch Neues: die Tirolerhüte, die jeder, auch der vornehmste Einwohner dieser einst so eleganten Stadt, jetzt trägt; die Pelze der kleinen Geschäftsfrauen, die früher nur Stoffmäntel besaßen; die Stiefel überall, wie man sie in England nicht kennt, von ledernen Schaftstiefeln bis zu hässlichen hohen Filzmodellen. Zu meiner Zeit zog man im Regen Galoschen an, aber nun regiert der Stiefel und verwandelt jede Frau in eine Lagerkommandantin oder in ein Straßenmädchen der Berliner Zwanzigerjahre."

36. In the earlier unpublished English version in "The Streets of Vineta" (22) in the Österreichisches Literaturarchiv, she draws parallels with the at-mosphere under the Austro-Fascists. The later version more clearly implicates Austrians in a National Socialist past.

37. "Der Antisemitismus—und damals war die Wiederkehr der Nazi-Schmierereien noch nirgends in Erscheinung getreten—herrsche nach wie vor. Dass sechs Millionen Juden ermordet worden waren, seien die sieben Millionen Österreicher, vermutlich sogar die ganze Welt, im Begriffe zu vergessen; sie nähmen es übel, daran erinnert zu werden, es gelte als taktlos. Zwar ziehe der Antisemitismus momentan die Krallen ein und drapiere sich mit Alibis, da mitunter kleinere Posten in nichtarische Hände kämen; auf die entscheiden-den würden Juden grundsätzlich nicht oder nur mit äußerstem Widerstreben berufen. Nach Rückkehrern, obschon man es offiziell nicht zugab, bestehe kein Verlangen, nach anerkannten am wenigsten; man wolle unter sich bleiben und sein angegriffenes Gewissen schonen." *Das Wunder des Überlebens* was first published in October, 1960 and then in December, 1961. I cite from the 1961 edition.

38. "Sie kamen als isolierte Individuen zurück, wurden aber von den an-deren als versprengte Teile eines imaginären Kollektivs wahrgenommen. Ihr Jude-Sein, ihre jüdische Identität war auf dieser Ebene somit nicht mehr frei bestimmbar, sondern festgelegt."

39. "Schäbig waren auch die Menschen gekleidet, scheel und misstrauisch

ihr Blick, wenn man mit ihnen ins Gespräch zu kommen suchte. Wir waren ja 'die reichen Amerikaner' und obendrein noch Juden. Alle Amerikaner waren Juden, dieser Herr Rosenfeld, wie die Nazis Roosevelt nannten, hatte ihnen Armut und zerbombte Städte eingebrockt. Die Chronologie war ihnen durcheinandergeraten" (1992, 133).

40. "Diesem von *Améry* beschriebenen 'Lebensmissverständnis' begegnen wir in den Berichten der von uns befragten Emigrantinnen und Emigranten allerdings erst im Zusammenhang mit der rückblickenden Bewertung ihres Beschlusses, zurückzukehren. . . . Offensichtlich hatten erst die Erfahrungen nach der Rückkehr jenen disillusionierenden Charakter und führten zur Artikulation jener tiefen Kränkung, von der *Améry* spricht."

41. "Mit wahrer Hast habe ich in einem ersten Band von Erinnerungen den Ablauf unseres Lebens seit Kriegsbeginn berichtet, jedoch nicht verraten, wie sehr seine Düsternis mich und meinen Mann im Inneren betroffen hat. Die Wahrheit ist, dass wir uns Seelenregungen versagen mussten. Angesichts der Ungeheuerlichkeit, die schon das alltägliche Morden aus der Luft und die latente Gefahr einer Invasion der Deutschen für uns darstellten, lange bevor der Abgrund menschlicher Teufelei, die 'Endlösung', an den Tag getreten war, *panzerten* wir uns bis zur *Stumpfheit* fast bis zur *Betäubung* unserer Sinne, wenn nicht bis zur *Lethargie*."

42. An overwhelming number of psychologists share a similar view despite the differences in their points of departure (Littlewood 1992, 53–54).

43. "Ich kehre an meinen Ursprung zurück, entfremdet durch langes Fortsein, gestählt durch manchen Verlust und bereit für eine harte, vermutlich schmerzliche Erfahrung."

44. "Im dunkelnden Licht stehe ich auf dem Pfarrplatz. Hier liegt meine Seele begraben. Wann immer ich in den zehn Jahren meiner Abwesenheit Heimweh hatte, war es nach diesem Ort. Wann immer ich gewisse Stellen von Beethoven oder Schubert hörte, erschien er vor meinem Blick. Ein kleiner Dorfplatz: links steht ein Bauernhaus, in dem die Eroica geschrieben wurde; ein anderes zur Rechten; und in der Mitte die kleine Kirche zu St. Jakob. . . . Im hölzernen Kirchtor hängen die Gemeindenachrichten wie zu meiner Zeit, aber ich bin von ihnen nicht betroffen. Wo meine Wurzeln tief in die Erde reichen wie nirgends sonst, bin ich eine völlig Fremde, so entrückt in Zeit und Raum wie ein geisterhafter Revenant."

45. "Alles angestaute Gefühl, jahrelang unterdrückt, als man seinen Mut für den Preis erkalteter Empfindung erkaufen musste—aller Kummer um die Erniedrigung meiner Heimat, alle Sorge um meine Kinder im Krieg, aller Schmerz um den Tod meines Vaters drängt jetzt hervor."

46. "Auch nach dem Ende des langen Winters, als die Türen und Fenster aufsprangen und wir hinausdrängten in die befriedete Wirklichkeit, lieferten wir uns den Emotionen noch nicht rückhaltlos aus. Einmal brach ich zusammen bei meiner ersten Rückkehr nach Wien, am Heiligenstädter Pfarrplatz, ich hatte es vorausgeahnt. Doch die ambivalente Lage, in der ich mich unter den Besatzern meiner einstigen Heimat befand, das Schwanken zwischen Zuversicht

und Zweifel, ob wir nun wahrhaft im englischen Raum Wurzeln geschlagen hatten und von den neuen Landsleuten vorbehaltlos aufgenommen wurden, war zu aufreibend, um auch noch heftig gefühlt zu werden. So drang denn alles wie durch einen Schleier zu uns."

47. Farrell suggests that trauma as a trope provided Germans with a mode of coping (1998, 23).

48. "Tatsächlich hat sich die Kluft zwischen den Hiergebliebenen—und damit sind auch solche gemeint, die ein reines Gewissen haben dürfen—und denen, die man davongejagt hat, nie wieder ganz geschlossen" (1992, 133).

49. "Meine Geburtsstadt, ja. Meine Heimatstadt? Zu tief war der Graben, der mich von den Menschen trennte."

50. "Am deutlichsten empfand ich das, wenn ich mit früheren oder neuen Bekannten über die jüngste Vergangenheit sprach. Wenn sie von der 'Katastrophe' sprachen, so meinten sie 1945. Für mich war die Katastrophe 1938 eingetreten, und 1945 war das Jahr der glückhaften Erfüllung. Menschen, deren politische und charakterliche Integrität über jedem Zweifel erhaben waren, hatten irgendwie nolens volens am Hitlerspuk teilgehabt, hatten das Schicksal Nazi-Deutschlands in guten wie in schlechten Zeiten geteilt. Manche waren als deutsche Besatzungsoffiziere in Paris, Athen oder Brüssel gewesen; überzeugt von ihrer eigenen Unschuld, erzählten sie ganz naiv von diesen 'guten' Zeiten, nicht ahnend, welchen verheerenden Eindruck solche Erzählungen bei allen jenen hervorrufen mussten, die den Krieg auf der anderen Seite erlebt hatten. Gewiss, die Angelegenheit war sehr kompliziert, es ist nicht leicht, die amerikanischen Bomben, die einem das Haus über dem Kopf zusammengeschlagen, als Schritt zur bevorstehenden Befreiung zu feiern. Aber die völlige Ahnungslosigkeit, mit der Österreicher—auch heute noch—sich mit dem Schicksal der deutschen Wehrmacht im Kriege identifizieren, lässt mir das Blut im Leib erstarren."

51. Thalberg's perceptions were not aberrations. He could have easily enumerated additional words that had assumed different meanings for the non-Jewish Austrians and the reémigrés. When the majority of Austrians spoke of refugees, they meant ethnic Germans forced to flee eastern Europe at the end of the war. "Returnees" were understood to be soldiers returning home, and both civilian and military populations laid claim to the word "victim." Moreover, when most Austrians said "we," they did not consider Jewish Austrians a part of this "we." Indeed, the experiences of Jewish Austrians were excluded from both public and private discourse. See Malina 1989, 161.

52. "Man hat in Österreich ganz offenbar niemals ernstlich erfasst, was in diesen Kriegsjahren wirklich vorgegangen ist, wie abgrundtief der Hass und die Verachtung ist, die die Welt für Hitler-Deutschland und alles, was damit zusammenhing, empfindet. Bis zum heutigen Tag kann ich, wenn von dieser Zeit gesprochen wird, mit einem Holländer, Norweger, mit einem Jugoslawen eher gemeinsamen Boden finden als mit meinen Landsleuten. Ein gedanklicher und gefühlsmäßiger Graben trennt mich in dieser Beziehung von meinem Land und seinen Leuten."

53. "Wie sehr ich später im Leben wieder in die österreichische Umgebung hineinwachsen werde—diese Ausgangslage nach dem verlorenen, gewonnenen Krieg wird eine Kluft zwischen mir und den anderen Bürgern bilden, die sich nie wieder schließt." See also 1989b, 194, 213 for similar sentiments.

54. "Wir waren nicht schuld daran, die meisten, so will man hoffen, auf der feindlichen Seite waren's nicht, doch fast alle drüben nahmen uns später übel, dass wir zu den Opfern gehört hatten, nicht zur Welt der Täter, und uns unter keinen Umständen die geringste Verantwortung für das jahrelange Grauen anzulasten war. Wie konnte uns dies jemals vergeben werden? Wie konnte man hoffen, dass eines Tages in der fernen Zukunft, wenn man wieder den Boden des Vaterlandes betrat oder gar sich von neuem in ihm niederließ, diese Kluft zwischen den Daheimgebliebenen und den Fortgegangenen, zumeist Fortgetriebenen, nicht jederzeit aufreißen mochte, zum Erstauen oder Entsetzen derer, die etwa gemeint hatten, die Entfremdung sei für immer vorbei."

55. My overview of memory and recall is based on Schacter 1996.

56. Studies include Ziegler and Kannonier-Finster 1993 (on Austrian memory); Safrian and Witek 1988 (on the events immediately following the *Anschluss* in Vienna); Wodak et al. 1990 (on anti-Semitic discourse in Austria particularly in the light of the Waldheim controversy); Mitten 1992 (on the Waldheim controversy); and Embacher, Lichtblau, and Sandner 1999 (on the *Wehrmacht* exhibition in Salzburg).

57. See Gorer 1965, esp. the introduction and conclusion.

58. Psychologist Schacter questions the assertion that traumatic memory is immutable, but nonetheless shares their general conclusions (1996, 205).

59. The necessity of telling in dealing with traumatic events is a common theme throughout the work on trauma. See esp. Dori Laub in Felman and Laub 1992 and Brison 1999.

CHAPTER 2

1. "Jede Sprache ist Teil einer Gesamtwirklichkeit, auf die man wohlbegründetes Besitzrecht haben muss, wenn man guten Gewissens und sicheren Schrittes in den Sprachraum eintreten soll" (1966, 90).

2. Billson borrows the term "histor" from Scholes and Kellogg (1966, 242–43). I prefer the term historian, finding it more illustrative than histor.

3. Scholes and Kellogg define literary narrative as characterized by "the presence of a story and a story-teller" (1966, 4). As discussed in the introduction, I find their terminology useful in looking at the ways in which Austrians construct narratives of national victimhood.

4. As a comparison, see Berger 1989.

5. Lepsius's study is quoted in numerous Austrian works: among others, Uhl 1997, 73; Ziegler and Kannonier-Finster 1993, 32–37.

6. In the efforts to highlight Austrian resistance, official offices largely overlooked the contributions of the Communists in favor of resistance among more conservative forces. Even if the earliest public ceremonies after the war commemorated the deeds of those in the resistance, official interest in this part

of the Austrian population soon waned. See Uhl 1997 for an in-depth discussion of the shifts in public perceptions of the years 1938–1945.

7. "Nur Unkenntnis der wahren Lage oder böser Wille kann das äußere Stimmungsbild dieser aufgewühlten Tage dem österreichischen Volke als Schuld anlasten."

8. "Es beruht auf einer falschen Perspektive, wenn sich heute Kritiker, die in diesen für Österreich so schweren Tagen und Jahren im sicheren Auslande saßen, das selbst Schritt um Schritt vor Hitler zurückwich, zu moralischen Richtern über dieses preisgegebene und gepeinigte österreichische Volk machen und von jedem 'Mann von der Straße' in Österreich nachträglich einen Heroismus verlangen, den die Welt damals selbst nicht aufgebracht hat."

9. See Eppel 1988 for a good overview of the flight, exile, and Austrian public opinion of those in exile.

10. "Es wäre ungerecht, wollte man . . . Okkuption etwa unter der Perspektive des persönlichen Verhaltens Einzelner oder der Augenblicks-Suggestion weiterer Kreise beurteilen."

11. For a discussion of the attacks on the World Jewish Congress during the Waldheim controversy, see Wodak et al. 1990, esp. 115–20.

12. In his memoirs *Im Glaspalast der Weltpolitik* (1985), Kurt Waldheim offers the perfect example of someone who conflates Austrian state and personal victimhood and combines public and private discourse to convince his audience of Austria's victim status.

13. " 'Gelt'n S', Herr Hofrat, dös müass'n aa Sie zugeb'n—dös Bombenschmeiß'n war do' nix wie'r a Barbarei!' Ich hätte sagen sollen: 'Es war die Konsequenz der Barbarei!', doch ich sagte dem Herrn Steindl gute Nacht, und damit ging der erste Tag unserer Rückkehr zu Ende."

14. "Dass sie uns, damals im März 1938, so schnöd behandelten, das haben sie völlig vergessen. Fast keiner von ihnen hat in diesen drei Monaten gefragt: 'Wie ist es Ihnen denn ergangen?' Sie sagen vielmehr und meinen es noch deutlicher, als sie es sagen, dass wir sehr wohl daran getan haben, uns bei Zeiten aus dem Staube zu machen. Es war sehr schlau von uns, damals."

15. "Die Leute selbst fühlten sich schuldlos, verraten, zu Unrecht vom Schicksal verfolgt. Dass sie—mindestens durch Schweigen, wenn nicht Mittun—ein Quentchen, ein Quentchen nur der Verantwortung, also der Schuld, gehabt hatten, hätten sie mit Empörung von sich gewiesen. Man raunzte, tat sich leid, beneidete die anderen um jedes Stück Brot, das größer war als jenes, das man selbst ergattert hatte, man wusste hinterher alles besser, behauptete aber, früher ahnungslos gewesen zu sein."

16. "Wir hatten keinen Hasskomplex gegen *die* Österreicher, *die* Wiener, *die* Arier. Wir ließen uns nicht von anderen anstecken. Was geschehen war, würde man nie vergessen können und dürfen. Aber Hass ist eine schlechte Bahn in eine neue Zeit."

17. See Bailer 1997 on the conflation of the civilian population and soldiers as the National Socialists' victims. Indeed, the use of "victim" has become so entrenched in Austrian discourse that even the Socialist Rosa Jochmann,

who had been interned in the concentration camp Ravensbrück, used the term "victim" to apply to the civilian population and soldiers as well as to those who had been murdered in concentration camps (106). There is no denying that the Austrian population suffered, but suffering cannot be equated with victimhood.

18. See Pelinka 1989.

19. "Ich trete aus dem Gegenlicht und er erkennt mich. Staunen und Schrecken treten in sein Gesicht, als hätte er mich erst im Jenseits wieder erwartet. Dann beginnt zu meinem Kummer eine Szene, wie sie mir in all ihren Einzelheiten von einem österreichischen Freund vorhergesagt wurde, der im Exil gestorben ist. Manchmal, im Internierungslager oder nach seiner Entlassung von der Isle of Man im Londoner Bombenhagel, hat er sich seinen Empfang im Herrenhof ausgemalt.

'Der Herr Doktor haben den Krieg im Ausland verbracht?' würde der Kellner ihn auf jene höflich indirekte Weise fragen, die seit Maria Theresia im Schwange ist. 'Das war aber gescheit vom Herrn Doktor. Da haben 'S sich viel Unannehmlichkeit erspart. Wenn der Herr Doktor wüssten, was uns alles passiert ist. Das Elend, das wir durchgemacht haben. Wie gut der Herr Doktor aussehen—wirklich, eine Freud!'

Enteignung, Demütigung, Verhaftung und Todesgefahr, illegale Flucht über versperrte Grenzen, Jahre des Exils, ein feindlicher Ausländer in einem vom Kriege zerrütteten Land—all das würde zunichte werden, würde sich in Luft auflösen, mit einem Fingerschnalzen weggeweht. So beginnt auch Herr Hnatek, von Mitleid mit sich selbst ergriffen, sein Schicksal und das Schicksal Wiens zu bejammern, dessen Staub ich so erfolgreich von meinen Schuhen geschüttelt habe.

'Die Frau Doktor haben gut daran getan, dass Sie fort sind. Allein die Luftangriffe—dreimal haben sie die ganze Stadt in Brand gesteckt.'"

20. Characteristic of much autobiographical literature but largely absent from the Austrian memoirs is a discussion of the fallibility of memory. Critchfield comments: "Exile autobiographies are in part characterized by reflections on the questionable nature of the highly subjective genre which is based on a person's ability to remember which is so incomplete and unreliable" (1984, 41–42). ("Exilautobiographien sind teilweise durch Reflexionen über die Fragwürdigkeit der höchst subjektiven Gattung gekennzeichnet, die auf dem so unzulänglichen und unzuverlässigen Erinnerungsvermögen eines Menschen beruht.")

21. "Noch heute stehen die Ereignisse in unverminderter Schärfe vor mir. Noch heute, nach über einem halben Jahrhundert" (1992, 76).

22. Compare with Greenspan's discussion on the ways in which Holocaust survivors retell their experiences: "Certain forms of recounting tend to evolve that are, simultaneously, more or less tellable by survivors and more or less hearable by others" (1998, 31).

23. "Dabei kam auch vieles an die Oberfläche, das ich gern vergessen hätte, das bis dahin im Unterbewusstsein hinter Schloss und Riegel gehalten worden war."

24. "Nichts bringt uns Menschen, Geschehnisse, die ganze Atmosphäre

näher als Erlebnisse, Charktere, Episoden, ohne jede Zeitordnung skizziert, so wie sie die Erinnerung in die Feder diktiert."

25. "Beschwören könnte ich nicht, ob das Erlebnisse oder wieder- und nacherlebte Erzählungen anderer waren. Dass Zeitungsberichte bei dieser Erinnerung eine große Rolle gespielt haben, ist selbstverständlich. Doch—nein! Die Erinnerung an den Versuch des Bürgermeisters, das Schlimmste zu verhüten, ist echt."

26. "Beim Schreiben habe ich die Augen für einen Augenblick geschlossen."

27. "Wer sich über die Genauigkeit meiner Erinnerungen wundert, möge bedenken, dass ich, wie schon gesagt, ein 'fotografisches' Gedächtnis habe. Meine 'Erinnerungs-Fotos' geben das Geschehen, je nach seiner Art Schwarzweiß oder in Farbe, wieder."

28. "Die Erinnerungen überfallen mich—ohne dass ich sie kalenderhaft und kontinuierlich aufgerufen hätte. Sie steigen herauf aus den Tiefen, in die ich sie gedrängt und verdrängt habe, als ob jede von ihnen verlangte, nicht vergessen zu werden. Sie fordern von mir, dass ich ihnen Wort und Gestalt gebe. In meinem Gedächtnis stoßen sich Gefühle, Gedanken, Träume und Wirklichkeiten, reihen sich zu Ketten aneinander, jagen und verfolgen mich. Ich müsste ganze Bände schreiben, um jeder dieser Aufgestiegenen, die zum Tag drängen, gerecht zu werden. Als ob ich ein Gefäß aus der Tiefe gehoben hätte, dessen Deckel sich nicht mehr schließen lässt. Sie belagern mich bis zur Erschöpfung, sie bedrängen mich, bis ich sie nicht mehr ertragen kann. Nur einer symbolischen Auslese kann ich Erscheinung geben. Doch auch diese spült mich an Ufer, an denen ich nicht landen wollte, weil mich dort nur Gestrüpp und Geröll erwarten."

29. "Ich habe versucht, diese versunkene Welt mit allen ihren Tugenden und Fehlern so zu schildern, wie ich sie erlebt habe. Dabei habe ich mich bemüht, mich nicht dem Vorwurf narzisstischer Selbstdarstellung oder der Selbstbemitleidung auszusetzen."

30. "Wenn dennoch Schmerz und Bitterkeit in den Text dieses ersten Teils eingeflossen sind, dann möge der geneigte Leser dies vergeben: ich kann ihm versichern, dass die erlebte Wirklichkeit unendlich viel schlimmer war, als sich dies mit Worten schildern lässt."

31. In their work with Holocaust survivors, Langer (1991) and Greenspan (1992; 1998) pinpoint a similar if not more extreme tension in the narratives. Langer writes of "parallel existence" and Greenspan of a "*simultaneity* of continuity and discontinuity." Greenspan notes a connection to Langer (1998, 175, n. 20). This also parallels George Steiner's discussion of irreconcilable "simultaneous experience" (1998, 156).

32. "Der letzte an mich gerichtete Brief, datiert vom 15.3.1941, erörtert zuerst die sich ständig verändernden Reiseschwierigkeiten, spiegelt aber im weiteren Verlauf so sehr den Widerstreit der Empfindungen wider, ist so sehr ein gültiges Dokument der Zeit, macht die stolze und gelassene Haltung Otto Hellers sichtbar, dass ich ihn zitieren will" (1992, 96).

33. "Indes sind all die Briefe, insgesamt zehn, . . . von einigem dokumentarischen Wert."

34. "Ich hatte einen Brief mitgebracht, den ich am 23. September 1939 an meine Eltern in Israel geschrieben hatte. Er gibt die Stimmung wieder, die nicht nur uns, politische Emigranten, sondern auch die Schweizer Bevölkerung nach dem Beginn des Blitzkrieges gegen Polen bewegte."

35. "Als der Zweite Weltkrieg ausbrach, müssen meine ehemaligen Mitschüler alle etwas über dreißig Jahre alt gewesen sein. Hat man auch den sanften Toni in eine Uniform gesteckt, hat auch er für das 'Tausendjährige Reich' kämpfen müssen, ist er davongekommen? Und die anderen, die mosaischer Konfession gewesen sind, konnten einige von ihnen der Vernichtung entgehen? Ich weiß es nicht. Ihre Spuren sind verweht" (1992, 43).

36. "Nach meiner Rückkehr nach Wien im Jahre 1947 habe ich vergeblich versucht, im Wiener Stadtschulrat und im Unterrichtsministerium zu erfahren, was aus der Maturaschule 'Universum' geworden war und ob man mir nicht den Namen des kommissarischen Leiters im Jahre 1938 eruieren könnte. Es gab nirgends Aufzeichnungen, viele Archive waren Opfer der Flammen geworden. Ich fürchte fast, dass der einzige Beweis, dass dieses 'Universum' im 9. Bezirk in der Garnisongasse 7 überhaupt existiert hat, das Verwendungszeugnis ist, welches mir Prof. Nathansky im März 1938 mit Schulstempel und Datum ausgestellt hat. Er selbst ist im KZ umgekommen."

37. "Es wäre wert, ihr ein Denkmal zu setzen. Ein Topf heißer Tee, wenn du frierst, ein Bett, in dem du ausschlafen kannst, dein Gewand, das neben dem Ofen trocknet, das kann dir den Mut zum Überleben geben.

Sie war viel älter als wir und lebt bestimmt nicht mehr, und ich möchte hier für sie einen Kranz niederlegen."

38. "Als ich im Oktober 1942 von Frankreich illegal über die Schweizer Grenze kam, lautete die Parole der Schweizer Behörden gegenüber Flüchtlingen: Das Boot ist voll. Es ist mir damals gelungen, der Auslieferung zu entgehen und so mein Leben zu retten. Das Andenken der Vielen, die den barbarischen Bestimmungen nicht entgehen konnten, gebietet es aber, dass über diese Dinge nicht der Mantel des Schweigens gebreitet wird. Das Drama jener Menschen, die gehetzt und verfolgt, nach größten Strapazen an der Schweizer Grenze ihren Häschern übergeben wurden, muss noch geschrieben werden. Es gehört in jenes Bild der Menschenverrohung, die Holocaust erst möglich gemacht hat."

39. "Man hat niemals mehr von ihm gehört."

40. "Sein Name kommt zwar in österreichischen Literaturgeschichten gelegentlich vor, als Vertreter des Expressionismus, doch der zweite Abschnitt seines Lebens, die nicht unbedeutenden Werke, die er in Frankreich geschaffen hat, seine sonstige Tätigkeit dort und sein tragisches Ende sind in Österreich weitgehend unbekannt geblieben" (1992, 83–84).

41. "Es ist mir ein Bedürfnis, seiner hier zu gedenken, denn es sind nicht mehr viele, die von der Begegnung mit ihm bestimmende Eindrücke empfingen. Und auch seiner Schriften und seines Wirkens für den österreichischen Geist erinnern sich zu wenige. Er teilt dieses Geschick mit anderen besten Österreichern des Geistes, die der tobende Ungeist in die Konzentrationslager verbannte."

42. "Meine Helfer waren Steffi und Hans Kunke. Ich freundete mich mit

Steffi an. Sie war Lehrerin und ein Prachtkerl: unbeschwert, heiter, aufgeschlossen. Sie hatte eine schöne Stimme. Ihre großen, glänzenden Augen sprachen eine so deutliche Sprache der Zuneigung und Begeisterung. (Beide wurden später grausam gefoltert und ermordet, er in Buchenwald, sie in Auschwitz, wohin man sie aus Ravensbrück brachte)."

43. Steffi Kunke appears in Austrian literature in Marie-Thérèse Kerschbaumer's book *Der weibliche Name des Widerstands.*

44. Indeed, much of the artifice of a text is meant to overcome the silence brought about by the traumatic experiences. Langer (1991) writes of the "imaginative space" separating the Holocaust witness from the listener or reader of the testimony.

45. "Symbolhaft und typisch für den Untergang des großbürgerlichen jüdischen Wiens war das tragische Schicksal des mütterlichen Teils meiner Familie."

46. "Von den mehreren Dutzend Kindern und Kindeskindern der 14 *Geschwister Kellner* sind fünf übriggeblieben. Sie leben über die Welt verstreut und schreiben einander gelegentlich Briefe."

47. "Von meiner großen, verzweigten, sehr aneinander hängenden Familie wurden 48 Menschen vom Moloch des Faschismus verschlungen.

Unter ihnen war Mischa, ein Jahr älter als ich, mit dem ich meine Kindheit verbracht habe, um die Wette rannte, Bäume erkletterte, mit dem ich herumtollte und Bücher las. Nein, lieber nicht daran denken."

48. "Meine Eltern erreichte er in Theresienstadt, wohin sie deportiert worden waren. Meine Geschwister sind in Jugoslawien umgekommen. Ich bin allein geblieben."

49. "Ich habe eine letzte Botschaft, die Monek Katz für dich hinterlassen hat. . . . Er hatte die Ermordung seiner Frau und seiner beiden Kinder überlebt, nun war er an der Reihe. Wir sassen im Dunkeln. Da schlug Monek vor, jeder möge Name und Adresse jener Person angeben, der man—sollte jemand durch ein Wunder überleben—eine letzte Nachricht zukommen lassen könnte."

CHAPTER 3

1. "Dann sprang ich auf und begann zu brüllen. Ich brüllte wie ein Tier. Ich brüllte den Herrgott an, der mir das angetan hatte. Das Brüllen wollte nicht mehr aufhören, wurde dann aber leiser, so dass nur noch ich allein es hören konnte. Ich aber höre es nun schon dreißig Jahre lang."

2. "Im Büro des Rechtsanwalts wurde ich freundlich empfangen und nach meinem Begehr gefragt. Aber es war mir völlig unmöglich auszudrücken, was mir wirklich am Herzen lag. Wie kann man in einer bürgerlichsatten, teuer eingerichteten Bibliothek eines freundlich, aber völlig verständnislos lächelnden Züricher Rechtsanwalts von Auschwitz, Krieg und Résistance sprechen?"

3. "Vielleicht klingt das alles zu gelassen, vielleicht ist das graue heulende Elend nicht darin, das darin war und jedes Rosa schwärzte. Mir liegt aber nicht daran, mit Qualen zu paradieren, die gemessen an den in Dachau und Belsen, Mauthausen und Gürs gelittenen immer noch Wonnen blieben."

4. My discussion of corporeality has been informed by Brison 1999; Culbertson 1995; Remmler 1994a and 1994b; and Scarry 1985.

5. "Man kennt zur Genüge die Bilder dessen, was uns erwartet hätte, wenn . . . Die alten Leute, die, auf den Knien rutschend, mit Bürsten und Seifenwasser die Krukenkreuze fortzuscheuern hatten unter den schadenfrohen Blicken und Zurufen von Vorbeikommenden" (1992, 77).

6. "Nur sehr gute Schwimmer konnten sich retten."

7. "Nirgendwo zu sein, war die Parole."

8. "Eine Selbstmordwelle hatte eingesetzt."

9. "*Marietta* schien besonders gefährdet, denn sie hatte vom Vater die dunklen Haare und Augen geerbt und sah 'jüdisch' aus. Ich selber fühlte mich sicherer, ich hatte helle Augen und Haare."

10. "Natürlich waren dies keine Todeslager und jeder Vergleich mit den Nazi-Lagern verbietet sich von selbst. Trotzdem, gerade die Leute, die aus einem wohlgeordneten, bürgerlichen Haushalt kamen, erlitten zunächst einen tiefen Schock; die Erniedrigung und Demütigung, die physische Belastung waren ungeheuer."

11. "In großen Autobussen verließen wir Colombes; eine schreiende und drohende Menge französischer Frauen wartete vor dem Stadion, bespuckte uns und warf mit Steinen: sie hielten uns für Nazis."

12. See Kranzler 1976, one of the first studies of Jewish communities in Shanghai. In the nineties, interest in Shanghai refugees has increased in Austria as well as Germany. In May 1995, Salzburg hosted a conference on Shanghai exiles; Berlin followed in 1997. Shanghai as a refuge has also been the subject of recent documentaries, including one by well-known German filmmaker Ulrike Ottinger.

13. "Die Jahre in Shanghai waren bittere Jahre. Sie waren wie ein Kelch, randvoll mit einem grausamen Schicksal angefüllt, den ich bis zum letzten Tropfen leeren musste."

14. "Der Hunger und die Entbehrungen hatten mich viel Kraft gekostet. Als ich endlich die weiße Schürze umgebunden und das weiße Häubchen aufgesetzt hatte, meine künftige Uniform für viele Jahre, war ich fast am Ende meiner Kräfte."

15. "Nun kam der große seelische Zusammenbruch. Ich weiß nicht mehr, wieviele Tage und Nächte ich von meinem Strohsack nicht aufstehen konnte. Einige Lagergenossen, darunter ein sehr harter Bursche, pflegten mich rührend. Als ich aus meinen Fieberträumen erwachte, hatte ich nur einen Wunsch, ehestens mit meinen Verwandten, die sich nach USA in Sicherheit und Wohlstand gerettet hatten, in Verbindung treten zu können, irgendwie doch noch Hilfe organisieren zu können."

16. "In der Nacht bekam ich plötzlich schreckliche Leibschmerzen."

17. "Für mich kamen kritische Stunden und Tage. Es schien also, dass es in meine Hand gegeben war, ob ich dieses keimende Leben bis zur Reife austragen wollte, oder ob ich es durch Turnübungen vor dem Eintritt in diese furchtbare Welt schützen sollte."

18. Compare Remmler 1994a. Her reading of Holocaust survivor Mali Fritz's memoir and her discussion of gender led me to consider how the writers possibly reclaimed limited subjectivity over their bodies.

19. "Ich habe mir eine neue Existenz, eine neue Familie, ein neues Leben geschaffen. Aber das alte Leben, das damals 1938 zu Ende ging, ist wie ein amputiertes Bein, das unendlich schmerzt, obwohl es längst nicht mehr da ist."

20. See Aberbach 1989, 9, 163.

21. "Heimweh ist eine unbeachtete Krankheit. Wer an ihr leidet, pflegt nicht davon zu reden. Sie kommt anfallsweise, wenn man sie am wenigsten erwartet. Ein Geruch kann sie auslösen, ein Lied, eine Straßenbiegung, ein Traum, ein Gesicht, ein Vogellaut, ein Glockenschlag. In derselben Sekunde zerbricht alles, die Erkenntnis der Vergeblichkeit steigt erstickend auf—jeder Anfall gleicht der Empfindung beim Tod eines Allernächsten, immer wieder stirbt einem wer. Mit der Zeit werden die Anfälle seltener, nie schwächer; im Gegenteil, sie nehmen an Vehemenz zu. Es ist eine unerforschte Krankheit, weshalb sie nicht als eine gilt. Manche aber sterben daran."

22. The same discussion can be found in Spitzer 1998, an excellent study.

23. "Auch er war der Todeskrankheit Emigration erlegen, denn man nenne es, wie man wolle, Herzschlag oder Selbstmord, die Herzen derer, die in der Ferne plötzlich zu schlagen aufhörten, die Seelen jener, die fernmüde zu sterben sich entschlossen, waren tödlich verbraucht."

24. "Zerstörte bauten sich Häuser in Heimwehland."

25. "Das Exil ist eine Krankheit, eine Gemütskrankheit, eine Geisteskrankheit, ja zuweilen eine körperliche Krankheit."

26. "Heimweh, das Gefühl des Ausgestoßenseins, des Unverstandenseins, der unüberbrückbaren Barrieren von Sprache, Tradition, Erziehung, Gewohnheit, familiären Bezügen, die den Emigranten von jenen trennen, unter denen er Asyl gefunden hat."

27. "Vor mir kauern zwei Kinder auf der Bank, sie sind kaum älter als ich und tuscheln miteinander in einem Idiom, das ich höre, aber nicht verstehe. Mit einem Mal läuft mir ein Schauer über den Rücken, denn ich erkenne: sie sprechen wienerisch. Sie sprechen wie meine Mitschülerinnen in Heiligenstadt, doch ich gehöre nicht mehr zu ihnen, ich weiß mich auf dänisch und auf friesisch auszudrücken, die Urlaute meines Volkes sind mir fremd.
Vorahnung künftiger Schrecken."

28. Her discussion offers interesting points of comparison with that of Améry. See also Strickhausen 1995 and Howells 1994. Strickhausen's article uses Spiel's internalized "schizophrenia" as the framework for interpreting Spiel's *Lisas Zimmer* and *Anna und Anna*. Howells offers a close reading of Spiel's essay on exile as a disease.

29. "Nur in Stichworten mag denn an meinen schizophrenen Seelenzustand dieser Wochen erinnert werden, an die Ankunft in Schwechat, in Nässe, Schlamm und schwarzem Schnee, an die Fahrt entlang der vier Friedhöfe, dieser Geistermetropole einer vom Tod besessenen Stadt."

30. "Wie sehr werden wir doch von Liedern geprägt! Ich kann alle Phasen

meines Lebens mit ihrer Hilfe verfolgen. Die Wienerlieder aus der Kremserschen Sammlung, die ich als kleines Kind in der Wollzeile sang. Die Brecht-Eisler-Lieder, die uns in unserer Solidarität mit den Armen, unserer Auflehnung gegen den drohenden Nationalsozialismus stärkten. Die so naiven wie oft rätselhaften Nursery rhymes, die wir mit den eigenen Kindern lernten. Die alten Volkslieder der Inseln, aus Irland und Schottland oft. Was bewegt mich nun mehr? 'Greensleaves' [sic] mit seinen Anklängen an die Elisabethaner, an Shakespeares Poesie? Oder das schlichte Heurigenlied 'Steht ein alter Nussbaum drunt in Heiligenstadt'? In diesem Zweifel ist die Schizophrenie meines Daseins beschlossen."

31. Fliedl 1995 convincingly argues that Spiel valued the positive effect writing in English had on her German. Fliedl also provides an insightful reading of *Anna und Anna*, interpreting it less as an obvious personification of Spiel's "schizophrenia" and more as a statement on the importance of language and the perversion of language in the *Ostmark*.

32. "Dann standen die drei im Haus am Bach, noch in halbleeren Zimmern, doch bald bekamen sie Gesellschaft. Dem Uhrkasten war die feinste zugedacht. Zwei Fauteuils im Louis-Seize-Stil, nicht echt wohl, aber nachgebaut vermutlich noch im vorigen Jahrhundert, denn auch hier war die Goldfassung an vielen Stellen längst abgeblättert oder verblasst, hatten sich im Wiener Dorotheum gefunden. Ein Sofa, mit nahezu dem gleichen Zierat und den gleichen kannelierten Armlehnen und Beinen, hatte im Schaufenster eines Trödelladens in der Chepstow Road lange auf einen Käufer gewartet; seine Verschiffung kostete mehr als es selbst. Vom Tapeziermeister Rechberger in Sankt Wolfgang einheitlich mit grünweißgestreiftem Seidendamast aus London bespannt, sahen die Möbel so aus, als hätten sie seit je zusammengehört, und der Uhrenkasten brauchte sich ihrer nicht zu schämen. Ein Barockluster an türkisch gedrechseltem Stiel war aus Salzburg hinzugekommen, und an den Wänden des kleinen Salons hingen Kupferstiche von Hogarth nebst vielen kleinen Londoner Veduten aus der gleichen Zeit."

33. "Denn wann immer wir gezweifelt haben, wo wir hingehören oder lieber hingehören wollen, ob es London wäre oder Wien: hier fühlten wir uns, meine Kinder und ich, in jedem Fall zu Hause."

34. "in Dingen zu leben, die uns Geschichten erzählen" (1966, 95).

35. "Hatten die Jahre 1934–1938 in mir Gefühle der Empörung, des Zornes, der Verachtung, der Trauer um Verlorenes geweckt und zum Aufruhr, zur Erkenntnis geführt, dass man um die verlorene Freiheit kämpfen muss, so lähmte mich 1938/39, weil ich meine eigene Ohnmacht kannte. Ich hatte Angst und schämte mich ihrer; Angst nicht nur um das eigene Leben, viel mehr: Da war die Furcht, dem Grauen nicht standhalten zu können, treulos zu werden, sich selbst und seinen eigenen Freunden gegenüber, die man in die eigene Not und Ausweglosigkeit hereinziehen könnte. Das KZ, die Gestapo, das braue Haus am Morzinplatz."

36. "Alles war zu Ende: das persönliche Glück, die Heimgeborgenheit, das

Heimatgefühl, die Zusammengehörigkeit—das ganze Leben. Was blieb, war panische Angst, würgende Atemlosigkeit, schwarze Ausweglosigkeit."

37. "Eine Tür fällt zu, endgültig zu. Es gibt keinen Ausgang mehr. . . . Ich will weg. Wo ist der Schlüssel? Er passt nicht.—Stöhnend erwache ich, fühle nur eines: ich muss weg!"

38. "Diese ersten paar Tage, die Menschen um mich, die vielen Amtswege eines Ausländers in seinem neuen Wohnland—das alles war so bestürzend und schattenhaft, so ungewohnt und ermüdend, dass ich wie ein Mechanismus meine Glieder gebrauchte, sprach, handelte. Ich war nicht dort, wo ich war. Ich war in einem Zwischenland, das kein Profil hatte. Ich verlor meines dabei. Eines war mir klar: das war '*die* Fremde,' von der die Dichter sprachen. . . . Ich entdeckte, dass ich die Sprache weder sprechen noch verstehen konnte, dass ich die Art der Menschen nicht fasste, ihre Einstellung nicht begriff, ihre Lebensgewohnheiten nicht verstand und—wie ich damals glaubte—nie annehmen würde."

39. "Irgendwie fand ich immer mehr zu meinem eigenen 'Ich' zurück. Ich arbeitete gern und beschloss, meine Freizeit . . . dazu zu verwenden, Masters of Arts in Cambridge oder Oxford zu werden."

40. "Eine neue Stella war ich in diesen beiden Jahren geworden. Ich hatte das Proletarierlos am eigenen Körper verspürt. . . . Von Arbeit zerrissene, wunde Hände sprachen eine andere Sprache als regelmäßig manikürte Finger und lackierte Nägel. Ich hatte Neues dazugelernt! Vor allem sprach ich jetzt englisches Englisch. Ich war toleranter geworden, gefestigt in meinen Anschauungen, aber bereit, die der anderen zu achten und sie zu verstehen. Ich war 'internationalisiert', war Österreicherin geblieben, aber weltoffener geworden. Die Schreckenstage des Naziregimes waren aus meinen Träumen verschwunden. Der Schock war behoben, das bewies mein Benehmen, meine Ruhe und Sorge für andere in den Tagen des 'Blitz' und später. Diese Stella wurde jetzt in eine erzieherische und berufliche Stellung versetzt, in der sie sich bewähren sollte und wollte."

41. Klein-Löw relates how she studied with Charlotte and Karl Bühler (1980, 56), and Willi and Anna Reich (58).

42. "Trauer und Leid sind dazu da, dass man auf ihnen Neues, Lebendiges, Beschwingendes baue."

43. "Als mein Mann und ich Arm in Arm in der kalten Winterluft nach Hause gingen, sahen wir die Umrisse der uns so vertrauten Gebäude der Inneren Stadt und ihre verträumten Plätze liebevoll und traurig an. Mir war zumute, als müsste ich jedes Haus und jeden Baum mit meinen Blicken streicheln. Ich hatte soeben begriffen, dass wir bald, sehr bald, würden Abschied nehmen müssen von der schönen und so geliebten Stadt. Mein Mann fühlte, was in mir vorging, und drückte fest meinen Arm."

44. See Spitzer's discussion of a print of St. Stephan's that had an honored place in his family's living room (1998, 75).

45. "Tatsächlich hat sich die Kluft zwischen den Hiergebliebenen—und damit sind auch solche gemeint, die ein reines Gewissen haben dürfen—und

denen, die man davongejagt hat, nie wieder ganz geschlossen. Und dennoch: Wie in einem Lied besungen, schäumte auf dem Heldenplatz der Flieder wie eh und je und wusste nicht, was sich hier zugetragen hatte; in der Prater-Hauptallee reckten die Kastanien die weißen und roten Kerzen in ihrer ganzen Pracht in die Luft, und das alles, wonach ich mich die ganzen Jahre gesehnt hatte, machte mich wehrlos gegen vieles andere" (1992, 133–34).

46. Compare with Fried 1963, 157. See Matti Bunzl 1996, 198 for a discussion of the ways in which young Jewish Austrians construct an ethnic identity through a consciously conceived spatial identity. Interestingly enough, they draw on the same traditions and institutions within Vienna to circumscribe their Jewish identity that the memoirists use to map out an Austrian identity.

47. "Die Menschen jüdischer Herkunft verschwanden über Nacht aus dem Alltagsleben, aus den Büros, aus den Kaffeehäusern und aus dem Straßenbild; jedermann wusste, was mit dem jüdischen Kaufmann vis à vis, mit dem jüdischen Arzt, mit dem jüdischen Nachbarn geschah, es war ganz offiziell in allen Gazetten zu lesen und konnte von jedermann auf den Straßen und Plätzen beobachtet werden. Unsere Nachbarn und Bekannten, Kollegen und Geschäftspartner gingen wie eh und je zur Arbeit und ins Büro, besuchten Kaffeehäuser und Theater, gingen in den Gottesdienst und fuhren in die Ferien, so als ob nichts geschehen wäre."

48. "Was ist eine Stadt? Eine von Menschenhand geschaffene Landschaft von Steinbauten, Verkehrswegen und einigen Grünflächen. Städte gewinnen erst Leben, wenn man sie mit Menschen verknüpfen kann. Sonst werden sie zu toten Steinhaufen, die einen Grabgeruch an sich tragen. So erschien mir Wien im Jahre 1945. Alle die Menschen, die ich gekannt und geliebt hatte, mit denen ich verwandtschaftlich oder freundschaftlich verbunden gewesen war, waren verschwunden: emigriert oder vergast. Jede Straßenecke, jede Parkbank in jener Gegend Wiens, in der ich gelebt hatte und die ich nun wieder aufsuchte, sprachen mir von dem Grauen der Vergangenheit."

49. "Jede Ecke, jedes Plätzchen, atmete Erinnerungen, sprach von Vergangenem, von einer anderen Welt, die ich und nur ich als letzter Überlebender meiner ersten Familie gekannt hatte. Entdeckungsfahrten durch Wien übten eine große nostalgische Anziehung auf mich aus, aber sie waren so unendlich schmerzlich, dass ich meist mitten drin abbrechen musste."

50. "Aus meiner persönlichen Sicht stellt sich jene Nachkriegsepoche in Österreich, die Gegenstand meiner Aufzeichnungen ist und die in der Ära *Kreisky* ihren Kulminationspunkt gefunden hat, als das Schlusslicht einer kulturhistorischen Epoche dar, die bereits am 11. März 1938 ihr grausames Ende gefunden hatte: der Strahl eines Sternes der längst erloschen war."

51. "[D]ie mühsam in uns verdrängte Heimat brach immer wieder hervor. Ich träumte von Heiligenstadt, von Spaziergängen im Prater mit unserem längst verstorbenen Hund Diemo, von den Konturen der Salesianerkirche am Rennweg und den Angsttraum von einem plötzlichen Aufwachen in Wien, fremd unter Feinden, mit englischem Geld in der Tasche, vogelfrei."

52. "Im dunkelnden Licht stehe ich auf dem Pfarrplatz. Hier liegt meine

Seele begraben. Wann immer ich in den zehn Jahren meiner Abwesenheit Heimweh hatte, war es nach diesem Ort."

53. "Samstag nachmittag ging ich in Heiligenstadt herum, im schmelzenden Schnee gegen halb fünf, in der Dämmerung, und es war hundertmal herzzerreißender, als ich je erwartet hatte. Ich ging in die kleine Pfarrkapelle und heulte 'einfach'."

54. "Welche Orte der Vergangenheit in den nächsten Tagen aufgesucht werden, bis hin zum topographisch genau bestimmbaron Ursprung meiner Einheit mit Wien, dem Pfarrplatz in Heiligenstadt, mag ich nicht noch einmal in allen Einzelheiten heraufbeschwören. Welche Menschen ich wiedersah—auch diese Reminiszenzen schmerzen nach all der inzwischen verstrichenen Zeit."

55. "Was in der Kindheit ein Wunschtraum gewesen war, wurde später zu einem Alpdruck."

56. "Viele meiner Freunde hatten dort gelebt und gearbeitet. Was in der unseligen Zeit der Judenverfolgungen geschehen war, konnte und wollte ich nicht vergessen, nicht verzeihen."

57. "In der Leopoldstadt wurde ich frei von Hemmungen, die mich gehindert hatten, zu schreiben. Hier warf ich die Scheu ab, mein vergangenes Leben in Erinnerungsrückblicken noch einmal zu erleben."

58. "Ich wurde frei von Vorurteilen, von Schuldgefühlen. Verdrängtes kam ans Licht. Einmal aus dem Verborgenen hervorgelockt, bedrückte es mich nicht mehr.

Ich änderte meine Einstellung zu Menschen. Alles Diskriminierende verschwand. Es blieb nur ein großes Staunen zurück, dass ich einmal einen Unterschied gemacht hatte zwischen Jiddisch und gepflegtes Deutsch sprechenden Menschen, zwischen Menschen aus orthodoxen und solchen aus assimilierten Familien."

59. "Wir fuhren die großartige Arlbergstraße talwärts, sie war nicht großartig. Das Eis brüchig, der Schnee beschmutzt, die geliebte Landschaft drohte."

60. At the end of his memoirs, Lothar refers to this period as the rape of Austria (438).

61. "Indem ich dies, fast an der Grenze, bedachte, zerstückte sich in mir jene Verbundenheit Stück für Stück der Straße, die ich fuhr. Alles, so empfand ich, hatte getäuscht. Die Großartigkeit war eine Kulisse für die Niedrigkeit, die Holdheit eine Schminke für das Gemeine. Ein Zuschauer bei einer Operation, sah ich mir zu, als ich mir Stück um Stück die Liebe meines Lebens aus dem Leibe riss."

62. "Unter dem schweigenden Flug der pfauenblauen Vögel, in der völligen, unverdorbenen Einsamkeit, im falschesten Augenblick am falschesten Ort packte mich ein Sehnsuchtsanfall nach der bescheidenen Majestät des Untersbergs, an dessen Fuss die kleine Morzger Kirche mit dem grünen Kirchturm steht."

63. "St. Anton, wo sie uns überfallen hatten. Landeck, von wo die SA-Männer gekommen waren. Immer wieder schob sich zwischen die ersehnten Anblicke eine untilgbare Erinnerung, die sie vereiste. In Kitzbühel, wo Mary,

die Kinder und ich am Schwarzsee drei Sommer Ferienglück genossen hatten, erkannte ich vor dem Bahnhof mehrere schon zu Schuschniggs Zeiten mit den Nazis einverstandene Leute."

64. "Beim Einfahren standen der Gaisberg, der Untersberg, die Hohen-Salzburg, die Türme und Kuppeln der Kirchen klar und herrlich gegen den Himmel. Jäh verschwand der Zwiespalt der Empfindungen, es zählte nicht, was sich der Wiedersehenslust entgegenwarf—die Wunder des Zurückgekehrtseins und des Überlebens geschahen wunderbarer, als man an sie geglaubt hatte. Im sacht ergrauten Licht zeichnete er sich ab, der stolz-bescheidene Untersberg, den Garten der Götter übertreffend; der waldige Gaisberg, lächerlich unscheinbar, gemessen an den Waldbergen von Maine, doch zauberischer als die geheimnislosen; ohne Drohung zackte die Hohensalzburg, die lieblichste der Festungen, sich empor; Kirchenuhren schlugen die neunte Stunde und Glocken läuteten mit einer Harmonie, die es sonst nirgends gab, weil sie Mozart hieß. Dass auf unserer Fluchtfahrt auch hier Spruchbänder des Hasses hingen, läuteten sie hinweg."

65. "Mir war bewusst geworden, wie falsch die Behauptung ist, das Erwartete bleibe hinter den Erwartungen zurück. . . . In dieser Stunde jedenfalls, einer der besten, vielleicht der besten meines Lebens, hatte das Erwartete die Erwartung übertroffen, weil ich erwartet hatte, von dem Entbehrten ergriffen zu werden, aber nicht von der Liebe dazu. Nur das eigene Leben lehrt die Wahrheiten. Die Wahrheit des Wiedersehens hängt von der Wahrheit des Wieder-Lieben-Könnens ab. Dass ich es konnte, machte mich froher als das, was uns bevorstand."

66. "der 'Augenblick im Paradiese' wird paradiesischer für jene, die der Hölle zu nahe kamen."

67. "Mit dem Schicksal hadern, zu spät hielt ein alltägliches Phänomen es mir vor den Augen, bleibt vergeblich; Schicksale sind Naturereignisse."

68. "Als ich zu Beginn des Septembers in Wien eintraf, wo meines Bleibens nunmehr sein sollte, fühlte ich, vom Franz-Josephs-Bahnhof kommend, angesichts der verfallenen, schäbigen Nussdorfer Straße die erste stürmische Lust des Wiedersehens. Vor dem Schuberthaus ließ ich halten, trat ein und war, mit einer Verspätung von drei Monaten, endlich angekommen."

69. "Ich aber ging, nach der Entscheidung, in den Wiener Volksgarten zum Denkmal eines großen Österreichers."

70. "Das Weltbild des Österreichers ist ohne sein Land nicht denkbar. Das Weltbild des Nationalsozialisten ist ohne Land denkbar. . . . Für den Nationalsozialisten gibt es das Gesetz des Blutes, für den Österreicher das Gesetz der Landschaft." Compare with Hilde Spiel's comments in Hermann (1992, 54).

71. " 'Übrigens kehre ich nicht zu Leuten zurück, sondern, entschuldigen Sie den pompösen Ausdruck, zu einer Landschaft, die ich zum Leben brauche.' "

CHAPTER 4

1. A few scholars who have stressed the connection between memory and/or past and identity are Egyptologist Assmann (1997); sociologists Berger

and Luckmann (1966); sociologist Halbwachs (1980); historian Lowenthal (1985); historian Maier (1988); psychologist Schacter (1996); and philosopher Warnock (1987).

2. "Ich war kein Ich mehr und lebte nicht in einem Wir. Ich hatte keinen Pass und keine Vergangenheit und kein Geld und keine Geschichte" (1966, 75).

3. Reinprecht 1992 discusses the tension between Jewish and Austrian identities for those returning (79–103).

4. Rozenblit 1983 argues that "if the urban environment facilitated cultural assimilation, it also provided the necessary demographic foundation for continued Jewish identity and the assertion of Jewish pride" (7). This may be true, but in the case of Spiel, Freundlich, and Thalberg, they draw on this cultural past to assert both an Austrian and a Jewish identity.

5. "Ein echtes Bummelleben müssen meine Eltern in ihren frühen Ehejahren geführt haben, damals, bald nach der Jahrhundertwende, knapp ein Dezennium trennte uns noch vom Ausbruch des Ersten Weltkriegs. Sie hatten 1905 geheiratet, 1906 war ich zur Welt gekommen und sollte ihr einziges Kind bleiben" (1992, 9).

6. "Wo immer ihr Abend begonnen hatte, er endete, so habe ich es jedenfalls erzählt bekommen, todsicher im längst legendär gewordenen Café Central" (9).

7. "Nach jenen Bummelnächten, lange vor Ausbruch des Ersten Weltkriegs, hielt der Vater trotz seines dauernden Schlafmankos eisern an seinem Acht-Uhr-Frühstück fest, während Mutter ihrem Schlafbedürfnis nachgeben durfte. Vater frühstückte also allein, wobei er sich in seine geliebte 'Arbeiter-Zeitung' vertiefte (neben der er auch die 'Neue Freie Presse' hielt, schon deshalb, damit sich Mutter über die ihrer Meinung nach ahnungslosen Musikkritiken von X und Y erbittern konnte, und auch darum, weil das eben ein Weltblatt war, dessen Einfluss bis in die fernsten Ecken der Monarchie reichte und weit darüber hinaus, kurz, weil es als unentbehrlich galt)" (11–12).

8. The percentage of Jewish Austrians and Austrians of Jewish heritage was very high among lawyers. See Beller 1989, 37 for a statistical breakdown.

9. "In die Vororte der Stadt, Dörfer noch vor nicht allzu langer Zeit, lagen die letzten Jahre des großen Friedens eingebettet wie sie selbst in die letzten Mulden des Wienerwaldes. Pötzleinsdorf war der mit dem ersten Augenaufschlag geschaute, aber nicht wahrgenommene Anfang; Sievering, gekannt und sogleich wieder vergessen, mit dem zweiten Lebensjahr schon vorbei; Heiligenstadt, sein Pfarrplatz, ein Haus und Garten in der Probusgasse, die bereits unverlierbare Landschaft einer Kindheit, in die noch vor dem dritten Jahr der Krieg einbrach."

10. See Rozenblit 1983 for a breakdown of Jewish population distribution in Vienna by district, esp. 71–98. Looking specifically at the district Döbling, where Heiligenstadt is located, we can see that the Jewish population steadily grew in the first part of the century. In 1900, the Jewish population was under 5 percent (77); by 1910, 7 percent of the population was Jewish (McCagg

1989, 210); and by 1923, it was estimated to be between 10 and 19 percent (Freidenreich 1991, 11).

11. "Als ich geboren wurde, herrschte in Wien Kaiser *Franz Joseph* und in Petersburg Zar *Nikolaus II.* Aus frühester Kindheit glaubte ich mich erinnern zu können, wie meine Kinderschwester Zita mich im Kinderwagen zur Wachablöse in den Inneren Burghof brachte; es war dies eine feierliche Angelegenheit, die jeden Tag um die Mittagsstunde stattfand und bei der auch der Kaiser am Fenster erschienen sein soll."

12. As Rozenblit writes, "[t]he Jews in Austria came to see themselves as Austrians, but it is not always clear what they meant by the term" (1992, 5). Before 1918, it "mostly indicated loyalty to the Habsburg dynasty and to the supra-national Habsburg state" (4).

13. "Niemand in meiner Familie, soweit ich sie noch erlebt habe, war sichtbar religiös. Dass der Glaube meiner Vorväter nicht der meiner war, blieb mir als Kind unbekannt. Mein Vater war, vielleicht als Student, katholisch geworden. Meine Mutter, deren beide Onkel ja bereits konvertiert hatten, folgte ihm ohne weiteres darin nach."

14. "Man hielt die österreichischen christlichen Feiertage, lebte und benahm sich so wie die anderen Mitbürger. Man war bewusst österreichisch, hatte Freud' und Leid mit diesem Land geteilt, im Kriege gedient und Vermögen durch Kriegsanleihen verloren, wie alle anderen Österreicher. . . . Das Judentum war etwas, das gerade noch in der Erinnerung lebte, an das man selten dachte, das sich vermutlich im Laufe der nächsten Generation in Nichts auflösen werde. Und doch . . ."

15. "eine warnende Mahnung, ein Element ewiger Unsicherheit."

16. Pauley writes of the Jewish population: "[o]n the eve of the *Anschluss,* 185,000 Jews (not counting the 34,500 classified as Jews by the Nazis in their Nuremberg Laws of 1935) lived in Austria. The country's Jewish population was little more than 11,000 shortly after the war" (1996, 492). See Freidenreich 1991, 213 for census figures from 1910, 1923, and 1934.

17. See John and Lichtblau 1990 for a history of migration to Vienna in the nineteenth and twentieth centuries.

18. "So bleibt mir nichts übrig, als den Seelenvogel zwischen diesen weißen Blättern aufzupflanzen; zu versuchen, Euer aller Leben der Vergessenheit zu entreißen, zu versuchen, es hier in diese Blätter zu bannen, damit Ihr Ruhe findet und damit auch meine Seele ruhiger werde. Möge ich die Kraft haben, Euch in diese Blätter zu ziehen und Euch hier noch einmal Leben zu geben, damit Ihr nicht nur einen Handvoll der sechs Millionen seid."

19. "Meine Mutter hieß als Mädchen Marie Gutfeld und entstammte einer Familie, die für das Entstehen einer gebildeten Menschenschicht jüdischer Herkunft, ihren bereits vollzogenen Eingang in das Wiener Sozialgefüge, beispielhaft war."

20. Spiel includes this photograph without a specific family reference and the photograph of her grandmother in her cultural history, *Vienna's Golden Autumn, 1866–1938.*

21. See Wistrich 1989, 583–620, for a discussion of Arthur Schnitzler and his literature in the context of the "Jewish question" at the turn of the century.
22. "Meine Mutter, ein schönes dunkles Mädchen, blieb von solchen Wirren der Seele und der Zeitläufte unberührt. Sie hatte von ihren Vorfahren heiteren Witz, guten Geschmack, Musikalität und eine gewisse träumerische Lässigkeit geerbt, die manchmal, aber nicht in ihrem Fall, mit kontemplativer Innenschau einher- oder dieser vorangeht. Anders als ihr Bruder war sie leichtlebig, so lange sie vom Schicksal ungeschoren blieb. An Wien hing sie innig und sehnte sich von allen Reisen, allen Ferien in ihre Stadt zurück. Sie hatte ein feines Näschen, einen feinen Mund. Ihre Freundinnen riefen sie Mizzi; der Schnitzlersche Name entsprach ihrem Gemüt."
23. See Pickus 1999 for an in-depth discussion of the *Corps,* German nationalistic fraternities (*Burschenschaften*), and Jewish student identity in nineteenth-century Germany (esp. 11, 43–51).
24. "bewahrten ihn später vor unverdienter Schmach."
25. "Der Schmach seiner Abkunft war auch er ausgesetzt, als man manche Wiener von anderen Wienern zu unterscheiden begann."
26. "Woher sie kamen, die Spiels, worauf ihre bürgerliche Existenz begründet war? Ich weiß es nicht. . . . Vermutlich war auch dieser Zweig der Familie seit geraumer Zeit in Wien ansässig gewesen."
27. "Drei Photographien aus dem Nachlass der Tante Lonny . . . geben spärliche Auskunft."
28. Schramm writes that Spiel repressed this side of the family. She speculates that Spiel's denial of her grandparents' roots in the Orthodox communities of Lemberg and Zuranow resulted from an atmosphere dominated by racial hatred (10).
29. "war Arzt, er war homosexuell, er nahm sich das Leben."
30. See Mitchell's discussion of "textual pictures" (1994, 109–81).
31. "Auf dem Bild sitzt er mit heiterer Miene, zeitunglesend, in einem Café. Auch an ihm sind jene Merkmale nicht zu endecken, die Menschen seiner Herkunft angeblich eignen: er könnte ein Sektionsrat im Verkehrsministerium sein, der einen Bericht von der Eröffnung einer neuen Eisenbahnlinie im Kronland Kroatien liest."
32. *Fanny von Arnstein* (1962; English translation, 1991) and *Vienna's Golden Autumn, 1866–1938* (1987).
33. "Der Beitrag der Juden zur Herausbildung einer eigenständigen österreichischen Kultur kann wohl kaum hoch genug veranschlagt werden. So eng war die Verflechtung der Juden mit dem österreichischen Geistesleben, so tief verwurzelt waren sie in ihrem Land, dass eine eigenständige österreichische Kultur ohne ihren Beitrag undenkbar geworden ist. So erstaunt es keineswegs, dass gerade jene, die die Existenz eines selbständigen Österreich und den Gedanken einer österreichischen Nation so vehement ablehnen, gleichzeitig die rabiatesten Antisemiten sind. Für die Nationalsozialisten stand die physische Vernichtung des österreichischen Judentums für das Verschwinden eines eigenständigen Österreich schlechthin."

34. See Schorske 1980 and Stefan Zweig's autobiography, *Die Welt von Gestern* (*The World of Yesterday*), which deals with this conflict.

35. "ein typischer Mann der Gründerjahre, ein Patriarch in seiner großen Familie, ein Renaissancemensch, der in einer Zeit der technischen und wissenschaftlichen Umwälzungen die Welt, seine österreichische Welt umformen wollte."

36. See Beckermann 1984 and her discussion of the photograph of an unknown Jewish family (9).

37. "Ich erinnere mich deutlich an das Atelier und den Fotografen, an meinen Unwillen bei den Vorbereitungen und der Prozedur selbst. Kompromisse mussten geschlossen werden. Die schön eingedrehten Locken verschwanden—bis auf eine einzige—auf mein unnachgiebiges Verlangen hin unter dem Hut. Meine Bereitschaft, weiße Schuhe und Strümpfe anzulegen, hatten sich meine Eltern mit einem Zugeständnis erkauft: den Stock—von einem Freunde geliehen—hielt ich, wie zur Abwehr, in der Hand.

Der arme Fotograf war verzweifelt: ich lächelte nicht, wie er es gern gehabt hätte; trotz seiner Bitten neigte ich meinen Kopf nicht nach links, um die Narbe zu verbergen; und das Kinn blieb unbescheiden vorgeschoben."

38. "Ich war anders als die anderen. Ich schämte mich."

39. " 'Die Narbe muss hinein, damit sie es gleich wissen!' Das war der Augenblick der Befreiung von einem Alpdruck!"

40. " 'Die Juden werden verfolgt, von vielen gehasst. Stelli, glaubst du, dass man sie und ihre Religion im Stich lassen sollte? Wäre das nicht feig?' "

41. "Meine Ablehnung, meine Wut waren so groß, dass ich mich ab meinem sechsten Lebensjahr krank stellte, um nicht mehr in das Dorf zu müssen."

42. "Ich fühlte mich fremd. . . . Man versuchte, mich ins Gespräch zu ziehen. Die Leute sprachen nicht meine, ich sprach nicht ihre Sprache. Sie bildeten einen festgefügten Kreis, ich stand außerhalb, war eine Außenseiterin."

43. "Da trat eine Frau ein, einfach gekleidet, unhübsch. 'Mundl,' der Obmann, erhob sich. Auch wir standen auf. Ein lautes 'Freundschaft!' klang uns entgegen. Wir (ich zählte mich also schon dazu) erwiderten diesen Gruß. Was war es, das mich von einem Augenblick zum anderen aus einer Außenseiterin zu einer 'Dazugehörenden' gemacht hat? Ich weiß es nicht."

44. "Vielleicht war es bei mir deswegen anders, weil ich in der Partei ein zweites Heim gehabt hatte, weil der Sozialismus starke Verwandtschaftsbande schafft."

45. "Ihr habt mir heute abend meine Heimat in Wien, in Österreich, in der Sozialistischen Partei vom neunen gegeben."

46. "Ich war heim- und heimatlos geworden. Am Beginn dieses neuen Lebensabschnitts hatte ich nur ein Ziel vor Augen: die Vergangenheit zu vergessen, in der Gegenwart zu leben, eine lebenswerte Zukunft zu gestalten."

47. "Viele meiner Mitglieder waren Juden, so manche unter ihnen fromme Juden, . . . alle klassenbewusst, alle arme Teufel, Proletarier und Jude—zwei Bürden, die es zu tragen gab. Denn es gab Antisemitismus."

48. "Bin ich noch immer eine Rebellin?"

49. Freidenreich 1991 describes the great diversity of the Jewish Socialists in the interwar period and highlights two ends of the spectrum: "Jewish Socialists," who "were Jews by birth but Socialists by conviction and did not generally involve themselves in Jewish affairs"; and "Socialist Jews," Jews who "remained involved in Jewish life as committed Socialists" (85).

50. "Ich bin am 10. Juli 1907 in Trembowla geboren. Zeit und Ort sind in meinem besonderen Fall von Bedeutung: Die Zeit, weil ich als ein Sieben-Monate-Kind in einer kühleren Jahreszeit wahrscheinlich gar keine Überlebenschance gehabt hätte, und der Ort, weil die ostgalizische Kleinstadt im nordöstlichen Zipfel der österreichisch-ungarischen Monarchie meine erste Kindheit und somit meine ganze Entwicklung richtunggebend mitgeprägt hat."

51. "Sie sahen in ihnen nicht Mitangehörige der Monarchie, sondern Fremde, von denen sich die Mehrzahl in Kleidung, Sprache und Gehaben unterschied. Es waren 'Zuagraste', und die haben schon damals wie noch heute in Wien und Österreich wenig Sympathien gefunden."

52. "Zuerst war ich das nette, artige Flüchtlingskind, das von so weit her kam und seine Heimat hatte verlassen müssen. Man war überall freundlich zu mir, man streichelte mich und schenkte mir dieses und jenes. Als die Zahl der Ostflüchtlinge wuchs, wurde ich als eine von ihnen zur 'Polischen' und schließlich, da die weit überwiegende Zahl der Ostflüchtlinge Juden waren, zur 'Jüdin' degradiert und als solche als 'Saujüdin' beschimpft."

53. "Wo gehöre ich dazu, wer bin ich, warum sind wir Juden so verschieden von den anderen?"

54. "Dieses erste Jahr im Schomer war beglückend für mich. Die quälende Identitätskrise war überwunden."

55. "Wir im Schomer wussten, dass es keine konfliktlose, heile Welt gibt und dass man lernen müsse, die eigene Zukunft und die der Welt in neu zu schaffende Bahnen zu lenken."

56. See Lichtblau and John 1999.

57. In his study on Karl Emil Franzos, Sommer situates Lachs's study (appearing under the name Schiffmann) as viewing Franzos's "Halb-Asien" in the tradition of "a liberal German-Jewish assimilationist" (1984, 3). In contrast, he defines Franzos as "an expansionist German nationalist of the post 1848, post-1870 period" (6).

58. This is a somewhat different strategy from that of their coreligionists in the interwar period. As historian Wistrich argues, "[a]fter the First World War the drift of Vienna Jews towards Social Democrats . . . became a flood and as a result the image of 'Red Vienna' literally fused in antisemitic circles with that of 'Jewish' subversion" (1987, 115). In the First Republic (1918–1934), "the so-called 'Jewish' leadership of the Austrian Social Democracy bent backwards to *dissociate* themselves from their former co-religionists" (117). This was no doubt a strategy on the part of the Jewish leaders to deal with rising anti-Semitism in Austria and the perception that "Red Vienna" was a Jewish creation.

59. "Meine ersten Erinnerungen sind aufgepflanzte Bajonette und eine Theatervorstellung" (9).

60. "Wenn ich daran zurückdenke, erscheinen mir diese ersten beiden Erinnerungen, vor denen ein absolutes Bewusstseins-Nichts liegt, kennzeichnend für mein Leben. Mit Bajonetten und dem Theater fing es an. Fast endete es so."

61. "Mit antiösterreichischen Demonstrationen in meiner Geburtsstadt Brünn hatte sie begonnen, die Zerreißung Österreichs war ihre Jugend, Österreichs Vergewaltigung und Schädigung die Mitte, Zorn und Qual durch Österreich, Hoffung auf Österreich und Sehnsucht nach Österreich waren die Emigration, Wiederkehr nach Österreich das Alter gewesen. Alles andere blieb Beiwerk. Beruf, vielleicht sogar Berufung, Abenteuer, Erfolg, versäumte und genützte Möglichkeiten, Enttäuschung, Wirken in Werken—alles Beiwerk. Auf Österreich gründete es sich oder stürzte, auf ein einziges Land, ob besser, ob schlechter als andere, blieb gleichgültig."

62. "Österreich-Ungarn ist nicht mehr. Anderswo möchte ich nicht leben. Emigration kommt für mich nicht in Frage. Ich werde mit dem Torso weiterleben und mir einbilden, dass es das Ganze ist."

63. Österreichs Geheimnis, Grillparzer hatte es gewusst und in seiner Selbstbiographie schonungslos enthüllt, liegt in der dämonischen Janusköpfigkeit: die Ziele erreicht man hier auf Umwegen, das Unbedingte durch das Bedingte. Doch noch immer sind Abgründe, über die man noch Hellbrunn kommt, der Wüste tausendmal vorzuziehen, durch die man nach Hollywood gelangt."

64. "Die Zeit, die ihn noch umgab, war ein Nichts. Aber mit dem Lande, dem er zugehörte, mit dem unzerstörbaren Wesen des Volkes, mit dem Weben der großen Geschicke—mit all dem wusste er sich verbunden."

65. "Der Abstammung nach. Der Konfession nach katholisch."

66. "Die Bedingungen, die den Menschen machen, sind die der Geographie, der Nationalität und der Rasse; von diesen drei empfängt er seine Gaben und seine Untugenden; sie abzuschütteln vermag er nur äußerlich. . . . Die Heimat legt man nicht ab wie ein Hemd, noch weniger seine Nationalität und am wenigsten seine Rasse."

67. "Taufwasser wäscht die Blutmischung nicht ab."

68. "am schönsten Maienmorgen des Jahres 1895."

69. "Wir hatten wieder ganz von vorne, mein Mann in einem neuen Beruf, beginnen müssen. Im Jahre 1922 bekam ich einen Sohn, einen echten Wiener. Zwanzig Jahre lebten wir in Wien ein arbeits- und erfolgreiches Leben."

70. "Alles hat er mit Auszeichnung gemacht, seine zwei Doktorate, seine Obliegenheiten als Geschäftsführer meines Vaters, seine Haltung als Offizier und Mensch. Ihm gebührte für alle seine Handlungen eine Auszeichnung, und eine ganz besondere als Mensch. Er hat sie als Doktor bekommen, als Mensch hat ihm das Schicksal fast alles versagt."

71. "Mein Sohn hatte sechzehn Jahre geglaubt, dass keine Macht der Welt ihn je bewegen könnte, Wien zu verlassen. Es gab jedoch eine diabolische Übermacht. Eines Tages kam er, am ganzen Leib bebend, am frühen Vormittag nach Hause. Man hatte ihn aus dem Gymnasium ausgestoßen. Nicht etwa wegen schlechter Lernerfolge oder wegen schlechten Betragens. Die Religionszugehörigkeit erwies sich als untragbar in den Augen der neuen Machthaber."

72. "Wir hatten viel Not gemeinsam ertragen, und das Elend hatte uns zusammengeschweißt. Die Armut hatte uns zu Brüdern und Schwestern gemacht, die wie Pech und Schwefel zusammenhielten."

73. "Ich hätte ersticken müssen, wenn ich nach Australien, Amerika oder sonst wohin gegangen wäre, da ja mein Sohn nach Wien zurückgekehrt ist. Ich wäre bestimmt an ewigem Heimweh zugrunde gegangen."

74. "Diese Frage meines Sohnes setzte den Schlusspunkt unter die Geschichte meiner Emigration und den Beginn zu einem neuen Lebensabschnitt in der Heimat."

CONCLUSION

1. "Der österreichische Diplomat Hans Thalberg schreibt in seinen Erinnerungen, dass er eher mit einem Holländer oder Jugoslawen eine gemeinsame Sichtweise über die Nazizeit finden könne als mit einem Österreicher. Ein gedanklicher und gefühlsmäßiger Graben trenne ihn von dem Land und den Leuten, denen er sich in seiner Jugend zugehörig gefühlt hat. In diesem Graben wurden wir geboren. In Familien, für die nichts mehr war wie früher."

REFERENCES

PRIMARY LITERATURE BY THE STUDIED MEMOIRISTS

Freundlich, Elisabeth. 1986. *Der Seelenvogel.* Vienna: Paul Zsolnay Verlag.
———. 1992. *Die fahrenden Jahre: Erinnerungen.* Ed. Susanne Alge. Salzburg: Otto Müller Verlag.
———. 1999. *The Traveling Years.* Trans. Elizabeth Pennebaker. Riverside, Calif.: Ariadne Press.
Klein-Löw, Stella. 1980. *Erinnerungen: Erlebtes und Gedachtes.* Vienna: Jugend und Volk.
Lachs, Minna. 1986. *Warum schaust du zurück: Erinnerungen 1907–1941.* Vienna: Europaverlag.
———. 1992. *Zwischen zwei Welten: Erinnerungen 1941–1946.* Vienna: Löcker Verlag.
Lothar, Ernst. 1944. *The Angel with the Trumpet.* Trans. Elizabeth Reynolds Hapgood. Garden City, N.Y.: Doubleday.
———. 1946. *Der Engel mit der Posaune.* London: Harrap.
———. 1945. *Heldenplatz.* Cambridge, Mass.: Schoenhof.
———. 1945. *The Prisoner.* Trans. James A. Galston. Garden City, N.Y.: Doubleday.
———. 1949. *Return to Vienna.* Garden City, N.Y.: Doubleday.
———. 1949. *Die Rückkehr.* Salzburg: Silberboot.
———. 1961. *Das Wunder des Überlebens Erinnerungen und Ergebnisse.* Vienna: Paul Zsolnay Verlag.
Spiel, Hilde. (No date) "Streets of Vineta," Manuscript, Österreichisches Literaturarchiv der Nationalbibliothek. Blatt II.
———. 1961. *The Darkened Room.* London: Methuen.
———. 1962. *Fanny von Arnstein oder die Emanzipation: Ein Frauenleben an der Zeitenwende 1758–1818.* Frankfurt a. M.: S. Fischer.
———. 1965. *Lisas Zimmer.* Munich: Nymphenburger Verlagshandlung GmbH.

———. 1968. *Rückkehr nach Wien: Ein Tagebuch.* Munich: Nymphenburger Verlagshandlung GmbH.

———. 1977. "Psychologie des Exils." In *Österreicher im Exil 1934 bis 1945: Protokoll des internationalen Symposiums zur Erforschung des österreichischen Exils von 1934 bis 1945,* ed. Dokumentationsarchiv des österreichischen Widerstandes und Dokumentationsstelle für neuere österreichische Literatur, xxii–xxxvii. Vienna: Österreichischer Bundesverlag.

———. 1987. *Vienna's Golden Autumn 1866–1938.* London: Weidenfeld and Nicolson.

———. 1989a. *Anna und Anna: Flüchten oder Hinnehmen? Eine Frage literarisch beantwortet.* Vienna: Kremayr & Scheriau.

———. 1989b. *Die hellen und die finsteren Zeiten: Erinnerungen 1911–1946.* Munich: List Verlag.

———. 1990. *Welche Welt ist meine Welt? Erinnerungen 1946–1989.* Munich: List Verlag.

———. 1991. *Fanny von Arnstein: A Daughter of the Enlightenment 1758–1818.* Trans. Christine Shuttleworth. New York: Berg.

———. 1999. "Heligenstadt Unchanged: Auszug aus Hilde Spiels Tagebuch vom 28. Jänner bis 19. Februar 1946." In *Hilde Spiel: Weltbürgerin der Literatur,* ed. Hans A. Neunzig and Ingrid Schramm, 80–86. Vienna: Paul Zsolnay Verlag.

Tausig, Franziska. 1987. *Shanghai Passage: Flucht und Exil einer Wienerin.* Vienna: Verlag für Gesellschaftskritik.

Thalberg, Hans J. 1984. *Von der Kunst, Österreicher zu sein: Erinnerungen und Tagebuchnotizen.* Vienna: Böhlau Verlag.

OTHER PRIMARY LITERATURE

Aichinger, Ilse. 1948. *Die größere Hoffnung.* Amsterdam: Bermann Fischer.

———. 1963. *Herod's Children.* Trans. Cornelia Schaeffer. New York: Atheneum.

Améry, Jean. 1966. *Jenseits von Schuld und Sühne: Bewältigungsversuche eines Überwältigten.* Munich: Szczesny Verlag. Reprint. 1977. Stuttgart: Klett-Cotta.

———. 1980. *At the Mind's Limits: Contemplations by a Survivor on Auschwitz and Its Realities.* Trans. Sidney Rosenfeld and Stella P. Rosenfeld. Bloomington: Indiana University Press.

Begov, Lucie. 1983. *Mit meinen Augen: Botschaft einer Auschwitz-Überlebenden.* Gerlinger: Bleicher Verlag.

Bruha, Antonia. 1984. *Ich war keine Heldin.* Vienna: Europaverlag.

Clare, George. 1981. *Last Waltz in Vienna: The Destruction of a Family 1842–1942.* London: Macmillan.

Deutsch, Gitta. 1993. *Böcklinstraßenelegie: Erinnerungen.* Vienna: Picus Verlag.

———. 1996. *The Red Thread.* Riverside, CA: Ariadne Press.

Drach, Albert. 1966. *Unsentimentale Reise: Ein Bericht.* Munich: A. Langen.

References

Fittko, Lisa. 1985. *Mein Weg über die Pyrenäen: Erinnerungen 1940/41.* Munich: Carl Hanser Verlag.

Flesch-Brunningen, Hans. 1988. *Die verführte Zeit: Lebenserinnerungen.* Ed. Manred Mixner. Vienna: Brandstatter.

Foster, Edith. 1989. *Reunion in Vienna.* Riverside, Calif.: Ariadne.

Frankl, Viktor E. 1946. *Ein Psychologe erlebt das Konzentrationslager.* Vienna: Jugend und Volk.

————. 1977. *Trotzdem ja zum Leben sagen: Ein Psychologe erlebt das Konzentrationslager.* Reprint, Munich: dtv.

————. 1959. *From Death-Camp to Existentialism: A Psychiatrist's Path to a New Therapy.* Boston: Beacon; *Man's Search for Meaning: An Introduction to Logotherapy.* Rev. ed. New York: Simon & Schuster, 1962.

Gessner, Adrienne. 1985. *Ich möchte gern was Gutes sagen.* Vienna: Amalthea.

Kerschbaumer, Marie-Thérèse. 1980. *Der weibliche Name des Widerstands.* Olten: Walter-Verlag. Film produced in 1981 by ORF and directed by Susanne Zanke.

Kreisky, Bruno. 1986. *Zwischen den Zeiten: Erinnerungen aus fünf Jahrzehnten.* Berlin: Siedler Verlag.

Lambert, Anna. 1992. *Du kannst vor nichts davonlaufen: Erinnerungen einer auf sich selbst gestellten Frau.* Trans. Alexander Potyka. Vienna: Picus Verlag.

Leichter, Henry O. 1995. *Eine Kindheit.* Trans. Susi Schneider. Vienna: Böhlau Verlag.

Maleta, Alfred. 1981. *Bewältigte Vergangenheit: Österreich 1932–1945.* Graz: Verlag Styria.

Pauli, Hertha. 1970. *Der Riss der Zeit geht durch mein Herz: Ein Erlebnisbuch.* Vienna: Paul Zsolnay Verlag.

Rattner, Anna. [1989?] "Der Zufall. Rückkehr einer Österreicherin." In *1938– Zuflucht Palästina: Zwei Frauen berichten,* ed. Helga Embacher. Vienna: Geyer.

Schiffer, Karl. 1988. *Über die Brücke: Der Weg eines linken Sozialisten ins Schweizer Exil.* Vienna: Verlag für Gesellschaftskritik.

Schwarz, Egon. 1979. *Keine Zeit für Eichendorff: Chronik unfreiwilliger Wanderjahre.* Königstein: Athenäum,; rev. ed. Frankfurt a. M.: Büchergilde Gutenberg, 1992.

Troller, Georg, Stefan. 1988. *Selbstbeschreibung.* Hamburg: Rasch und Röhung.

Verkauf-Verlon, Willy. 1983. *Situationen: Eine autobiographische Wortcollage.* Vienna: Verlag für Gesellschaftskritik.

Waldheim, Kurt. 1985. *Im Glaspalast der Weltpolitik.* Düsseldorf: Econ Verlag.

————. 1986. *In the Eye of the Storm: A Memoir.* Bethesda, Md.: Adler & Adler.

Waller, Lore Lizbeth. 1993. *View from a Distance.* Riverside, Calif.: Ariadne.

Wander, Fred. 1996. *Das gute Leben: Erinnerungen.* Munich: Carl Hanser Verlag.

Zaloscer, Hilde. 1988. *Eine Heimkehr gibt es nicht.* Vienna: Löcker Verlag.

Zweig, Stefan. 1943. *The World of Yesterday.* New York: Viking.

————. 1944. *Die Welt von Gestern.* Stockholm: Bermann Fischer.

SECONDARY LITERATURE

Alge, Susanne. 1992. "Nachwort." In *Die fahrenden Jahre*, by Elisabeth Freund-lich, 175–86. Salzburg: Otto Müller Verlag.

Applegate, Celia. 1990. *A Nation of Provincials: The German Idea of "Heimat."* Berkeley: University of California Press.

Assmann, Jan. 1997. *Das kulturelle Gedächtnis: Schrift, Erinnerung und politi-sche Identität in frühen Hochkulturen.* Munich Verlag C. H.: Beck.

Aberbach, David. 1989. *Surviving Trauma: Loss, Literature and Psychoanalysis.* New Haven: Yale University Press.

Bailer, Brigitte. 1997. "They Were All Victims: The Selective Treatment of the Consequences of National Socialism." In *Austrian Historical Memory and National Identity*, ed. Günter Bischof and Anton Pelinka, 103–15. Con-temporary Austrian Studies 5. New Brunswick: Transaction Publishers.

Bal, Mieke, Jonathan Crewe, and Leo Spitzer, eds. 1999. *Acts of Memory: Cultural Recall in the Present.* Hanover: University Press of New England.

Beckermann, Ruth. 1987. *Die papierene Brücke.* Vienna: filmladen.

———. 1989. *Unzugehörig: Österreicher und Juden nach 1945.* Vienna: Löcker Verlag.

———. 1994. "Jean Améry and Austria." In *Insiders and Outsiders: Jewish and Gentile Culture in Germany and Austria*, ed. Dagmar C. G. Lorenz and Gabriele Weinberger, 73–86. Detroit: Wayne State University Press.

———., ed. 1984. *Die Mazzesinsel: Juden in der Wiener Leopoldstadt 1918–1938.* Vienna: Löcker Verlag.

Beller, Steven. 1989. *Vienna and the Jews 1867–1938: A Cultural History.* Cambridge: Cambridge University Press.

Berger, Karin. 1989. "Aus Angst, uns ein Bild zu zerstören." In *"Man hat ja nichts gewusst!" Frauen im Krieg und im Faschismus von 1939–1945. Auf—Eine Frauenzeitschrift.* Vol.65 (September): 3–4.

Berger, Karin, et al., eds. 1985. *Der Himmel ist blau. Kann sein: Frauen im Widerstand. Österreich 1938–1945.* Vienna: promedia.

———. 1987. *Ich geb Dir einen Mantel, dass Du ihn noch in Freiheit tragen kannst. Widerstehen im KZ. Österreichische Frauen erzählen.* Vienna: pro-media.

Berger, Peter L., and Thomas Luckmann. 1966. *The Social Construction of Reality: A Treatise on the Sociology of Knowledge.* New York: Doubleday.

Berkley, George E. 1988. *Vienna and Its Jews: The Tragedy of Success 1880s–1980s.* Cambridge, Mass.: Abt Books.

Billson, Marcus. 1977. "The Memoir: New Perspectives on a Forgotten Genre." *Genre* 10.2: 259–82.

Bischof, Günter. 1997. Introduction to *Austrian Historical Memory and Na-tional Identity*, ed. Günter Bischof and Anton Pelinka. Contemporary Austrian Studies 5. New Brunswick: Transaction Publishers.

Bischof, Günter, and Anton Pelinka, eds. 1997. *Memory and National Identity.* Contemporary Austrian Studies 5. New Brunswick: Transaction Publish-ers.

Bolkosky, Sidney M. 1987. "Interviewing Victims Who Survived: Listening for the Silences that Strike." *Annals of Scholarship: Metastudies of the Humanities and Social Sciences* 4.2: 33–51.

Borneman, John, and Jeffrey M. Peck. 1995. *Sojourners: The Return of German Jews and the Question of Identity.* Lincoln: University of Nebraska Press.

Brison, Susan J. 1999. "Trauma Narratives and the Remaking of Self." In *Acts of Memory: Cultural Recall in the Present,* ed. Mieke Bal et al., 39–54. Hanover: University Press of New England.

Bruckmüller, Ernst. 1998. "The Development of Austrian National Identity." In *Austria, 1945–95: Fifty Years of the Second Republic,* ed. Kurt Richard Luther and Peter Pulzer, 83–108. Aldershot, Eng.: Ashgate.

Bukey, Evan B. 1989. "Popular Opinion in Vienna after the *Anschluss.*" In *Conquering the Past: Austrian Nazism Yesterday and Today,* ed. F. Parkinson, 151–64. Detroit: Wayne State University Press.

———. 2000. *Hitler's Austria: Popular Sentiment in the Nazi Era, 1938–1945.* Chapel Hill: University of North Carolina Press.

Bunzl, John and Bernd Marin. 1983. *Antisemitismus in Österreich: Sozialhistorische und soziologische Studien.* Vergleichende Gesellschafsgeschichte und politische Ideengeschichte der Neuzeit 3. Innsbruck: Inn-Verlag.

Bunzl, John. 1987. *Der lange Arm der Erinnerung. Jüdisches Bewusstsein heute.* Vienna: Böhlau Verlag.

Bunzl, Matti. 1996. "The City and the Self: Narratives of Spatial Belonging among Austrian Jews." *City and Society*: 50–81.

Campbell, Karlyn Kohrs. 1982. *The Rhetorical Act.* Belmont, Calif.: Wadsworth.

Caruth, Cathy, ed. 1995. *Trauma: Explorations in Memory.* Baltimore: Johns Hopkins University Press.

Critchfield, Richard. 1984. "Einige Überlegungen zur Problematik der Exilautobiographik." *Exilforschung: Ein internationales Jahrbuch* 2: 41–55.

———. 1994. *When Lucifer Cometh: The Autobiographical Discourse of Writers and Intellectuals Exiled During the Third Reich.* Literature and the Sciences of Man 7. New York: Peter Lang.

Culbertson, Roberta. 1995. "Embodied Memory, Transcendence, and Telling: Recounting Trauma, Re-establishing the Self." *New Literary History* 26: 169–95.

Daviau, Donald G., and Jorun B. Johns. 1989. "Ernst Lothar." In *Deutschsprachige Exilliteratur seit 1933: New York,* ed. John M. Spalik and Joseph Strelka, 2: 520–53. Bern: Francke Verlag.

Des Pres, Terrence. 1976. *The Survivor: An Anatomy of Life in the Death Camps.* New York: Oxford University Press.

Embacher, Helga. 1995. *Neubeginn ohne Illusionen: Juden in Österreich nach 1945.* Vienna: Picus Verlag.

Embacher, Helga, Albert Lichtblau, and Günther Sandner, eds. 1999. *Umkämpfte Erinnerung: Die Wehrmachtausstellung in Salzburg.* Salzburg: Residenz.

Embacher, Helga, and Margit Reiter. 1997. Mythos Shanghai? Geschlechterbeziehungen in Extremsituationen: Österreichische und deutsche Frauen in Shanghai der 30er und 40er Jahre. Manuscript. Final Report for the National Bank Project. Fall.

Eppel, Peter. 1988. "Österreicher im Exil 1938–1945." In *NS-Herrschaft in Österreich 1938–1945*, ed. Emmerich Tálos, et al. 553–70. Vienna: Verlag für Gesellschaftskritik.

Epstein, Helen. 1979. *Children of the Holocaust: Converations with Sons and Daughters of Survivors*. New York: Putnam's Sons.

Erikson, Kai. 1995. "Notes on Trauma and Community." In *Trauma: Explorations in Memory*, ed. Cathy Caruth, 183–99. Baltimore: Johns Hopkins University Press.

Exil und Reimgration. 1991. Special issue of *Exilforschung* 9.

Farrell, Kirby. 1998. *Post-traumatic Culture: Injury and Interpretation in the Ninties*. Baltimore: Johns Hopkins University Press.

Felman, Shoshana. 1992. "Education and Crisis, or the Vicissitudes of Teaching." In *Testimony: Crises of Witnessing in Literature, Psychoanalysis, and History*, ed. Shoshana Felman and Dori Laub. New York: Routledge.

Fliedl, Konstanze. 1995. "Hilde Spiel's Linguistic Rights of Residence." Trans. Francis James Finlay. In *Austrian Exodus: The Creative Achievements of Refugees from National Socialism*, ed. Edward Timms and Ritchie Robertson, 78–93. Austrian Studies 6. Edinburgh: Edinburgh University Press,

Foley, Barbara. 1982. "Fact, Fiction, Fascism: Testimony and Mimesis in Holocaust Narratives." *Comparative Literature* 34.4: 330–60.

Freidenreich, Harriet Pass. 1991. *Jewish Politics in Vienna, 1918–1938*. Bloomington: Indiana University Press.

Fried, Marc. 1963. "Grieving for a Lost Home." In *The Urban Condition: People and Policy in the Metropolis*, ed. Leonard J. Duhl, 151–71. New York: Basic Books.

Friedlander, Saul, ed. 1992. *Probing the Limits of Representation: Nazism and the "Final Solution."* Cambridge: Harvard University Press.

Gilman, Sander. 1991. *The Jew's Body*. New York: Routledge.

———. 1999. "Introduction: The Frontier as a Model for Jewish History." In *Jewries at the Frontier: Accommodation, Identity, Conflict*, ed. Sander Gilman and Milton Shain, 1–25. Urbana: University of Illinois Press.

Gilman, Sander, and Milton Shain, eds. 1999. *Jewries at the Frontier: Accommodation, Identity, Conflict*. Urbana: University of Illinois Press.

Gorer, Geoffrey. 1965. *Death, Grief, and Mourning in Contemporary Britain*. London: Cresset Press.

Greenspan, Henry. 1992. "Lives as Texts: Symptoms as Modes of Recounting in the Life Histories of Holocaust Survivors." In *Storied Lives: The Cultural Politics of Self-Understanding* ed. George C. Rosenwald and Richard L. Ochberg, 145–64. New Haven: Yale University Press.

———. 1998. *On Listening to Holocaust Survivors: Recounting and Life History*. Westport, Conn.: Praeger.

Grinberg, León, and Rebeca Grinberg. 1989. *Psychoanalytic Perspectives on Migration and Exile.* Trans. Nancy Festinger. New Haven: Yale University Press.

Halbwachs, Maurice. 1980. *The Collective Memory.* Trans. Francis J. Ditter, Jr. and Vid Yazdi Ditter. New York: Harper and Row.

Haslinger, Josef. 1987. *Politik der Gefühle: Ein Essay über Österreich.* Darmstadt: Luchterhand.

Heinemann, Marlene E. 1986. *Gender and Destiny: Women Writers and the Holocaust.* New York: Greenwood.

Herman, Judith Lewis. 1992. *Trauma and Recovery.* New York: Basic Books.

Hermann, Ingo, ed. 1992. *Hilde Spiel, Die Grande Dame: Gespräch mit Anne Linsel in der Reihe "Zeugen des Jahrhunderts."* Göttingen: Lamuv Verlag.

Hertling, Viktoria. 1992. "' . . . irgendwie doch einen Erfolg gehabt': Die *Austro-American Tribune* in New York (1942–1945)." In *Die Resonanz des Exils: Gelungene und misslungene Rezeption deutschsprachiger Exilautoren,* ed. Dieter Sevin, 34–50. Amsterdam: Rodopi.

———. 1997. "Exil und Post-Exil: Elisabeth Freundlichs Erinnerungsbuch *Die fahrenden Jahre." Modern Austrian Literature* 30.1 : 102–16.

Hirsch, Julia. 1981. *Family Photographs: Content, Meaning, and Effect.* New York: Oxford University Press.

Hirsch, Marianne. 1997. *Family Frames: Photography, Narrative and Postmemory.* Cambridge: Harvard University Press.

Howells, Christa Victoria. 1994. "Heimat und Exil: Ihre Dynamik im Werk von Hilde Spiel." Ph.D. diss., Rice University.

Jochum, Manfred. 1985. "Die Vierziger Jahre. Ein Überblick." In *Wien 1945 davor/danach,* ed. Liesbeth Waechter-Böhm, 215–37. Vienna: Verlag Christian Brandstätter.

John, Michael, and Albert Lichtblau. 1993. *Schmelztiegel Wien—Einst und Jetzt: Zur Geschichte und Gegenwart von Zuwanderung und Minderheiten.* Vienna: Böhlau Verlag.

Jüdische Schicksale: Berichte von Verfolgten. 1993. Ed. Dokumentationsarchiv des österreichischen Widerstandes. Vienna: Österreichischer Bundesverlag.

Jung, Jochen, ed. 1983. *Vom Reich zu Österreich: Kriegsende und Nachkriegszeit in Österreich erinnert von Augen- und Ohrenzeugen.* Salzburg: Residenz Verlag.

———. 1988. *Reden an Österreich: Schriftsteller ergreifen das Wort.* Salzburg: Residenz Verlag.

Kaes, Anton. 1989. *From "Hitler" to "Heimat": The Return of History as Film.* Cambridge: Harvard University Press.

Kenyon, Gary M., and William L. Randall. 1997. *Restorying Our Lives: Personal Growth through Autobiographical Reflection.* Westport, Conn.: Praeger.

Knight, Robert. 1992. " 'Neutrality,' Not Sympathy: Jews in Post-War Austria." In *Austrians and Jews in the Twentieth Century: From Franz Joseph to Waldheim,* ed. Robert S. Wistrich, 220–233. New York: St. Martin's Press.

————., ed. 1988. *"Ich bin dafür, die Sache in die Länge zu ziehen"*: *Wortprotokolle der österreichischen Bundesregierung von 1945–52 über die Entschädigung der Juden*. Frankfurt a. M.: Athenäum.

Koebner, Thomas, and Erwin Rotermund, eds. 1990. *Rückkehr aus dem Exil: Emigranten aus dem Dritten Reich in Deutschland nach 1945*. Marburg: edition text und kritik.

Konzett, Matthias. 1998. "The Politics of Recognition in Contemporary Austrian Jewish Literature." *Monatshefte* 90.1: 71–88.

Kranzler, David. 1976. *Japanese, Nazis, & Jews: The Jewish Refugee Community of Shanghai, 1938–1945*. New York: Yeshiva University Press.

Krystal, Henry. 1995. "Trauma and Aging: A Thirty-Year Follow-Up." In *Trauma: Explorations in Memory*, ed. Cathy Caruth, 76–99. Baltimore: Johns Hopkins University Press.

Langer, Lawrence L. 1991. *Holocaust Testimonies: The Ruins of Memory*. New Haven: Yale University Press.

Die Leiche im Keller: Dokumente des Widerstandes gegen Dr. Kurt Waldheim. 1988. Vienna: Picus Verlag.

Lejeune, Philippe. 1989. *On Autobiography*. Trans. Katherine Leary, ed. Paul John Eakin. *Theory and History of Literature* 52. Minneapolis: University of Minnesota Press.

Lichtblau, Albert and Michael John. 1999. "Jewries in Galicia and Bukovina, in Lemberg and Czernowitz: Two Divergent Examples of Jewish Communities in the Far East of the Austro-Hungarian Monarchy." In *Jewries at the Frontier: Accommodation, Identity, Conflict*, ed. Sander Gilman and Milton Shain, 29–66. Urbana: University of Illinois Press.

Liessmann, Konrad Paul. 1998. "Überlebenserinnerungen. Zu den Autobiographien von Günther Anders, Jean Améry und Hilde Spiel." In *Autobiographien in der österreichischen Literatur: Von Franz Grillparzer bis Thomas Bernhard*, ed. Klaus Amann und Karl Wagner, 203–16. Innsbruck: StudienVerlag.

Littlewood, Janet. 1992. *Aspects of Grief: Bereavement in Adult Life*. London: Tavistock/Routledge.

Lixl-Purcell, Andreas, ed. 1988. *Women of Exile: German-Jewish Autobiographies since 1933*. New York: Greenwood.

Lorenz, Dagmar C. G. 1992a. "Hilde Spiel: *Lisas Zimmer*: Frau, Jüdin, Verfolgte." *Modern Austrian Literature* 25.2: 79–95.

————. 1992b. *Verfolgung bis zum Massenmord: Holocaust-Diskurse in deutscher Sprache aus der Sicht der Verfolgten*. Ed. Jost Hermand. *German Life and Civilization* 11. New York: Peter Lang.

Lorenz, Dagmar C. G., and Gabriele Weinberger, eds. 1994. *Insiders and Outsiders: Jewish and Gentile Culture in Germany and Austria*. Detroit: Wayne State University Press.

Lowenthal, David. 1985. *The Past Is a Foreign Country*. Cambridge: Cambridge University Press.

Maier, Charles. 1988. *The Unmasterable Past: History, Holocaust, and German National Identity.* Cambridge: Harvard University Press.

Malina, Peter. 1989. "Nach dem Krieg." In *Österreicher und der Zweite Weltkrieg,* ed. Dokumentationsarchiv des österreichischen Widerstandes and Dr. Wolfgang Neugebauer, 145–69. Vienna: Österreichischer Bundesverlag.

Maynes, Mary Jo. 1989. "Gender and Narative Form in French and German Working-Class Autobiographies." In *Interpreting Women's Lives: Feminist Theory and Personal Narratives,* ed. Personal Narratives Group, 103–17. Bloomington: Indiana University Press.

McCagg Jr., William O. 1989. *A History of Habsburg Jews, 1670–1918.* Bloomington: Indiana University Press.

McVeigh, Joseph. 1988. *Kontinuität und Vergangenheitsbewältigung in der österreichischen Literatur.* Vienna: Braumüller.

Middleton, David, and Derek Edwards. 1990. Introduction to *Collective Remembering,* ed. David Middleton. London: Sage Publications.

Mitchell, W. J. T. 1994. *Picture Theory: Essays on Verbal and Visual Representation.* Chicago: University of Chicago Press.

Mitscherlich, Alexander, and Margarete Mitscherlich. 1967. *Die Unfähigkeit zu trauern: Grundlagen kollektiven Verhaltens.* Munich: Piper.

———. 1975. *The Inability to Mourn: Principles of Collective Behavior.* Trans. Beverley R. Placzek. New York: Grove Press.

Mitten, Richard. 1992. *The Politics of Antisemitic Prejudice: The Waldheim Phenomenon in Austria.* Boulder: Westview Press.

"Moscow Conference." 1971. In *Henry Steel Commager Documents of American History,* 9th ed., 2: 479. New York: Meredith.

Neunzig, Hans A., and Ingrid Schramm, eds. 1999. *Hilde Spiel: Weltbürgerin der Literatur.* Vienna: Paul Zsolnay Verlag.

Der Novemberpogrom 1938. Die "Reichskristallnacht" in Wien. 1988. Vienna: Museum der Stadt Wien.

Oxaal, Ivar, Michael Pollak, and Gerhard Botz, eds. 1987. *Jews, Antisemitism and Culture in Vienna.* London: Routledge and Kegan Paul.

Papisch, Peter. 1985. "Hilde Spiels *Rückkehr nach Wien*—eine besondere Thematik der Exilliteratur." In *Exil: Wirkung und Wertung: Ausgewählte Beiträge zum fünften Symposium über deutsche und österreichische Exilliteratur,* ed. Donald G. Daviau and Ludwig M. Fischer, 173–83. Columbia: Camden House.

Parkes, Colin Murray. 1986. *Bereavement. Studies of Grief in Adult Life.* 2d ed. London: Tavistock Publications.

Parkinson, F., ed. 1989. *Conquering the Past: Austrian Nazism Yesterday and Today.* Detroit: Wayne State University Press.

Pauley, Bruce F. 1992. *From Prejudice to Persecution: A History of Austrian Anti-Semitism.* Chapel Hill: University of North Carolina Press.

———. 1996. "Austria." In *The World Reacts to the Holocaust,* ed. David S. Wyman, 473–513. Baltimore: Johns Hopkins University Press.

Pelinka, Anton. 1987. "Der verdrängte Bürgerkrieg." In *Das große Tabu,* ed. Anton Pelinka and Erika Weinzierl, 143–53. Vienna: Verlag der Österreichischen Staatsdruckerei.

———. 1989. "SPÖ, ÖVP, and the 'Ehemaligen': Isolation or Integration?" In *Conquering the Past: Austrian Nazism Yesterday and Today,* ed. F. Parkinson, 245–56. Detroit: Wayne State University Press.

———. 1990. *Zur österreichischen Identität: Zwischen deutscher Vereinigung und Mitteleuropa.* Vienna: Ueberreuter.

Pelinka, Anton, and Erika Weinzierl, eds. 1987. *Das große Tabu.* Vienna: Verlag der Österreichischen Staatsdruckerei.

Personal Narratives Group. 1989. *Interpreting Women's Lives: Feminist Theory and Personal Narratives.* Bloomington: Indiana University Press.

Pfäfflin, Friedrich. 1988. "Jean Améry: Daten zu einer Biographie." *Text + Kritik* 99: 56–69.

Pickus, Keith H. 1999. *Constructing Modern Identities: Jewish University Students in Germany, 1815–1914.* Detroit: Wayne State University Press.

Prutsch, Ursula, and Manfred Lechner, eds. 1997. *Das ist Österreich: Innensichten und Außensichten.* Vienna: Döcker Verlag.

Rapaport, Lynn. 1997. *Jews in Germany after the Holocaust: Memory, Identity, and Jewish-German Relations.* Cambridge: Cambridge University Press.

Reinprecht, Christoph. 1992. *Zurückgekehrt: Identität und Bruch in der Biographie österreichischer Juden.* Ed. Hilde Weiss. Sociologica 3. Vienna: Braumüller.

Reitani, Luigi. 1992. "Appunti sull' identità ebraica nella Vienna della Seconda Repubblica." In *Studia austriaca,* 73–95. Milan: Edizioni dell'arco.

Remmler, Karen. 1994a. "Gender Identities and the Remembrance of the Holocaust. *Women in German Yearbook* 10: 167–87.

———. 1994b. "Sheltering Battered Bodies in Language: Imprisonment Once More?" In *Displacements: Cultural Identities in Question,* ed. Angelika Bammer, 216–32. Bloomington: Indiana University Press.

———. 1996. *Waking the Dead: Correspondences between Walter Benjamin's Concept of Remembrance and Ingeborg Bachmann's "Ways of Dying."* Riverside, Calif.: Ariadne Press.

Ringel, Erwin. 1984. *Die österreichische Seele: Zehn Reden über Medizin, Politik, Kunst und Religion.* Vienna: Böhlau Verlag.

Rot-Weiß-Rot-Buch: Gerechtigkeit für Österreich: Darstellungen, Dokumente und Nachweise zur Vorgeschichte und Geschichte der Okkupation Österreichs (nach amtlichen Quellen). 1946. Ed. under the direction of Dr. Karl Gruber. Vienna: Österreichische Staatsdruckerei.

Rozenblit, Marsha L. 1983. *The Jews of Vienna, 1867–1914: Assimilation and Identity.* Ed. Paula E. Hyman and Deborah Dash Moore. SUNY Series in Modern Jewish History. Albany: State University of New York Press.

———. 1992. "The Jews of Germany and Austria: A Comparative Perspective." In *Austrians and Jews in the Twentieth Century: From Franz Joseph to Waldheim,* ed. Robert S. Wistrich, 1–18. New York: St. Martin's.

Safrian, Hans, and Hans Witek. 1988. *Und keiner war dabei: Dokumente des alltäglichen Antisemitismus in Wien 1938*. Vienna: Picus Verlag.

Scarry, Elaine. 1985. *The Body in Pain: The Making and Unmaking of the World*. New York: Oxford University Press.

Schacter, Daniel L. 1996. *Searching for Memory: The Brain, the Mind, and the Past*. New York: Basic Books.

Schama, Simon. 1995. *Landscape and Memory*. New York: Alfred A. Knopf.

Scholes, Robert, and Robert Kellogg. 1966. *The Nature of Narrative*. New York: Oxford University Press.

Schorske, Carl E. 1980. *Fin-de-Siècle Vienna: Politics and Culture*. New York: Knopf.

Schramm, Ingrid. 1999. "Welche Welf war ihre Welt? Ein literarisches Leben Zwischen hellen und finsteren Zeiten." In *Hilde Spiel: Welfbürgerin der Literatur*, ed. Hans A. Neunzig and Ingrid Schramm, 9–22. Vienna: Paul Zsolnay Verlag.

Schwarz, Egon. 1994. "Jews and Anti-Semitism in Fin-de-Siècle Vienna." In *Insiders and Outsiders: Jewish and Gentile Culture in Germany and Austria*, ed. Dagmar Lorenz and Gabriele Weinberger, 47–65. Detroit: Wayne State University Press.

Sebald, W. G. 1988. "Verlorenes Land: Jean Améry und Österreich." *Text + Kritik* 99: 20–29.

Secher, H. Pierre. 1993. *Bruno Kreisky, Chancellor of Austria: A Political Biography*. Pittsburgh: Dorrance.

———. 1994. "Kreisky and the Jews." In *The Kreisky Era in Austria*, ed. Günter Bischof and Anton Pelinka, 10–31. Contemporary Austrian Studies 2. New Brunswick: Transaction Publishers.

Seeber, Ursula, ed. 1998. *Ein Niemandsland, aber welch ein Rundblick! Exilautoren über Nachkriegs-Wien*. Vienna: Picus Verlag.

Seeber-Weyrer, Ursula. 1997. " 'Ergötze dich am längst nicht mehr Vorhandenen': Österreich-Bilder des Exils." In *Das ist Österreich: Innensichten und Außensichten*, ed. Ursula Prutsch and Manfred Lechner, 123–40. Vienna: Döcker Verlag.

Sichrovsky, Peter. 1985. *Wir wissen nicht was morgen wird, wir wissen wohl was gestern war: Junge Juden in Deutschland und Österreich*. Cologne: Kiepenheuer & Witsch.

Sommer, Fred. 1984. *"Halb-Asien": German Nationalism and the Eastern European Works of Emil Franzos*. Ed. Ulrich Müller et al. Stuttgarter Arbeiten zur Germanistik 145. Stuttgart: Akademischer Verlag Hans-Dieter Heinz.

Spitzer, Leo. 1998. *Hotel Bolivia: The Culture of Memory in a Refuge from Nazism*. New York: Hill and Wang.

———. 1999. "Back Through the Future: Nostalgic Memory and Critical Memory in a Refuge from Nazism." In *Acts of Memory: Cultural Recall in the Present*, ed. Mieke Bal et al., 87–104. Hanover: University Press of New England.

Stadler, Friedrich, and Peter Weibel, eds. 1995. *Vertreibung der Vernunft: The Cultural Exodus from Austria.* Vienna: Springer-Verlag.

Steiner, George. 1998. *Language and Silence: Essays on Language, Literature, and the Inhuman.* New Haven: Yale University Press.

Steiner, Gertraud. 1987. *Die Heimat-Macher: Kino in Österreich 1946–1966.* Vienna: Verlag für Gesellschaftskritik.

Strickhausen, Waltraud. 1995. " 'Das Exil ist eine Krankheit': Zu Hilde Spiels Darstellung der psychischen Auswirkungen des Exils." *Zwischenwelt* 4: 141–58.

———. 1996. *Die Erzählerin Hilde Spiel: oder, 'Der weite Wurf in die Finsternis.'* New York: Peter Lang.

Tálos, Emmerich, Ernst Hanisch, and Wolfgang Neugebauer, eds. 1988. *NS-Herrschaft in Österreich 1938–1945.* Vienna: Verlag für Gesellschaftskritik.

Uhl, Heidemarie. 1997. "The Politics of Memory: Austria's Perception of the Second World War and the National Socialist Period." In *Austrian Historical Memory and National Identity,* ed. Günter Bischof and Anton Pelinka, 64–94. Contemporary Austrian Studies 5. New Brunswick: Transaction Publishers.

van Amerongen, Martin. 1977. *Kreisky and seine unbewältige Gegenwart.* Trans. Gerhard Hartmann. Graz: Styria.

van der Kolk, Bessel A., and Onno van der Hart. 1995. "The Intrusive Past: The Flexibility of Memory and the Engraving of Trauma." In *Trauma: Explorations in Memory,* ed. Cathy Caruth, 158–82. Baltimore: Johns Hopkins University Press.

Vansant, Jacqueline. 1994a. "Challenging Austria's Victim Status: National Socialism and Austrian Personal Narratives." *The German Quarterly* 67.1: 38–57.

———. 1994b. "Wieviel Kanon braucht der Mensch?" In *Die einen raus—die anderen rein. Kanon und Literatur: Vorüberlegungen zu einer Literaturgeschichte Österreichs,* ed. Wendelin Schmidt-Dengler, Johann Sonnleitner, and Klaus Zeyringer, 161–71. Berlin: Erich Schmidt Verlag.

Waechter-Böhm, Liesbeth, ed. 1985. *Wien 1945: davor/danach.* Vienna: Verlag Christian Brandstätter.

Warnock, Mary. 1987. *Memory.* London: faber and faber.

Weinzierl, Erika. 1969. *Zu wenig Gerechte: Österreicher und Judenverfolgung, 1938–1945.* Graz: Styria.

Whiteman, Dorit Bader. 1993. *The Uprooted: A Hitler Legacy: Voices of Those Who Escaped the "Final Solution".* New York: Plenum Press.

Wiesinger-Stock, Sandra. 1996. *Hilde Spiel: Ein Leben ohne Heimat?* Vienna: Verlag für Gesellschaftskritik.

Wilder-Okladek, F. 1969. *The Return Movement of Jews to Austria after the Second World War.* Publications of the Research Group for European Migration Problems 16. The Hague: Martinus Nijhoff.

Wimmer, Adi. 1996. "Austria's Jewish Exiles and Their Narratives of Trauma."

In *Ethnic Literature and Culture in the U.S.A., Canada, and Australia,* ed. Igor Maver, 161–75. Frankurt a. M.: Peter Lang.

————., ed. 1993. *Die Heimat wurde ihnen fremd, die Fremde nicht zur Heimat: Erinnerungen österreichischer Juden aus dem Exil.* Vienna: Verlag für Gesellschaftskritik.

Wistrich, Robert S. 1982. *Socialism and the Jews: The Dilemmas of Assimilation in Germany and Austria-Hungary.* Rutherford, Fairleigh Dickinson University Press.

————. 1987. "Social Democracy, Antisemitism and the Jews of Vienna." In *Jews, Antisemitism and Culture in Vienna,* ed. Ivar Oxaal, et al, 111–20. London: Routledge and Kegan Paul.

————. 1989. *The Jews of Vienna in the Age of Franz Joseph.* Oxford: Oxford University Press

————., ed. 1992. *Austrians and Jews in the Twentieth Century: From Franz Joseph to Waldheim.* New York: St. Martin's Press.

Wodak, Ruth, et al. 1990. *"Wir sind alle unschuldige Täter": Diskurshistorische Studien zum Nachkriegsantisemitismus.* Frankfurt a. M.: Suhrkamp.

Wyman, David S., ed. 1996. *The World Reacts to the Holocaust.* Baltimore, Johns Hopkins University Press.

Yates, Frances A. 1966. *The Art of Memory.* Chicago: University of Chicago Press.

Young, James. 1988. *Writing and Rewriting the Holocaust.* Bloomington: Indiana University Press.

Zernatto, Guido. 1939. *Die Wahrheit über Österreich.* New York: Longmans, Green.

Ziegler, Meinrad, and Waltraud Kannonier-Finster. 1993. *Österreichisches Gedächtnis: Über Erinnern und Vergessen der NS-Vergangenheit.* Böhlaus Zeitgeschichtliche Bibliothek 25. Vienna: Böhlau Verlag.

Index

Page numbers of photographs are in italic.